T0205963

Communications
in Computer and Information Science   2104

Editorial Board Members

Joaquim Filipe ⓘ, *Polytechnic Institute of Setúbal, Setúbal, Portugal*
Ashish Ghosh ⓘ, *Indian Statistical Institute, Kolkata, India*
Lizhu Zhou, *Tsinghua University, Beijing, China*

Rationale

The CCIS series is devoted to the publication of proceedings of computer science conferences. Its aim is to efficiently disseminate original research results in informatics in printed and electronic form. While the focus is on publication of peer-reviewed full papers presenting mature work, inclusion of reviewed short papers reporting on work in progress is welcome, too. Besides globally relevant meetings with internationally representative program committees guaranteeing a strict peer-reviewing and paper selection process, conferences run by societies or of high regional or national relevance are also considered for publication.

Topics

The topical scope of CCIS spans the entire spectrum of informatics ranging from foundational topics in the theory of computing to information and communications science and technology and a broad variety of interdisciplinary application fields.

Information for Volume Editors and Authors

Publication in CCIS is free of charge. No royalties are paid, however, we offer registered conference participants temporary free access to the online version of the conference proceedings on SpringerLink (http://link.springer.com) by means of an http referrer from the conference website and/or a number of complimentary printed copies, as specified in the official acceptance email of the event.

CCIS proceedings can be published in time for distribution at conferences or as postproceedings, and delivered in the form of printed books and/or electronically as USBs and/or e-content licenses for accessing proceedings at SpringerLink. Furthermore, CCIS proceedings are included in the CCIS electronic book series hosted in the SpringerLink digital library at http://link.springer.com/bookseries/7899. Conferences publishing in CCIS are allowed to use Online Conference Service (OCS) for managing the whole proceedings lifecycle (from submission and reviewing to preparing for publication) free of charge.

Publication process

The language of publication is exclusively English. Authors publishing in CCIS have to sign the Springer CCIS copyright transfer form, however, they are free to use their material published in CCIS for substantially changed, more elaborate subsequent publications elsewhere. For the preparation of the camera-ready papers/files, authors have to strictly adhere to the Springer CCIS Authors' Instructions and are strongly encouraged to use the CCIS LaTeX style files or templates.

Abstracting/Indexing

CCIS is abstracted/indexed in DBLP, Google Scholar, EI-Compendex, Mathematical Reviews, SCImago, Scopus. CCIS volumes are also submitted for the inclusion in ISI Proceedings.

How to start

To start the evaluation of your proposal for inclusion in the CCIS series, please send an e-mail to ccis@springer.com.

Hans-Georg Fill ·
Francisco José Domínguez Mayo ·
Marten van Sinderen · Leszek A. Maciaszek
Editors

Software Technologies

18th International Conference, ICSOFT 2023
Rome, Italy, July 10–12, 2023
Revised Selected Papers

 Springer

Editors
Hans-Georg Fill
University of Fribourg
Fribourg, Switzerland

Francisco José Domínguez Mayo
University of Seville
Seville, Sevilla, Spain

Marten van Sinderen
University of Twente
Enschede, The Netherlands

Leszek A. Maciaszek
Macquarie University and Wrocław
University of Economics and Business
Wrocław, Poland

ISSN 1865-0929   ISSN 1865-0937 (electronic)
Communications in Computer and Information Science
ISBN 978-3-031-61752-2   ISBN 978-3-031-61753-9 (eBook)
https://doi.org/10.1007/978-3-031-61753-9

This Springer imprint is published by the registered company Springer Nature Switzerland AG
The registered company address is: Gewerbestrasse 11, 6330 Cham, Switzerland

If disposing of this product, please recycle the paper.

Preface

The present book includes extended and revised versions of a set of selected papers from the 18th International Conference on Software Technologies (ICSOFT 2023), held in Rome, Italy, from 10 to 12 July 2023.

ICSOFT 2023 received 129 paper submissions from 37 countries, of which 5% were included in this book.

The papers were selected by the event chairs and their selection was based on a number of criteria that included the classifications and comments provided by the program committee members, the session chairs' assessment and also the program chairs' global view of all papers included in the technical program. The authors of selected papers were then invited to submit revised and extended versions of their papers having at least 30% innovative material.

The purpose of the International Conference on Software Technologies is to bring together researchers, engineers and practitioners interested in software technologies. The conference areas were "Software Engineering and Systems Development", "Software Systems and Applications" and "Foundational and Trigger Technologies".

The papers selected to be included in this book contribute to the understanding of relevant trends of current research on Software Technologies, including: Empirical Software Engineering, Software and Systems Modeling, Data Mining and Data Analysis, Open-Source Development, Requirements Engineering, Quality Management, Model-Driven Software Engineering, High-Performance Computing, Data-Driven Software Engineering and Automated Software Engineering.

We would like to thank all the authors for their contributions and also the reviewers who have helped to ensure the quality of this publication.

July 2023

Hans-Georg Fill
Francisco José Domínguez Mayo
Marten van Sinderen
Leszek A. Maciaszek

Organization

Conference Chair

Leszek Maciaszek — Macquarie Univ., Australia and Wroclaw Univ. of Economics and Business, Poland

Program Co-chairs

Hans-Georg Fill — University of Fribourg, Switzerland
Francisco José Domínguez Mayo — University of Seville, Spain
Marten van Sinderen — University of Twente, Netherlands

Program Committee

Rodina Ahmad — University of Malaya, Malaysia
Paulo Alencar — University of Waterloo, Canada
Marco Autili — University of L'Aquila, Italy
Davide Basile — ISTI CNR Pisa, Italy
Hubert Baumeister — Technical University of Denmark, Denmark
Jorge Bernardino — Polytechnic of Coimbra - ISEC, Portugal
Paul E. Black — National Institute of Standards and Technology, USA
Dominique Blouin — Télécom Paris, France
Thomas Buchmann — Hof University, Germany
Alejandro Calderón — University of Cádiz, Spain
Ana Castillo — Universidad de Alcalá, Spain
Anis Charfi — Carnegie Mellon University, Qatar
Alberto Coen-Porisini — Università degli Studi dell'Insubria, Italy
Estrela Cruz — Instituto Politécnico de Viana do Castelo, Portugal
João Cunha — Polytechnic of Coimbra, Coimbra Institute of Engineering, Portugal
Sergiu Dascalu — University of Nevada, Reno, USA
Cléver Ricardo de Farias — University of São Paulo, Brazil
Giuseppe Di Lucca — University of Sannio Benevento, Italy
João Dias — University of Porto, Portugal
Gencer Erdogan — SINTEF, Norway

Morgan Ericsson	Linnaeus University, Sweden
Letha Etzkorn	University of Alabama in Huntsville, USA
Eduardo Fernandez	Florida Atlantic University, USA
Alessio Ferrari	CNR, Italy
Kehan Gao	Eastern Connecticut State University, USA
Vinicius Garcia	Federal University of Pernambuco, Brazil
Felix Garcia Clemente	University of Murcia, Spain
Paola Giannini	University of Piemonte Orientale, Italy
Jose Gonzalez	University of Seville, Spain
Des Greer	QUB, UK
Christiane Gresse von Wangenheim	Federal University of Santa Catarina, Brazil
Hatim Hafiddi	INPT, Morocco
Jean Hauck	Universidade Federal de Santa Catarina, Brazil
Mercedes Hidalgo-Herrero	Universidad Complutense de Madrid, Spain
Andreas Hinderks	Universidad de Sevilla, Germany
Ralph Hoch	TU Wien, Austria
Andreas Holzinger	Medical University Graz, Austria
Jang-Eui Hong	Chungbuk National University, South Korea
Miloslav Hub	University of Pardubice, Czech Republic
Thomas Hupperich	University of Münster, Germany
Zbigniew Huzar	Wroclaw University of Science and Technology, Poland
Judit Jasz	University of Szeged, Hungary
Florian Johannsen	University of Applied Sciences Schmalkalden, Germany
Francisco José Domínguez Mayo	University of Seville, Spain
Hermann Kaindl	TU Wien, Austria
Takashi Kobayashi	Tokyo Institute of Technology, Japan
Jun Kong	North Dakota State University, USA
Herbert Kuchen	University of Münster, Germany
Rob Kusters	Open Universiteit Nederland, Netherlands
Youness Laghouaouta	INPT, Morocco
Giuseppe Lami	Consiglio Nazionale delle Ricerche, Italy
Claude Laporte	École de Technologie Supérieure, Canada
Konstantin Läufer	Loyola University Chicago, USA
Gary Leavens	University of Central Florida, USA
Pierre Leone	University of Geneva, Switzerland
Patricio Letelier	Technical University of Valencia, Spain
Letitia Li	BAE Systems, USA
Horst Lichter	RWTH Aachen University, Germany
David Lorenz	Open University, Israel

Daniel Lucrédio	Federal University of São Carlos, Brazil
Ivan Lukovic	University of Belgrade, Serbia
Chung-Horng Lung	Carleton University, Canada
Stephane Maag	Télécom SudParis, France
Tomi Männistö	University of Helsinki, Finland
Federico Mari	University of Rome Foro Italico, Italy
Stuart Marshall	Victoria University of Wellington, New Zealand
Manuel Mazzara	Innopolis University, Russian Federation
Andreas Meier	Zurich University of Applied Sciences, Switzerland
Antoni Mesquida Calafat	Universitat de les Illes Balears, Spain
Gergely Mezei	Budapest University of Technology and Economics, Hungary
Ali Mili	NJIT, USA
Mª Ángeles Moraga	University of Castilla-La Mancha, Spain
Elisa Nakagawa	University of Sao Paulo, Brazil
Takako Nakatani	Open University of Japan, Japan
Paolo Nesi	University of Florence, Italy
Toacy Cavalcante de Oliveira	Federal University of Rio de Janeiro, Brazil
Marc Oriol	Universitat Politècnica de Catalunya - BarcelonaTech, Spain
Jennifer Pérez	Universidad Politécnica de Madrid, Spain
Dana Petcu	West University of Timisoara, Romania
Alexander Petrenko	ISPRAS, Russian Federation
Giuseppe Polese	Università degli Studi di Salerno, Italy
Mohammad Mehdi Pourhashem Kallehbasti	University of Science and Technology of Mazandaran, Iran
Stefano Quer	Politecnico di Torino, Italy
Andres Rodriguez	UNLP, Argentina
Antonio Rodriguez-Diaz	Universidad Autónoma de Baja California, Mexico
Colette Rolland	Université Paris 1 Panthéon-Sorbonne, France
António Rosado da Cruz	Instituto Politécnico de Viana do Castelo, Portugal
Gunter Saake	Institute of Technical and Business Information Systems, Germany
Gwen Salaün	Grenoble INP, Inria, France
Johannes Sametinger	Johannes Kepler University Linz, Austria
Christian Schlegel	Technische Hochschule Ulm, Germany
Asma Sellami	University of Sfax, Tunisia
Istvan Siket	Hungarian Academy of Science, Hungary
Harvey Siy	University of Nebraska at Omaha, USA
Ketil Stolen	UiO, Norway

Hiroki Suguri	Miyagi University, Japan
Rosa Sukamto	Universitas Pendidikan Indonesia, Indonesia
Angelo Susi	Fondazione Bruno Kessler, Italy
Francesco Tiezzi	University of Camerino, Italy
Claudine Toffolon	Université du Mans, France
Davide Tosi	Università dell'Insubria, Italy
Porfirio Tramontana	University Federico II of Naples, Italy
Juan Vara Mesa	University Rey Juan Carlos, Spain
Tullio Vardanega	University of Padua, Italy
Tony Wasserman	Software Methods and Tools, USA
Dietmar Winkler	Vienna University of Technology, Austria
Dinghao Wu	Pennsylvania State University, USA
Carlos Mario Zapata-Jaramillo	Universidad Nacional de Colombia, Colombia

Additional Reviewers

Matthias Kollenbroich	University of Münster, Germany
Vinh Le	University of Nevada, Reno, USA
Jonathan Neugebauer	WWU Münster, Germany
Ferenc Somogyi	Budapest University of Technology and Economics, Hungary
Laura Troost	University of Münster, Germany
Hendrik Winkelmann	University of Münster, Germany

Invited Speakers

Jordi Cabot	Luxembourg Institute of Science and Technology, Luxembourg
Agnes Koschmider	University of Bayreuth, Germany
Wolfgang Maaß	Saarland University, Germany

Contents

Green Evolutionary Algorithms and JavaScript: A Study on Different Software and Hardware Architectures

Juan J. Merelo-Guervós[1]([✉]), Mario García-Valdez[2], and Pedro A. Castillo[1]

[1] Department of Computer Engineering, Automatics and Robotics and CITIC,
University of Granada, Granada, Spain
`jjmerelo@gmail.com`
[2] Department of Graduate Studies, National Technological Institute of Mexico, Tijuana, Mexico

Abstract. Energy-aware computing is the design and operation of hardware and software systems to minimize their energy consumption. This requires consideration of many variables and parameters, making it necessary to focus on a single one or a few to obtain meaningful results; this is why, in this paper, we will investigate the energy consumption of three JavaScript interpreters (bun, node.js, and deno) for evolutionary algorithms (EAs), a type of population-based stochastic optimization algorithm. We expect different energy budgets for running the same EA workload on these interpreters due to their different conceptual designs. We will also compare the energy consumption of the different operators and functions of the EA, to see if there are differences in the energy consumption of the different interpreters. Additionally, we will perform these measurements across different architectures, homogeneous (Intel) and heterogeneous (ARM), to profile their energy consumption. To obtain these results, we will test different tools to measure per-process energy consumption accurately. After choosing a tool, we will perform experiments on a workload similar to an EA to measure the energy consumption of EA-specific functions and operators for different problem sizes. Finally, we will draw a conclusion on which JavaScript interpreter and architecture are the most energy-efficient for EA workloads if energy is a limited concern.

Keywords: Green computing · Metaheuristics · JavaScript · Energy-aware computing · Evolutionary algorithms

1 Introduction

Green computing [20] refers to the design of hardware and/or software systems that are first conscious, and then minimize the environmental impact for a given workload. There are no fixed rules that apply to any field, which is why researchers usually settle on a specific field with well-known sets of algorithms and specific operators, such as evolutionary algorithms or metaheuristics [34]. Even within a narrow field, there are many possible choices. The language used to implement the algorithms is one of them, because implementation matters [30]. Even within a language, there are many possible implementations, including simply the different versions that are periodically published; in some cases, different interpreters or compilers created by different teams with different intents or assumptions will also be available.

© The Author(s), under exclusive license to Springer Nature Switzerland AG 2024
H.-G. Fill et al. (Eds.): ICSOFT 2023, CCIS 2104, pp. 1–18, 2024.
https://doi.org/10.1007/978-3-031-61753-9_1

Our group has a 25-year-long history of working with JavaScript [11,13,15,24,28, 38]. Despite its overall performance not being as good as other languages, given the availability of libraries such as NodEO [28] and the expressiveness and abundance of support for the JavaScript language, the time from idea inception to solution in production can actually be faster than with other languages. Also, given the fact that it can readily run on the browser, it is a good (and probably the only) choice for volunteer computing [23,25].

Its evolution from a single-browser implementation to the many existing today makes it an attractive language to experiment with green computing. This evolution has taken it from a language designed in the late nineties for simple browser widgets and client-side validations [9,14], to being the one most widely used by developers, measured by their GitHub repositories [36], occupying this position since 2014 [35], this popularity is because JavaScript its almost the exclusive language needed for front-end programming (its only competition being mobile application development languages, such as Swift or Kotlin, or languages transpiled to JavaScript, such as Dart or TypeScript), while at the same time being strong for full-stack development, with solid support for the back end, including application servers, middleware, and database programming. Other popularity indices, such as TIOBE[1], that take into account other factors besides lines of code production, currently (October 2023) rank it as the sixth, although it was also the most popular language in 2014. It can be claimed, then, that it is among the most popular, if not the most popular language among developers.

Due to its popularity and the fact that it has a continuously updated standard [7], there have traditionally been different virtual machines (or interpreters) that are able to run JS. In its initial decade, browsers were the only mainstream platform available[2]; however, the introduction of Node.js running on the V8 JavaScript Engine [44] in 2009 gave it the mainstream support it has today. The wide adoption of node.js, along with the ECMA standard, inspired the development new interpreters like deno [6] (written in Rust) and, more recently, bun [45], programmed in the Zig, a relatively new language for systems programming.

No wonder, then, that JavaScript is also a popular language for implementing metaheuristics, especially evolutionary algorithms (EA). EAs [8] are population-based stochastic optimization algorithms based on the representation of a problem as a "chromosome", and the *evolution* of a population of these "chromosomes" by random change (via so-called "genetic" operators such as mutation and crossover), evaluation of those chromosomes by what is often called the "fitness" function, and selection for reproduction of those that achieve the best fitness values, emulating the survival of the fittest of natural evolution. From the early implementations in the browser [12,22,42], whole libraries [40], through complete implementations geared towards volunteer computing [26]. After choosing the language [30], choosing an interpreter is the next decision that will impact whatever objective the researcher wants to reach, whether performance or energy efficiency; this will one of the main focuses of this paper.

---

[1] https://www.tiobe.com/tiobe-index/.

[2] Although there were interpreters such as SpiderMonkey or Rhino available; they were not, however, as popular and mostly unused in production environments.

Since the architecture of the different JS virtual machines is different, and are created with languages with different focus (Rust is focused on memory safety [33], while Zig is centered on simplicity and performance [17]), different energy consumption profiles should be expected. All three interpreters can (roughly) run the same, unmodified source code. What we intend with this paper is to find a rule of thumb on which JS interpreter might give the lowest power consumption, the maximum performance, or both, so that EA practitioners can use it for deploying their applications to production.

In the first version published of this line of research [29], we established a methodology for choosing an energy profile and performance measures in the versions of the interpreters that were current at that time. In this paper we will update the methodology and the results, using the current versions of the interpreters, and extend the methodology to other architectures, namely Apple Silicon, which allows us to gather some insight also on how energy results are achieved for the different virtual machines.

The rest of the paper follows this plan: next, we will present the state of the art; then we will describe the experimental setup in Sect. 3; results will be presented next in Sect. 4, and we will end with a discussion of results, conclusions and future lines of work.

2   State of the Art

The power efficiency of CPUs (computations per kilowatt-hour) has doubled roughly every year and a half from 1946 to 2009 [19], this improvement has been mainly a by-product of Moore's law, the trend of chip manufacturers to decrease in half the size and distance between transistors every two years. Unfortunately, the physical limits of electronics imply that performance is no longer the single metric a processor is judged by; energy efficiency is at least as important an important driver for current innovation; creating the challenge of building more power-efficient systems [39].

This challenge can be addressed at the hardware and software levels. At the hardware level, it is leading towards the development of heterogeneous CPU topologies that typically include two types of cores: "performance" and "efficiency"; while the former vie for executing workloads as fast as possible, the latter are geared towards running them without incurring in high energy costs [2]. Most modern processors, such as the Apple Silicon family, as well as other ARM-based architectures, adopt this kind of architecture. We also find increasingly processors that are designed with machine learning workloads in mind, especially for trained models, such as the Google TPU or the Apple Neural Engine [48]. As the cited paper points out, integrating these elements into algorithm implementations to increase speed and efficiency presents a challenge.

These new challenges are tackled at the software level, with developers proposing increasingly more energy-efficient algorithm implementations. Algorithm comparatives nowadays include power efficiency as a performance metric, these include encryption algorithms [32,43], estimation models for machine learning applications [10] and genetic programming (GP) [5], and code refactoring [37]. Since metaheuristics are so extensively used in machine learning applications, its interest in research has grown in parallel to its number of applications. Many papers focus on analyzing how certain metaheuristics parameters have an impact on energy consumption.

Díaz-Álvarez et al. [4] study how the population's size in genetic programming influences power consumption. In an earlier work, centered on genetic algorithms (GAs) [47], power-consumption of battery-powered devices was measured for various parameter configurations including chromosome and population sizes. The experiments used the OneMax and Trap function benchmark problems, and they concluded that execution time and energy consumption do not linearly correlate and there is a connection between the GA parameters and power consumption. In GAs, the mutation operator appears to be a power-hungry component according to Abdelhafez et al. [1], in their paper, they also report that in a distributed evaluation setting, the communication scheme has a greater impact. Fernández de Vega et al. [46] experimented with different parameters for a GP algorithm and concluded that hand-held devices and single-board computers (SBCs) require an order of magnitude less energy to run the same algorithm.

Of course, it is also a challenge to check how the software and hardware architecture interact so that effectively the most efficient configuration is used for every kind of workload. This is why, in this paper, we will focus on the software side of the equation, and check how different JS interpreters perform when running the same workload, as well as how they interact with the "performance" and "efficiency" hardware cores of the Apple Silicon M1 processor.

3   Methodology and Experimental Setup

In this section, we will first present what can be measured and how it can be done in the two platforms targeted in this paper, Intel and Apple Silicon; then we will briefly describe how the experiments are run and the output is processed in Subsect. 3.3.

3.1   Measurements on an Intel-Based Platform

There are many ways to measure the consumption of applications running in a computer; besides measuring directly from the power intake, those running as applications and tapping the computer sensors fall roughly into two fields: power monitors and energy profilers [3]. Power monitors need additional hardware to measure the power drawn by the whole machine; besides being expensive, their setup is difficult, and it is complicated to measure precisely how much a specific process consumes.

On the other hand, energy profilers are programs that draw information from hardware sensors [41], generally exposed through kernel calls or higher-level wrapper libraries, to pinpoint consumption by specific processes in a time period. Tools that give these measures, either with a graphic or a command line interface, have been available for some time already, and have become more popular lately. One of the mainstream processor architectures, Intel, includes an interface called RAPL, or Running Average Power Limit [16]. Essentially, it consists of a series of machine-specific registers (MSRs) that contain information on the wattage drawn by different parts of the architecture; the content of these registers will be processed (through the corresponding library) and consumed by different command line utilities. We will use these command-line utilities since they produce an output that can be automatically processed and evaluated, which is what we are looking for in this paper[3].

Energy profiles, as measured by RAPL or other APIs, include different *domains* [18], essentially the computing devices or peripherals requiring the reported amount of energy. DRAM or dynamic RAM, CORE, or GPU will report what happens on those specific devices, with a core being every one of the computing units within the central processing unit; other domains, like PKG or package, will report what happens in the "package", or CPU together with other devices in the chipset.

Different measuring command line tools were tested in [29], finally choosing pinpoint [21] (available from https://github.com/osmhpi/pinpoint), which is a tool that uses the RAPL interface, as well as the NVIDIA registers, and reports the power consumed by these devices.

3.2 Measurements on the Apple Silicon Platform

The Apple Silicon processor line is a series of ARM-based processors designed by Apple for their laptops and desktop computers. The architecture is fundamentally different from the x86 one that we have mentioned above, and has been designed with energy efficiency in mind. The processor has two kinds of cores: performance cores (or P-Cores) which include hyperthreading and are designed mainly for high-performance workloads, and efficiency cores (or E-Cores) which use less power. Which processors run the actual process is up to the operating system; besides the GPU, Apple Silicon also includes something called the Apple Neural Engine, which is a kind of tensor processing unit that works under some very specific conditions. These last two subsystems are not relevant for the purposes of this paper, but we are anyway interested in the kind of sensors that are available to measure power consumption for our workload.

The operating system has a set of parameters that fall under the management of the so-called IOReport subsystem. This includes access to many different metrics, but also to the ones we are interested in general power consumption, as well as the activity of P- and E- cores. As in the case of the RAPL metrics, there are several command-line tools that can be used to record them during the execution of our workload:

- powermetrics is a command line tool that can be used to record the power consumption of the whole system, as well as the activity of the P- and E-cores. It's not designed to record specific commands, but it can be run in the background while we run other processes, showing measures with the sampling rate that is desired.
- pinpoint, in its most recent versions[4], is also able to capture these metrics, with an output that has the same format as it does for other platforms and uses the same metrics.

---

[3] Systems based on the AMD architecture have a similar power profiling system called AMP with its corresponding command line tool. However, we found that it was not well documented, and excessively complicated for the purposes of this article. Although not as complete, AMD processors also include the aforementioned MSRs so RAPL-based utilities can run on them.

[4] As a matter of fact, the code was incorporated in October 2023.

Of these two, we will use pinpoint for the same reasons as in the case of the Intel platform: it is easier to process the output, with no need to start and stop the process before and after the command we are measuring finishes, incurring thus in a certain amount of overhead. We can also leverage all the scripts that we had created for processing the other platform's output.

3.3 Running the Experiments and Processing the Results

A Perl script was created to perform the experiments; it launched the scripts and collected results by analyzing the standard output and putting it in a CSV format that would allow examination of the experiments.

The initial experiment consisted of a script that used the saco-js library to perform the union of "bags", sets that can hold several copies of the same item. 1024 sets were generated; these sets had 1024, 2048, 4096 elements. Then, a union of bags was performed on pairs of sets until there was only one left. This is similar to some operations performed by EAs, mainly related to merging populations. They do not involve floating-point operations in any way.

The scripts that launched every kind of tool were slightly different, mainly because the output needed to be processed in different ways (and different kinds of information extracted). Additionally, pinpoint, which is the only tool that does not need superuser privileges, sometimes returned 0 in energy measures. This was an error, and those runs were discarded.

Finally, the scripts performed an additional task: since it is not possible to disaggregate the readings for our program from the energy consumed by other processes running at the same time, what we did was to run every program 15 times, compute the average time, and then use the same tool to measure the energy consumption for the sleep program during the average amount of time. The energy readings shown are the result of subtracting this measurement from every one of the 15 other measurements taken so that we can analyze the differential of energy that has been consumed by our programs; the result is clipped at 0, since negative energy differentials would make no sense.

4   Experimental Results

On the JavaScript side, we used three different interpreters:

- bun version 1.0.7
- deno version 1.37.2, which includes the v8 library version 11.8.172.13 and typescript 5.2.2
- node.js version 20.9.0

bun and nodejs are fully compatible, so they run exactly the same code. The code for deno needed a small modification: the path to the library had to be changed (since it does not use the node_modules to host installed modules), and it uses a different library for processing the command line arguments. Other than that, the business logic was exactly the same.

These were running in an Ubuntu version 20.04.1 with kernel version 5.15.0-69. The processor is an AMD Ryzen 9 3950X 16-Core. Since we will not be testing in a pure Intel architecture, the complete RAPL API is not going to be available; that is also why we will be experimenting with different tools so that we can have an adequate coverage of energy consumption for the commands we will be measuring.

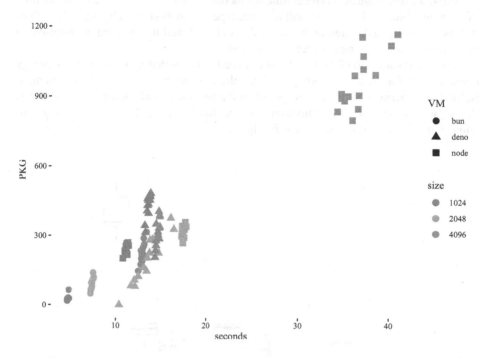

Fig. 1. Boxplot of energy consumption vs. time taken for all three sizes and VMs.

As was done in [27], which was focused on wall clock performance, the experiments will be focused on the key operations performed by an EA: evaluation of fitness and "genetic" operators like mutation and crossover. We will first measure again the performance of the three interpreters involved, and then compare these new measurements to old versions of the same VMs.

4.1 Comparing Performance of JS Interpreters

We will repeat the setup in the initial exploration, to check the energy consumption for the processing of 40000 chromosomes, a number chosen to take a sizable amount of memory, but also on the ballpark of the usual number of operations in an EA benchmark, it is also compact enough to avoid issues with garbage collection in memory, something that was detected after the initial exploration. Experiments were repeated for the same chromosome size as before, 1024, 2048, and 4096, and for the three JS virtual machines used. Although the business logic is exactly the same for the experiments, the script has two versions, one for deno and the other for bun/node, due to the different way they have of reading command-line arguments. This does not affect the overhead in any way. Code, as well as the data resulted from the experiments and analyzed in this paper, are released with a free license (along with this paper) from the repository https://github. com/JJ/energy-ga-icsoft-2023.

First, we will evaluate a typical fitness function, OneMax, which counts the number of ones in a binary (1 s and 0 s) string. This type of function, which check the values of bits in a string and assign an integer value to it, is found in many papers focused on evaluating EAs, including parallel versions [31].

The results are shown in Fig. 1. This already shows that time, as well as energy consumption, for node is higher; just check the separation of the squares representing individual experiments in that interpreter to the rest of the values for the same color; this separation increases with chromosome size. But this paper focuses on energy consumption, which we summarize next in Fig. 2.

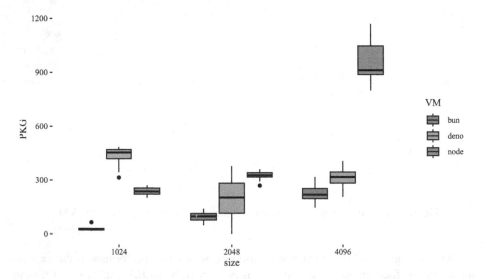

Fig. 2. Boxplot of PKG measurements for the OneMax problem and the three different virtual machines.

The figure shows the almost-flat growth of energy consumption for bun. How consumption grows for deno is weird, since it takes less energy when the chromosome is bigger (4096). Once again, node is the bigger energy guzzler, consuming up to 3 times more than deno on average, and more than 6 times as much as bun. We will see how this is reflected in monetary terms, taking into account that the cost in Spain today is around 0.2/kWh. This cost, shown in Table 1, reaches almost one-hundredth of a euro for the most "expensive" VM, node; that gives you an idea of the kind of cost the algorithms have, and also how this cost decreases almost an order of magnitude if bun is used.

Table 1. Estimated cost of the OneMax runs for every VM and size, in-cents.

size	VM	average	sd
1024	bun	0.0001539	0.0000619
1024	deno	0.0024187	0.0002792
1024	node	0.0013258	0.0001140
2048	bun	0.0005347	0.0001334
2048	deno	0.0010807	0.0005901
2048	node	0.0017962	0.0001288
4096	bun	0.0012538	0.0002453
4096	deno	0.0017395	0.0003150
4096	node	0.0053656	0.0006608

The crossover operation involves copy operations between strings, as well as the creation of new strings. We will again generate 40K chromosomes and group them in pairs; these strings will be crossed by interchanging a random fragment from one to the other and back. The resulting pairs will be stored in an array, which is eventually printed. The result of every experiment is shown in an energy vs. wall clock time chart in Fig. 3.

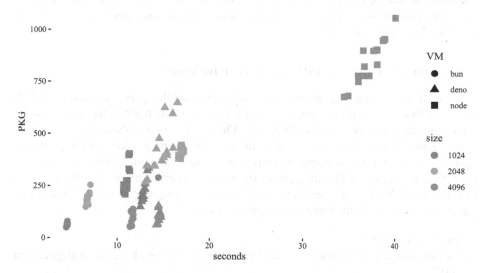

Fig. 3. PKG consumption, in Joules, vs. time in seconds, for the crossover and the three different virtual machines.

The scenario is remarkably similar to the one shown in Fig. 1. In the two cases, bun achieves the top performance and lowest energy consumption, and node is the worst. Average energy consumption is shown as a boxplot in Fig. 4.

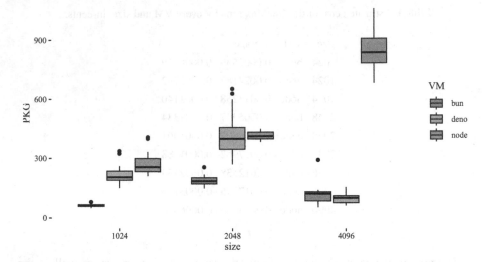

Fig. 4. Boxplot of PKG measurements for the crossover operator and the three different virtual machines.

Here we can see again the surprising fact that deno takes the same amount of energy, on average, as node for size 2048, in a similar case to what happened for OneMax (shown in Fig. 2). The difference between the thriftiest, bun, and the heaviest consumer, node, is approximately three times, in this case, less than in the case of the OneMax fitness function.

4.2 Comparison Between Different Interpreter Versions

Since [29] was written, the interpreters used in that and this paper have evolved; bun has gone from beta to production with its 1.0 version, while node.js has gone from its LTS (long-term support) version 18 to 20. While new versions always try to improve performance, it is not a given that they do so while keeping a low-energy profile or optimizing for energy consumption in any way. In this subsection, we will compare the energy consumption of the different versions of the interpreters used in the previous installment of this line of research to see if there are any significant differences. In that paper, the versions for the three JS interpreters were:

- bun version 0.5.8
- deno version 1.32.1, which includes the v8 library version 11.2.214.9 and typescript 5.0.2
- node.js version 18.5.0

Current versions, up-to-date by November 1st 2023, are shown above in Sect. 4.

In Table 2, we can see the ratio of energy consumption for these old versions vs. the new ones; it is obvious that there are changes, and mostly improvements, making new versions better for green computing; however, there are differences across interpreters,

Table 2. Ratio of PKG energy consumption, new version vs. old version for OneMax and crossover.

VM	Size	OneMax	Crossover
1024	bun	0.1409633	0.5152208
1024	deno	1.5822899	1.2619724
1024	node	0.5890714	1.0223690
2048	bun	0.3585723	1.1748255
2048	deno	0.2919937	0.7837860
2048	node	0.4859071	0.9041335
4096	bun	0.7590040	0.3560366
4096	deno	0.5565258	0.2731623
4096	node	0.5658727	0.8536361

sizes, and the workload involved. While in general bun spends less energy, sometimes remarkably so, like in the case of the OneMax function and the smallest size, there are cases, like Crossover for the medium size, where it can be slightly worse. deno is the interpreter that has the most irregular energy consumption changes; while it is remarkably worse for the smallest size, it shows very good improvements in the others. node.js shows a more consistent improvement, improving energy consumption by roughly 50% in the case of OneMax, and slight improvements of around 10% in the case of Crossover.

This tells us that, in general, we should always try to use the latest version of the interpreter, as it will most likely be more energy efficient. However, benchmarking these new versions is still necessary, as there are cases where the new version is not better than the old one. At the same time, these results confirm that bun, even after the introduction of the 1.0 version, is still the most energy-efficient interpreter, and it is probably a reasonable rule-of-thumb to make it our first choice when dealing with evolutionary algorithms workloads.

As has been indicated earlier, Apple Macs have a different architecture, called Apple Silicon, using heterogeneous cores, the "P" and "E" cores. The chosen tool, pinpoint, yields measurements for every code subset, as well as DRAM; we have performed a series of measurements with these interpreter versions:

- bun version 1.0.9
- deno version 1.36.4
- node.js version 20.9.0

As in the previous cases, we have performed measurements for the OneMax fitness function and the Crossover operator; the platform was a MacBook Air M1 with 16 GB of RAM and macOS Ventura 13.2.1. The results are shown in Fig. 5 and Fig. 6.

The situation shown in that figure is remarkably similar, in the sense that node.js consumes more energy than the other two, and bun is at the same time faster and consumes less energy. There are, however, some specifics in how Apple Silicon measures

Fig. 5. Boxplot of energy consumption for the OneMax fitness function: RAM (left), "efficiency" CPUs (middle), "performance CPUs" (right) vs. time taken for all three sizes and VMs, in a Mac.

and spends the energy; from left to right, we can see that the *scale* of the three charts is quite different: the bulk of the energy is spent by the "P" cores, that is, the performance cores. The same happens in the case of Crossover, shown in Fig. 6. This implies that, for this workload, the "E" cores are used at a very low level, if at all. The total energy spent by the cores is also much higher than the one spent by the RAM.

Fig. 6. Boxplot of energy consumption for the crossover operator in RAM (left), "efficiency" CPUs (middle), "performance CPUs" (right) vs. time taken for all three sizes and VMs, in a Mac.

We will try to compare this energy profile with the one obtained previously in an Unix machine with an AMD processor. Although they are not entirely comparable, PKG is equivalent to the sum of P and E cores.

What we see in Table 3 is that, in all cases, the workload under study consumes less energy in the Apple Silicon architecture than in the desktop machine. A priori, this should be expected, since energy management is one of the features of portable machines, and is probably not exclusive of Apple Silicon. What is surprising, however, is that in some cases the improvement is quite significant: the crossover operation performed by node.js can spend 9 times less energy in the Apple Silicon device; One-Max more or less the same in deno. Even bun, characterized by the lowest energy profile, can spend even less energy in this case; for instance, on average bun will

Table 3. Ratio of CPU energy consumed by the desktop machine over the MacAir with Apple Silicon M1.

VM	Size	OneMax	Crossover
1024	bun	1.468400	3.320168
1024	deno	9.516335	4.865280
1024	node	7.786783	9.003350
2048	bun	3.199349	6.283378
2048	deno	3.051165	6.642003
2048	node	5.788639	7.373402
4096	bun	4.018065	2.065695
4096	deno	5.287960	1.674841
4096	node	3.981288	3.492605

spend 18.8713333 J in the MacBook Air for OneMax with 1024 bits, while the desktop machine will spend 27.7106667 J.

What is remarkable, in this case, is also that the laptop is *faster*, with the workload taking on average 3.297769 s on the MacBook Air for OneMax with 1024 bits, and 4.7860919 in the other case; all across the board, the MacBook Air is faster.

5   Conclusions

This paper investigates the energy efficiency of various JavaScript interpreters and architectures under Evolutionary Algorithm (EA) workloads. We analyze the energy consumption of brief scripts extensively used within these algorithms and how these energy expenses scale as the chromosome size increases. We have developed a methodology that enables the precise measurement of energy consumption for individual processes; we also adopted a multi-platform tool, `pinpoint`, that can give accurate estimations of sensor readings, discarding experiments where that estimation was not adequate; we calibrated this tool by comparing its readings with other tools, which were also evaluated for the same purpose and eventually discarded. Further, we adopted a benchmarking strategy akin to the one used to measure performance, enabling us to pinpoint energy expenditure for specific operations while discarding the noise produced by executing a complete algorithm. Such an approach excludes the interference of different operations, applied in different proportions, that could obfuscate actual energy costs when blended within the whole algorithm. Testing short code paths, consistent with the suggestions of [16], makes it easier to understand their individual contribution to the overall consumption of the algorithm, thus paving the way for more targeted optimization-either by refining the code itself or by adjusting its frequency within the algorithm.

During the exploratory data analysis, we have established that, in Linux and MacOS machines, `pinpoint` can be profitably used to measure per-process energy consumption, as long as these measurements are repeated and the process themselves include short snippets of business logic; this tool should be preferred over others that are either less accurate or simply take into account different aspects of energy consumption.

The core objective of this paper, however, was to check which JavaScript interpreter and computing architecture are optimal for minimizing energy consumption; the experiments have reliably confirmed bun to be the superior interpreter across all tested architectures. It not only consumes less energy for all the range of chromosome sizes; it also exhibits enhanced time efficiency and can run applications written for Node (mostly) unmodified; its consumption also scales better with problem size. These advantages may stem from its design philosophy and the use of Zig. This language prioritizes compile-time safety and manual memory allocation by default and avoids hidden control flow. With bun recently achieving its 1.0 milestone, it is our pick for workloads of this kind.

If using bun is an issue, deno might be a good alternative. Except in very specific cases, it is going to be faster and consume less energy than node, even more so when memory requirements are high. According to our initial exploration, it will also consume less energy *per second*; thus for workloads that take roughly the same time, it will be a better candidate than node. As an inconvenience, it needs minor modifications for the code to run, at least if you need core or other kinds of external libraries; its core library modules are different from those used in node/bun, although that need not be a disadvantage per se, since it is not complicated to design algorithmic code that is interpreter-independent.

The previous two points imply that energy-wise (or even performance-wise), there are no good reasons to use node.js for running EAs. Except if the business logic uses specific, early-adoption, or some features that, for some reason, do not work with bun yet, we advise anyone to keep using bun for these kinds of workloads.

By testing different versions of the interpreters, we can affirm also that the advantage of bun over the other interpreter is consistent in time; in some cases there are dramatic reductions in consumption in new versions. However, it is also true that bun has gone from beta to production, so the same kind of reductions might not be expected in the near future. Since it is impossible to preview whether energy consumption optimization will proceed at the same rate for every other interpreter, we will still need to test new versions, maybe under a reduced benchmark. The interpreter architecture, which is based in three different languages, might still give some edge for bun over deno and for this one over node.js. But in absence of any principled certainty on this, we can only advice to keep benchmarking new versions of the interpreters for the workloads we are interested with, maybe in small samples so that decisions can be made quickly.

As we have indicated in the experimental section, the extensive advantage that bun has over the other interpreters does not leave much room for adopting different benchmarks that could make that ranking vary; at any rate, these experiments have shown how much faster and energy-saving bun is (from 1/3 to 1/6 the energy consumed by node). Still, it would be interesting to know what happens to this gap under different operations like selection or a different kind of mutation.

Another interesting avenue of research is the way different architectures affect energy consumption, not only at the processor design level but also at the machine design level. Other computers with different cooling strategies, passive or active, will spend energy differently and interact with workloads and interpreters in non-trivial ways. Even an architecture, like the Apple Silicon M1, in a non-professional laptop can outperform a professional workstation desktop computer and consume less energy in the process. Since researchers generally have different kinds of computers available, our measurements here indicate that, whenever possible, the Apple Silicon M1 architecture should be preferred.

Although Evolutionary Algorithms (EAs) typically do not rely on GPUs, certain fitness functions operating on floating-point numbers may benefit from GPU acceleration. Investigating how JavaScript interpreters manage such tasks when leveraging GPU capabilities presents an intriguing avenue for future research; how interpreters work in this area could be an interesting future line of work; additionally to GPUs, Apple includes what is called the Apple Neural Engine. Although this is geared mainly towards tensor processing, implementing EAs on this platform is a challenge due to its specialized focus. Nonetheless, exploring its application in this context and assessing the impact on energy consumption would be a valuable contribution to the field.

In this paper, mutation is not examined as a micro-operation, it will likely not have much influence; however, other operations like selection, with more complexity, require energy expenses that scale in a wholly different way. In general, building up a more general instance of a single generation in an evolutionary algorithm will give us a broader perspective on energy profiles without losing sight of the individual operations that make it up and the specific energy costs of each of them. At the same time, in this paper, we have experimented with a single data structure to represent the chromosomes; current EAs use additional data structures, and they will have different energy profiles. Fixing other parameters (like interpreters and architecture) and working on them will also give us a path for making evolutionary algorithms greener.

Acknowledgements. This work is supported by the Ministerio Español de Economía y Competitividad (Spanish Ministry of Competitivity and Economy) under project PID2020-115570GB-C22 (DemocratAI::UGR) and Project 18186.23-P of 2023 TecNM research grants.

References

1. Abdelhafez, A., Alba, E., Luque, G.: A component-based study of energy consumption for sequential and parallel genetic algorithms. J. Supercomput. **75**, 6194–6219 (2019)
2. Ali, Z., Tanveer, T., Aziz, S., Usman, M., Azam, A.: Reassessing the performance of arm vs x86 with recent technological shift of apple. In: 2022 International Conference on IT and Industrial Technologies (ICIT), pp. 01–06 (2022). https://doi.org/10.1109/ICIT56493.2022.9988933
3. Cruz, L.: Tools to measure software energy consumption from your computer, July 2021. https://luiscruz.github.io/2021/07/20/measuring-energy.html
4. Díaz-Álvarez, J., Castillo, P.A., Fernandez de Vega, F., Chávez, F., Alvarado, J.: Population size influence on the energy consumption of genetic programming. Measur. Control **55**(1–2), 102–115 (2022)
5. Diaz Alvarez, J., Castillo Martínez, P.A., Rodríguez Díaz, F.J., Fernández de Vega, F., et al.: A fuzzy rule-based system to predict energy consumption of genetic programming algorithms (2018)
6. Doglio, F.: Introducing Deno

7. ECMA: 262: ECMAScript language specification. ECMA (European Association for Standardizing Information and Communication Systems), pub-ECMA: adr (1999)
8. Eiben, A.E., Smith, J.E.: What is an evolutionary algorithm? In: Introduction to Evolutionary Computing. NCS, pp. 25–48. Springer, Heidelberg (2015). https://doi.org/10.1007/978-3-662-44874-8_3
9. Flanagan, D.: JavaScript. O'Reilly (1998)
10. García-Martín, E., Rodrigues, C.F., Riley, G., Grahn, H.: Estimation of energy consumption in machine learning. J. Parallel Distrib. Comput. **134**, 75–88 (2019)
11. García-Valdez, M., Trujillo, L., Fernández de Vega, F., Merelo Guervós, J.J., Olague, G.: EvoSpace: a distributed evolutionary platform based on the tuple space model. In: Esparcia-Alcázar, A.I. (ed.) EvoApplications 2013. LNCS, vol. 7835, pp. 499–508. Springer, Heidelberg (2013). https://doi.org/10.1007/978-3-642-37192-9_50
12. González, J., Merelo, J.J., Castillo, P.A., Rivas, V., Romero, G.: Optimizing web newspaper layout using simulated annealing. In: Mira, J., Sánchez-Andrés, J.V. (eds.) IWANN 1999. LNCS, vol. 1607, pp. 759–768. Springer, Heidelberg (1999). https://doi.org/10.1007/BFb0100543
13. González, J., Rojas, I., Pomares, H., Salmerón, M., Merelo-Guerv'os, J.J.: Web newspaper layout optimization using Simulated Annealing. IEEE Trans. Syst. Man Cybern. B **32**(5), 686–690 (2002). http://ieeexplore.ieee.org/iel5/3477/22189/01033189.pdf
14. Goodman, D., Morrison, M., Eich, B.: JavaScript® Bible. Wiley, New York, NY, USA (2007)
15. Guervós, J.J.M., Castillo, P.A., Mora, A.M., Esparcia-Alcázar, A.I., Santos, V.M.R.: Assessing different architectures for evolutionary algorithms in JavaScript. In: Arnold, D.V., Alba, E. (eds.) Genetic and Evolutionary Computation Conference, GECCO 2014, Vancouver, BC, Canada, 12–16 July 2014. Companion Material Proceedings, pp. 119–120. ACM (2014). https://doi.org/10.1145/2598394.2598460
16. Hähnel, M., Döbel, B., Völp, M., Härtig, H.: Measuring energy consumption for short code paths using RAPL. SIGMETRICS Perform. Eval. Rev. **40**(3), 13–17 (2012). https://doi.org/10.1145/2425248.2425252
17. Kelley, A.: Introduction to the zig programming language, February 2019. https://andrewkelley.me/post/intro-to-zig.html
18. Khan, K.N., et al.: Energy profiling using IgProf. In: 2015 15th IEEE/ACM International Symposium on Cluster, Cloud and Grid Computing, pp. 1115–1118. IEEE (2015)
19. Koomey, J.G., Berard, S., Sanchez, M., Wong, H.: Web extra appendix: implications of historical trends in the electrical efficiency of computing. IEEE Ann. Hist. Comput. **33**(3), S1–S30 (2011)
20. Kurp, P.: Green computing. Commun. ACM **51**(10), 11–13 (2008)
21. Köhler, S., et al.: Pinpoint the joules: unifying runtime-support for energy measurements on heterogeneous systems. In: 2020 IEEE/ACM International Workshop on Runtime and Operating Systems for Supercomputers (ROSS), pp. 31–40 (2020). https://doi.org/10.1109/ROSS51935.2020.00009
22. Langdon, W.B.: Global distributed evolution of L-systems fractals. In: Keijzer, M., O'Reilly, U.-M., Lucas, S., Costa, E., Soule, T. (eds.) EuroGP 2004. LNCS, vol. 3003, pp. 349–358. Springer, Heidelberg (2004). https://doi.org/10.1007/978-3-540-24650-3_33
23. Laredo, J.L.J., et al.: Designing robust volunteer-based evolutionary algorithms. Genet. Programm. Evolvable Mach. **15**(3), 221–244 (2014). https://doi.org/10.1007/s10710-014-9213-5
24. Merelo, J.J., Castillo, P., Laredo, J., Mora, A., Prieto, A.: Asynchronous distributed genetic algorithms with JavaScript and JSON. In: WCCI 2008 Proceedings, pp. 1372–1379. IEEE Press (2008). http://atc.ugr.es/I+D+i/congresos/2008/CEC_2008_1372.pdf

25. Merelo, J.J., García, A.M., Laredo, J.L.J., Lupión, J., Tricas, F.: Browser-based distributed evolutionary computation: performance and scaling behavior. In: GECCO 2007: Proceedings of the 2007 GECCO Conference Companion on Genetic and Evolutionary Computation, pp. 2851–2858. ACM Press, New York, NY, USA (2007). https://doi.org/10.1145/1274000.1274083

26. Merelo, J.J., García-Valdez, M., Castillo, P.A., García-Sánchez, P., de las Cuevas, P., Rico, N.: NodIO, a JavaScript framework for volunteer-based evolutionary algorithms: first results. ArXiv e-prints, January 2016. http://arxiv.org/abs/1601.01607

27. Merelo, J.J., et al.: Benchmarking languages for evolutionary algorithms. In: Squillero, G., Burelli, P. (eds.) EvoApplications 2016. LNCS, vol. 9598, pp. 27–41. Springer, Cham (2016). https://doi.org/10.1007/978-3-319-31153-1_3

28. Merelo Guervós, J.J.: NodEO, a evolutionary algorithm library in node. Technical report, GeNeura group, March 2014. https://doi.org/10.6084/m9.figshare.972892. http://figshare.com/articles/nodeo/972892

29. Merelo-Guervós, J.J., García-Valdez, M., Castillo, P.A.: An analysis of energy consumption of JavaScript interpreters with evolutionary algorithm workloads. In: Fill, H., Mayo, F.J.D., van Sinderen, M., Maciaszek, L.A. (eds.) Proceedings of the 18th International Conference on Software Technologies, ICSOFT 2023, Rome, Italy, 10–12 July 2023, pp. 175–184. SCITEPRESS (2023). https://doi.org/10.5220/0012128100003538

30. Merelo, J.J., Romero, G., Arenas, M.G., Castillo, P.A., Mora, A.M., Laredo, J.L.J.: Implementation matters: programming best practices for evolutionary algorithms. In: Cabestany, J., Rojas, I., Joya, G. (eds.) IWANN 2011. LNCS, vol. 6692, pp. 333–340. Springer, Heidelberg (2011). https://doi.org/10.1007/978-3-642-21498-1_42

31. Merelo Guervós, J.J., Valdez, J.M.G.: Performance improvements of evolutionary algorithms in Perl 6. In: Aguirre, H.E., Takadama, K. (eds.) Proceedings of the Genetic and Evolutionary Computation Conference Companion, GECCO 2018, Kyoto, Japan, 15–19 July 2018, pp. 1371–1378. ACM (2018). https://doi.org/10.1145/3205651.3208273. http://doi.acm.org/10.1145/3205651.3208273

32. Mota, A.V., Azam, S., Shanmugam, B., Yeo, K.C., Kannoorpatti, K.: Comparative analysis of different techniques of encryption for secured data transmission. In: 2017 IEEE International Conference on Power, Control, Signals and Instrumentation Engineering (ICPCSI), pp. 231–237. IEEE (2017)

33. Noseda, M., Frei, F., Rüst, A., Künzli, S.: Rust for secure IoT applications: why C is getting rusty. In: Embedded World Conference 2022, Nuremberg, 21–23 June 2022. WEKA (2022)

34. Novoa-Hernández, P., Puris, A., Pelta, D.A.: Measuring the environmental cost in the evaluation of metaheuristics. In: 19th World Congress of the International Fuzzy Systems Association (IFSA), 12th Conference of the European Society for Fuzzy Logic and Technology (EUSFLAT), and 11th International Summer School on Aggregation Operators (AGOP), pp. 203–210. Atlantis Press (2021)

35. O'Grady, S.: The RedMonk programming language rankings: January 2014. Tecosystems blog, January 2014. http://redmonk.com/sogrady/2014/01/22/language-rankings-1-14/

36. O'Grady, S.: The RedMonk programming language rankings: January 2023. Tecosystems blog, May 2023. https://redmonk.com/sogrady/2023/05/16/language-rankings-1-23/

37. Ournani, Z., Rouvoy, R., Rust, P., Penhoat, J.: Tales from the code# 1: the effective impact of code refactorings on software energy consumption. In: ICSOFT 2021-16th International Conference on Software Technologies (2021)

38. Peñalver, J.G., Merelo, J.J.: Optimizing web page layout using an annealed genetic algorithm as client-side script. In: Eiben, A.E., Bäck, T., Schoenauer, M., Schwefel, H.-P. (eds.) PPSN 1998. LNCS, vol. 1498, pp. 1018–1027. Springer, Heidelberg (1998). https://doi.org/10.1007/BFb0056943. http://www.springerlink.com/link.asp?id=2gqqar9cv3et5nlg

39. Richard, C.: System Architecture and Integration, pp. 155–174. Apress, Berkeley, CA (2023). https://doi.org/10.1007/978-1-4842-8847-4_8
40. Rivas, V.M., Guervós, J.J.M., López, G.R., Arenas-García, M., Mora, A.M.: An object-oriented library in JavaScript to build modular and flexible cross-platform evolutionary algorithms. In: Esparcia-Alcázar, A.I., Mora, A.M. (eds.) EvoApplications 2014. LNCS, vol. 8602, pp. 853–862. Springer, Heidelberg (2014). https://doi.org/10.1007/978-3-662-45523-4_69
41. Sinha, A., Chandrakasan, A.P.: JouleTrack: a web based tool for software energy profiling. In: Proceedings of the 38th Annual Design Automation Conference, pp. 220–225 (2001)
42. Smith, J., Sugihara, K.: GA toolkit on the web. In: Proceedings of the First Online Workshop on Soft Computing, p. 12 (1996). http://citeseerx.ist.psu.edu/viewdoc/summary?doi=10.1.1.48.8320
43. Thakor, V.A., Razzaque, M.A., Khandaker, M.R.: Lightweight cryptography algorithms for resource-constrained IoT devices: a review, comparison and research opportunities. IEEE Access 9, 28177–28193 (2021)
44. Tilkov, S., Vinoski, S.: Node.js: using JavaScript to build high-performance network programs. IEEE Internet Comput. 14(6), 80–83 (2010). https://doi.org/10.1109/MIC.2010.145
45. Tomar, D.: Bun JS: a brand-new, lightning-quick JavaScript runtime. Medium (2022). https://devangtomar.medium.com/bun-a-brand-new-lightning-quick-javascript-runtime-e42119a306ca
46. de Vega, F.F., et al.: A cross-platform assessment of energy consumption in evolutionary algorithms. In: Handl, J., Hart, E., Lewis, P.R., López-Ibáñez, M., Ochoa, G., Paechter, B. (eds.) PPSN 2016. LNCS, vol. 9921, pp. 548–557. Springer, Cham (2016). https://doi.org/10.1007/978-3-319-45823-6_51
47. Fernández de Vega, F., Díaz, J., García, J.Á., Chávez, F., Alvarado, J.: Looking for energy efficient genetic algorithms. In: Idoumghar, L., Legrand, P., Liefooghe, A., Lutton, E., Monmarché, N., Schoenauer, M. (eds.) EA 2019. LNCS, vol. 12052, pp. 96–109. Springer, Cham (2020). https://doi.org/10.1007/978-3-030-45715-0_8
48. Verhelst, M., Shi, M., Mei, L.: ML processors are going multi-core: a performance dream or a scheduling nightmare? IEEE Solid-State Circuits Mag. 14(4), 18–27 (2022). https://doi.org/10.1109/MSSC.2022.3201783

Low-Modeling of Software Systems

Jordi Cabot[1,2(✉)]

[1] Luxembourg Institute of Science and Technology, Esch-sur-Alzette, Luxembourg
jordi.cabot@list.lu
[2] University of Luxemrbourg, Esch-sur-Alzette, Luxembourg

Abstract. There is a growing need for better development methods and tools to keep up with the increasing complexity of new software systems. New types of user interfaces, the need for intelligent components, sustainability concerns, ... bring new challenges that we need to handle. In the last years, model-driven engineering has been key to improving the quality and productivity of software development, but models themselves are becoming increasingly complex to specify and manage. In this paper, we present the concept of *low-modeling* as a solution to enhance current model-driven engineering techniques and get them ready for this new generation of software systems.

Keywords: Low-modeling · Low-code · DSL · Artificial Intelligence · Model-Driven

1 Introduction

Current software development projects face a growing demand for advanced features. Including support for new types of user interfaces (augmented reality, virtual reality, chat and voice interfaces, ...), intelligent behaviour to be able to classify/predict/ recommend information based on user's input or the need to face new security and sustainability concerns, among many other new types of requirements.

To tame this complexity, software engineers typically choose to work at a higher abstraction level [2] where technical details can be ignored, at least during the initial development phases. *Low-code platforms* are the latest incarnation of this trend, promising to accelerate software delivery by dramatically reducing the amount of hand-coding required. Low-code can be seen as a continuation or specific style of other model-based[1] approaches [4], where high-level software specifications are used to (semi)automatically generate the running software system.

Nevertheless, even software models are becoming more and more complex due to the increasing complexity of the underlying systems being modeled. Beyond "classical" data and behavioural aspects we now need to come up with new models to define the new types of UIs or all the smart features of the software. Note that AI elements are hard to specify [14], architect, test and verify [15] and low-code systems have so far paid little attention to the modeling and development of smart systems.

---

[1] Here we are referring to *software models* (*e.g.*, state machine diagrams), not Machine Learning models.

© The Author(s), under exclusive license to Springer Nature Switzerland AG 2024
H.-G. Fill et al. (Eds.): ICSOFT 2023, CCIS 2104, pp. 19–28, 2024.
https://doi.org/10.1007/978-3-031-61753-9_2

In this sense, we argue for the need of *low-modeling* techniques that accelerate the modeling process from which then the system will be generated.

The next sections define the concept of low-modeling (Sect. 2) and describe a number of low-modeling strategies (Sect. 3). We then illustrate the benefits of low-modeling through a specific case study (Sect. 4) and provide a very brief introduction of an ongoing low-modeling platform project (Sect. 5).

2   Low Modeling Definition

The Forrester Report [16] states that low-code application platforms accelerate app delivery by dramatically reducing the amount of hand-coding required. Similarly, we define *low-modeling* as the *set of strategies that accelerate the modeling of a software system by dramatically reducing the amount of hand-modeling required.*

Often, a low-modeling platform will also follow a low-code approach to generate the final software code from the (semi)automatically generated models.

Low-modeling can also improve the adoption of modeling in companies and organizations. It is well accepted that the adoption challenge is a complex sociotechnical problem [10]. And it is aggravated when considering that software is now being developed by multidisciplinary teams, e.g to deal with the specification and development of the intelligent components embedded in most new systems. In this sense, the goal of low-modeling is not only to increase the productivity of developer teams, but also to contribute to the democratization of software development by enabling all types of professionals to participate in the development process and even build their own applications beyond what low-code, no-code and template-based approaches offer.

3   Low Modeling Strategies

This section gives a short overview of several strategies that could be employed to put in place a low-modeling strategy. Similarly to low-code approaches where code is semi-automatically generated from "earlier" sources (i.e. models in that case), in a low-modeling approach we will see how models are generated also from other input sources, such as existing knowledge or (un)structured documents.

Note that many of the techniques employed to do so are not new but they will need to be adapted and extended to cover the new types of models required to specify today's systems (e.g. its smart capabilities or new types of interfaces as exemplified in the next section).

The list does not aim to be exhaustive. And any modeling strategy will probably employ a combination of techniques, where the right combination and specific type of low-modeling approach will depend on the specific needs of the system-to-be and the resources already available in the organization (e.g. existing information, how standard is the domain we are modeling, how simple/complex are their features, ...).

According to the low-modeling definition, the goal of these techniques is to create initial versions of models (or more complete versions of existing ones) to be then validated and refined by modeling experts. The goal is NOT to replace the need for modeling but to let modelers focus on the more creative and key aspects of the modeling activity instead of wasting time on boilerplate modeling.

3.1 Heuristic-Based Model Generation

Convention over configuration is a software design paradigm used by software frameworks that attempts to decrease the number of decisions that a developer using the framework is required to make without necessarily losing flexibility and don't repeat yourself (DRY) principles[2]. We could use this principle at the modeling level to reduce the number of modeling decisions a designer has to make (hence, being more low-modeling).

In particular, convention over configuration and the use of heuristics can help us to create basic models for parts of the system from other existing models. A good example is the automatic generation of behavioural models [1] or user interface models [18] from static models. The key idea is that any data model will require a number of basic CRUD (create/read/update/delete) operations to visualize and manipulate the data specified in the model. This operations can be deduced from an analysis of the static model elements and relationships by systematically applying a number of heuristics. This is similar to the scaffolding features offered by most web programming frameworks. Obviously, this generated behaviuor must then be refined and new behaviours, that go beyond the CRUD core elements, added to complete the model. Still, this represents a minor percentage of the total model size and creation time (the Pareto rule also applies here) (Fig. 1).

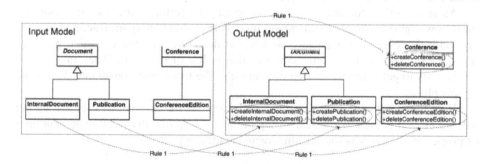

Fig. 1. CRUD-driven operation generation, taken from [1].

3.2 Knowledge-Based Model Enrichment

For many domains, there is plenty of structured knowledge already available. From simple thesaurus to general ontologies like Cyc [11]. This knowledge can be used to enrich a partial model with alternative concepts related to those already present in the model (e.g. based on the distance, in the ontology hierarchy, between the existing models and potentially new ones). For some domains, more specific ontologies, targeting the knowledge of that particular domain, could exist and produce better results. An

---

[2] https://en.wikipedia.org/wiki/Convention_over_configuration.

even more extreme approach can involve the derivation of the target model by pruning all the superfluous concepts (for the system at hand) from an initial ontology [7].

Knowledge can also come from previous models created as part of previous modeling projects in the same domain. Either by the same company or by others but contributed to a common model repository [8, 17]. As before, these previous models could be compared with the current one to suggest ways to enrich it.

Regardless of the specific method, the key idea is to reuse existing knowledge, already formalized by other individuals or whole communities, to speed up the creation of new models for the same domain. And not only that, this knowledge-reuse can also improve the overall quality. Differences between the model and the existing knowledge-bases could suggest errors in the model. These potential errors would then need to be revised by the expert so conclude whether the error is true or it is just that for this specific system we are deviating from more common specifications.

3.3 ML-Based Model Inference

The last group of techniques deal with the variety of ML techniques and applications that could help to infer models [3] from unstructured sources. This ranges from the automatic derivation of models from the textual analysis of documents to the creation of modeling assistants (similar to what GitHub copilot offers to programmers) thanks to the use of Generative AI techniques [6].

As all the other domains where AI is applied, these techniques end up being the most powerful ones (as they can extract models from completely unstructured sources and with the least human intervention) but at the same time the ones that pose the highest risk as there are no guarantees in the quality of the result. They may be the fastest way to get some results but they are also the most time-consuming during the review phase.

Note that the quality of the results largely depends on the datasets used during the ML training. It is then worth mentioning initiatives targeting the creation and curation of proper model datasets for machine learning, such as [12].

4   Case Study: Low Modeling of Conversational Interfaces

As an example of how these low-modeling strategies could be combined to accelerate the development of smart components and systems, we illustrate their role in a specific scenario: the automatic development of chatbots to talk to (open) data sources.

In real-world applications, the most common data type is tabular data. With the rise of digital technologies and the exponential growth of data, the number of tabular data sources is constantly increasing and is expected to continue to do so in the future. In particular, tabular data is also the underlying mechanism used by all kinds of public administrations to publish public data sets, known as open data. Indeed, a quick search in any of the public administration open data and transparency portals reveals the large number of data sources published[3] and the popularity of CSV and other similar tabular data formats to publish those. Despite its importance, there is a lack of methods and tools that facilitate the exploration of tabular data by non-technical users.

Conversational User Interfaces (CUI), embedded in chatbots and voicebots, have been proven useful in many contexts to automate tasks and improve the user experience, such as automated customer services, education and e-commerce. We believe they could also play a major role in the exploitation of tabular data sources. Until now, such chatbots for tabular data were either manually created (an option that it is not scalable) or completely relying on pure English-to-SQL translational approaches (with limited coverage and with a risk of generating wrong answers). We have been working on a new, fully automated, approach where bots are automatically derived based on an analysis of the tabular data description and contents.

The low-level technical details of the solution are described in [9] but in this section we expand on the key role of low-modeling in the generation of such bots.

4.1 From Tabular Data to Data Models

We aim to generate CUIs to interrogate tabular data sources. Tabular data is structured into rows, each of which contains information about some observation. Each row contains the same number of cells (they could be empty), which provide values of properties of the observation described by the row. In tabular data, cells within the same column provide values for the same property of the observations described by each row [20].

A static analysis of the tabular data columns and contents, enables us to infer enough information to fill a simple data model as the one in Fig. 2. From the structure of the dataset we will gather the list of columns/fields (with their names). From the analysis of the dataset content, we will infer the data type of each field (numeric, textual, date-time, ...) and its diversity (number of different values present in that specific column). Based on a predefined (but configurable) diversity threshold, we automatically classify as *categorical* those fields under the threshold.

We can enrich this data model with additional information, e.g. adding synonyms based on thesaurus to improve the bot comprehension capabilities and the use of ontologies to detect semantic relationships between the fields.

4.2 From Data Models to Conversational Models

Chatbots conversation capabilities are designed as a set of *intents*, where each intent represents a possible user goal when interacting with the bot. The bot then tries to match any user utterance (i.e., user's input question) to one of its intents. As part of the

---

[3] Just the EU portal https://data.europa.eu/ registers over 1.5M.

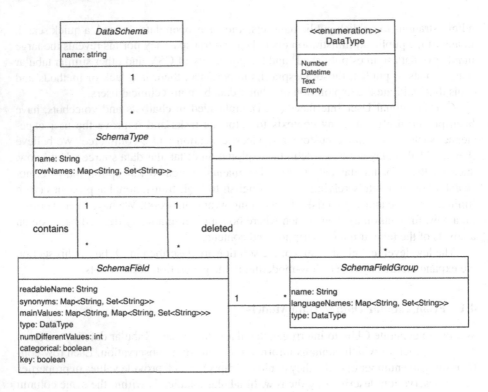

Fig. 2. DataSchema metamodel.

match, one or more parameters (also called *entities* in bot terminology) in the utterance can also be recognized, in a process known as *named entity recognition* (NER). When there is a match, the bot back-end executes the required behaviour.

We have then defined a set of heuristics [9] that are iteratively applied to the data model to generate a conversation model compliant with the conversation metamodel partially depicted in Fig. 3.

4.3   From Conversational Models to the Actual Chatbot

This last step is straightforward as it just involves a model-to-text transformation to go from an initial tabular data source to an actual running chatbot via a couple of intermediate models in a fully automated way thanks to the use of a combination of low-modeling strategies.

Note that even if an initial working version of the models is automatically generated, all models are explicit and can be manually refined at every step if needed.

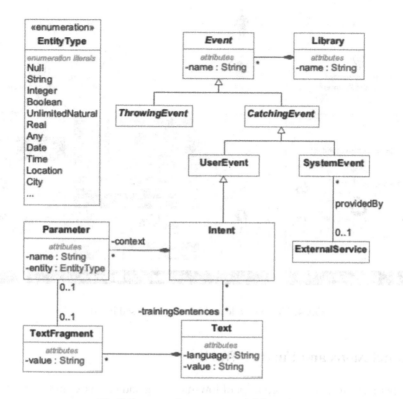

Fig. 3. Intent package metamodel from [13].

5 BESSER: A Low-Code Low-Modeling Platform

We will continue exploring these ideas as part of the *BESSER* platform, a low-code and low-modeling platform to speed up the definition of high quality smart software. BESSER is a 5-years project. As part of the project results, we are developing an open-source platform implementing the project results, available in our GitHub organization[4].

BESSER will extend the low-code architecture depicted in Fig. 4 with low-modeling components able to generate (partial) versions of all the models for smart software from (un)structured data sources using a variety of static analysis, knowledge engineering and ML-based model inference techniques such as those mentioned in the previous sections.

Note how these inference techniques will need to target each type of model separately (the traditional models, the smart front-end ones such as the conversational models we have just seen, the smart back-end ones, etc.) but also the interaction between them to ensure they behave in a consistent way.

---

[4] https://github.com/besser-pearl.

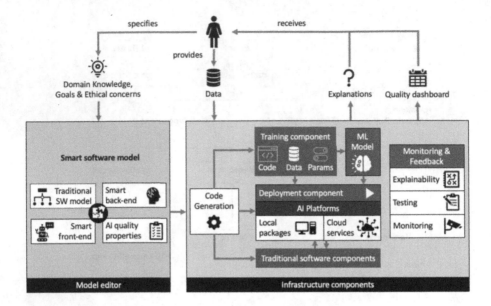

Fig. 4. The low-code architecture proposed in [5].

6   Conclusions and Further Work

This paper has introduced the concept of low-modeling and given examples of different types of low-modeling strategies that could be used to improve the development of complex systems, such as smart software systems, following a model-driven approach. This is just a first step in this direction, as the community is still proposing new types of languages and models to cover all aspects required to precisely define such smart systems. New low-modeling strategies will be needed to accelerate the development of these new kinds of models.

Beyond this challenge, we also believe that modeling languages themselves will need to be more flexible and integrate as first-class elements, new modeling concerns. For instance, we believe uncertainty modeling [19] should be considered a first-level concern. Not only AI systems are full of uncertainty per se (at all levels, at the data level, at the ML model level, ...) but the result of most low-modeling strategies comes with its own level of confidence. Moreover, low-modeling strategies may generate partial models that may need to dynamically evolve if the environment changes. Finally, low-modeling will need to go beyond the inference of the key data and behavioural elements of the system being modeled and become able to also suggest initial models for other system aspects such as the security concerns or even the ethical constraints.

Acknowledgements. This project is supported by the Luxembourg National Research Fund (FNR) PEARL program, grant agreement 16544475.

References

1. Albert, M., Cabot, J., Gómez, C., Pelechano, V.: Generating operation specifications from UML class diagrams: a model transformation approach. Data Knowl. Eng. **70**(4), 365–389 (2011)
2. Booch, G.: The history of software engineering. IEEE Softw. **35**(5), 108–114 (2018). https://doi.org/10.1109/MS.2018.3571234
3. Burgueño, L., Cabot, J., Wimmer, M., Zschaler, S.: Guest editorial to the theme section on AI-enhanced model-driven engineering. Softw. Syst. Model. **21**(3), 963–965 (2022). https://doi.org/10.1007/s10270-022-00988-0
4. Cabot, J.: Positioning of the low-code movement within the field of model-driven engineering. In: Companion Proceedings of MODELS 2020, pp. 76:1–76:3. ACM (2020). https://doi.org/10.1145/3417990.3420210
5. Cabot, J., Clarisó, R.: Low code for smart software development. IEEE Softw. **40**(1), 89–93 (2022)
6. Cámara, J., Troya, J., Burgueño, L., Vallecillo, A.: On the assessment of generative AI in modeling tasks: an experience report with ChatGpt and UML. Softw. Syst. Model. **22**(3), 781–793 (2023). https://doi.org/10.1007/s10270-023-01105-5
7. Conesa, J., Olivé, A.: A method for pruning ontologies in the development of conceptual schemas of information systems. In: Spaccapietra, S., Atzeni, P., Chu, W.W., Catarci, T., Sycara, K.P. (eds.) Journal on Data Semantics V. LNCS, vol. 3870, pp. 64–90. Springer, Heidelberg (2006). https://doi.org/10.1007/11617808_3
8. France, R., Bieman, J., Cheng, B.H.C.: Repository for model driven development (ReMoDD). In: Kühne, T. (ed.) MODELS 2006. LNCS, vol. 4364, pp. 311–317. Springer, Heidelberg (2007). https://doi.org/10.1007/978-3-540-69489-2_38
9. Gomez, M., Cabot, J., Clarisó, R.. Towards the automatic generation of conversational interfaces to facilitate the exploration of tabular data (2023)
10. Hutchinson, J.E., Whittle, J., Rouncefield, M.: Model-driven engineering practices in industry: social, organizational and managerial factors that lead to success or failure. Sci. Comput. Program. **89**, 144–161 (2014). https://doi.org/10.1016/j.scico.2013.03.017
11. Lenat, D.B.: CYC: a large-scale investment in knowledge infrastructure. Commun. ACM **38**(11), 33–38 (1995)
12. López, J.A.H., Izquierdo, J.L.C., Cuadrado, J.S.: ModelSet: a dataset for machine learning in model-driven engineering. Softw. Syst. Model. **21**(3), 967–986 (2022). https://doi.org/10.1007/s10270-021-00929-3
13. Planas, E., Daniel, G., Brambilla, M., Cabot, J.: Towards a model-driven approach for multiexperience AI-based user interfaces. Softw. Syst. Model. **20**, 997–1009 (2021)
14. Rahimi, M., Guo, J.L., Kokaly, S., Chechik, M.: Toward requirements specification for machine-learned components. In: 2019 IEEE 27th International Requirements Engineering Conference Workshops (REW), pp. 241–244 (2019). https://doi.org/10.1109/REW.2019.00049
15. Riccio, V., Jahangirova, G., Stocco, A., Humbatova, N., Weiss, M., Tonella, P.: Testing machine learning based systems: a systematic mapping. Empir. Softw. Eng. **25**(6), 5193–5254 (2020). https://doi.org/10.1007/s10664-020-09881-0
16. Richardson, C., Rymer, J.R., Mines, C., Cullen, A., Whittaker, D.: New development platforms emerge for customer-facing applications. Forrester: Cambridge, MA, USA **15** (2014)
17. Rocco, J.D., Ruscio, D.D., Iovino, L., Pierantonio, A.: Collaborative repositories in model-driven engineering. IEEE Softw. **32**(3), 28–34 (2015). https://doi.org/10.1109/MS.2015.61

18. Rodriguez-Echeverria, R., Preciado, J.C., Sierra, J., Conejero, J.M., Sanchez-Figueroa, F.: AutoCRUD: automatic generation of crud specifications in interaction flow modelling language. Sci. Comput. Program. **168**, 165–168 (2018)
19. Troya, J., Moreno, N., Bertoa, M.F., Vallecillo, A.: Uncertainty representation in software models: a survey. Softw. Syst. Model. **20**(4), 1183–1213 (2021). https://doi.org/10.1007/s10270-020-00842-1
20. W3C: Model for tabular data and metadata on the web (2015)

Model-Driven Security Smell Resolution in Microservice Architecture Using LEMMA

Philip Wizenty[1], Francisco Ponce[2,3], Florian Rademacher[4],

Jacopo Soldani[5], Hernán Astudillo[2,3], Antonio Brogi[5],

and Sabine Sachweh[1]

[1] IDiAL Institute, University of Applied Sciences and Arts Dortmund, Dortmund, Germany
{philip.wizenty,sabine.sachweh}@fh-dortmund.de
[2] Universidad Técnica Federico Santa María, Valparaíso, Chile
[3] ITiSB, Universidad Andrés Bello, Viña del Mar, Chile
francisco.ponceme@sansano.usm.cl, hernan@inf.utfsm.cl
[4] Software Engineering, RWTH Aachen University, Aachen, Germany
rademacher@se-rwth.de
[5] University of Pisa, Pisa, Italy
{jacopo.soldani,antonio.brogi}@unipi.it

Abstract. Effective security measures are crucial for modern Microservice Architecture (MSA)-based applications as many IT companies rely on microservices to deliver their business functionalities. Security smells may indicate possible security issues. However, detecting security smells and devising strategies to resolve them through refactoring is difficult and expensive, primarily due to the inherent complexity of microservice architectures.

This paper proposes a Model-driven approach to resolving security smells in MSA. The proposed method uses LEMMA as a concrete approach to model microservice applications. We extend LEMMA's functionalities to enable the modeling of microservices' security aspects. With the proposed method, LEMMA models can be processed to automatically detect security smells and recommend the refactorings that resolve the identified security smells.

To test the effectiveness of the proposed method, the paper introduces a proof-of-concept implementation of the proposed LEMMA-based, automated microservices' security smell detection and refactoring.

Keywords: Microservice architecture · Model-driven engineering · Security · Bad smells

1 Introduction

Microservice Architecture (MSA) [19] is an architectural style for distributed and service-based software systems. MSA has gained popularity over the recent years for realizing enterprise applications. Companies like Amazon[1], Netflix[2], and Twitter[3]

---

[1] https://www.amazon.com/.

[2] https://www.netflix.com/.

[3] https://twitter.com/.

© The Author(s), under exclusive license to Springer Nature Switzerland AG 2024
H.-G. Fill et al. (Eds.): ICSOFT 2023, CCIS 2104, pp. 29–49, 2024.
https://doi.org/10.1007/978-3-031-61753-9_3

already rely on MSAs to deliver their business functions. The popularity of microservices is mainly due to their cloud-native nature, which enables microservice applications to fully exploit the potential of cloud computing. Additionally, microservices are natively aligned with increasingly popular DevOps practices [3].

MSA, or microservice architecture, is a service-oriented architecture that follows a set of design principles. These principles enable microservice applications to be highly distributed, dynamic, and fault-tolerant. However, MSA inherits security concerns and practices from service-oriented architectures and presents new security challenges. These challenges include the so-called *security smells*, which were first identified in a study on microservice security published in [22].

Microservice security smells can be symptoms of unintentional bad design decisions that can affect an application's overall security [22]. To mitigate the impact of these smells, known refactorings can be applied to secure the application without altering its functionalities provided to clients. Additionally, improving security may require effort, and refactoring security issues can improve overall application quality [5].

Detecting security smells in microservices and resolving them is difficult, expensive, and prone to errors. This is mainly due to the fact that the microservices architecture tends to be complicated, with many interrelated microservices within an application [21]. This paper aims to explore the possibility of automated detection and refactoring of common microservices security smells, as identified by [22]. To achieve this, we propose to use Model-Driven Engineering (MDE) [7] by expanding the *Language Ecosystem for Modeling Microservice Architecture*[4] (LEMMA) [23]. LEMMA is a tool that was specifically designed to apply MDE in microservice design, development, and operation and has the potential to detect and address security smells in microservices.

The paper extends our work published in [36] by using Software Architecture Reconstruction (SAR) [5] to automatically construct the viewpoint-specific architecture models used in the security smell resolution process. Moreover, we introduced the Food to Go Restaurant microservice-based software system as an additional validation for our approach. The main contributions of this paper are[5]:

- We introduce LEMMAs software architecture reconstruction functionalities to recover the architectural design of the software system in viewpoint-specific models tailored to different stakeholders in the software engineering process for MSA, e.g., domain experts, software developers, and service operators.
- Our proposed approach presents the steps towards resolving microservice security smells using MDE. Specifically, our approach involves expanding LEMMA to include the security aspects of microservices. Therefore, we present a method for

---

[4] https://github.com/SeelabFhdo/lemma.

[5] This contribution extends our approach described in [36] by providing an extended version of the microservice security smell resolution process including Software Architecture Reconstruction (cf. Sect. 2.3) and LEMMAs Microservice Reconstruction Framework (cf. Sect. 4.1). Additionally, we introduced the Foot to Go Restaurant software system as a case study to validate our extended approach (cf. Sect. 3 and Sect. 5). To include the results from our extended approach, we adapted Sect. 5 to include all detected security smells and Sect. 6 and Sect. 8 to include new results of our research.

automatically analyzing LEMMA models to identify common security smells and suggest appropriate refactorings to resolve their effects.
– We assessed the feasibility of our proposed method with a proof-of-concept implementation. It facilitates detecting and refactoring microservice security issues in LEMMA models of third-party applications.

The remainder of the paper is organized as follows. Section 2 provides preliminaries on microservice security smells and LEMMA. Section 3 introduces a case study to illustrate our approach. Section 4 introduces our method to detect and refactor microservice security smells in LEMMA models, whose proof-of-concept implementation is in Sect. 5. Sections 6 to 8 discuss our approach, present related work, and draw some concluding remarks, respectively.

2 Preliminaries

We introduce LEMMA as a concrete approach to viewpoint-based microservices modeling (Sect. 2.1) and present preliminary information on microservice security smells in the following subsection (Sect. 2.2). Additionally, we introduce Software Architecture Reconstruction to derive the architectural design of a software system from its current implementation in Sect. 2.3.

2.1 Viewpoint-Based Microservice Modeling with LEMMA

The complexity of MSA engineering presents various challenges in architecture design, implementation, and operation [8,16,30]. For example, the capabilities of microservices must be balanced to ensure that they are distinct yet not too granular, allowing for targeted scaling and avoiding excessive communication between microservices (design challenge). The independence of microservices can lead to a high degree of technology heterogeneity, which increases maintenance costs and learning curves (implementation challenge). To ensure the successful adoption of MSA, the structure of the development organization must be aligned with the software architecture, involving the coordination of MSA team interactions to facilitate knowledge sharing (organizational challenge).

A possibility to address these challenges is that researchers can explore using Model-Driven Engineering (MDE) [7] to facilitate the engineering of MSA by providing a targeted and viewpoint-specific abstraction from complexity. However, the resulting modeling approaches are highly varied, and the majority focus on a single phase of MSA engineering, such as microservice design [13,15], implementation [14,34], or operation [14,29]. Consequently, these approaches do not enable an integrated model-based expression of concerns across different phases of MSA engineering nor facilitate a consistent sharing of knowledge among MSA teams.

In order to address the challenges associated with model-driven microservice architecture engineering, the LEMMA MDE ecosystem was developed [23]. LEMMA offers a range of modeling languages to capture different aspects of MSA engineering from a stakeholder-oriented architecture perspective. Models created with these languages can be combined using an import mechanism that allows elements of other models to be linked, thus facilitating reuse and increasing the amount of information captured in the various perspectives. The proposed approach to resolving security smells in microservice architectures is based on the following LEMMA modeling languages.

Technology Modeling Language (TML). The Technology Viewpoint of LEMMA's TML is focused on microservice technology decisions. It enables the creation of models that capture technology decisions related to microservices and their deployment, such as communication protocols and deployment technologies. Furthermore, the TML allows for defining technology aspects that apply to certain concepts in LEMMA models, for example, modeled microservices and their interfaces or infrastructure nodes like databases. These aspects of technology can be used to add metadata to LEMMA models, such as the authorization protocol of a specific microservice [23].

Service Modeling Language (SML). The SML of LEMMA addresses the Service Viewpoint in MSA engineering. This is realized by providing modeling concepts to define microservices, their interfaces, operations, and endpoints in service models. Furthermore, SML is integrated with TML, allowing LEMMA service models to import LEMMA technology models. This enables the specification of protocol-dependent communication endpoints, such as HTTP addresses, along with the methods available to operate on them [23].

Operation Modeling Language (OML). The operation viewpoint and, therefore, the deployment specification is addressed by LEMMAs OML. This allows the specification and configuration of microservice containers and infrastructure nodes, such as those used for service discovery or load balancing, in operation models [23]. The Operation Modeling Language (OML) integrates with the Technology Modeling Language (TML) to address the technology heterogeneity of MSA with regards to microservice operation and deployment [16]. Technology models can be used to flexibly specify the technologies used for microservice deployment and infrastructure usage.

In addition to providing a model-based description of microservices and their operations, LEMMA enables model processing [23]. It has already been used to facilitate the integration of the MSA team through model transformation [31] and to improve the efficiency of microservice development through code generation [24]. Here, we take advantage of LEMMA's model processing capabilities to detect security smells in service and operation models through static analysis and suggest resolution strategies through interactive model refactoring.

2.2 Smells and Refactorings for Microservice Security

A security smell can indicate a poor decision that may have been made unintentionally, which could negatively influence the software system's security [22]. Refactoring the application or its services without changing the functionality provided to customers can help fix the effects of security smells [5]. However, this process requires effort from development teams, which can increase development costs. Nevertheless, it can improve the overall quality of the application. The two most common security smells for microservices, according to [22], are *Publicly Accessible Microservices* and *Insufficient Access Control*, and their effects and possible refactoring as described below.

Insufficient Access Control. The *Insufficient Access Control* smell is a security issue that arises when the microservices in a software system do not enforce proper access control. This can lead to confidentiality breaches, as attackers can exploit a service to access data or perform operations they should not be able to. The *"confused deputy problem"* [11] is a particular vulnerability where an attacker can deceive a service into revealing confidential information or executing unauthorized operations. Traditional identity control models may not be enough for microservice applications, as client permissions must be verified at each application level, and each microservice must have a system to accept or reject requests automatically. To address this, it is suggested to delegation framework such as OAuth 2.0[6] as a mechanism that provides suitable access control to the microservices forming the software systems. OAuth 2.0 is a token-based access control system that allows a resource owner to grant a client access to a specific resource on their behalf.

Publicly Accessible Microservices. The security smell of *Publicly Accessible Microservices* occurs when the microservices that comprise a software system are directly exposed to external users or third-party systems. To reduce the risk of confidentiality violations and improve maintainability and usability, each publicly accessible microservice should be guarded behind a centralized access point. This decreases the attack surface, making the application less vulnerable overall.

A potential refactoring is the integration of an API Gateway that acts as a central entry point for the whole software system. The gateway can be used to access the APIs of the formerly exposed microservices, allowing authentication to be performed centrally and reducing the application's attack surface. It simplifies authentication auditing tasks, and development teams can use the gateway to secure the software system by blocking all external requests to internal microservices through a firewall.

2.3 Software Architecture Reconstruction

This section introduces a four-phased process for recovering the architecture design of a software system utilizing LEMMA reconstruction functionalities. The reconstruction of a software systems architectural design leveraging architecture models is a complex and tool-dependent process [5] that generally requires a set of different functionalities to support the different kinds of source code artifacts of the development process, for example, programming languages, deployment specifications, and runtime dependencies. Therefore, the reconstruction requires a set of tools to recover the architectural design.

The SAR reconstruction process includes four phases with specific steps and results:

1. *Raw View Extraction* is the first phase of the SAR process with a strong focus on obtaining architecture information about the software system, mainly from source code artifacts, deployment specifications, and service interactions [5, 10].
2. The *Database Construction* phase consists of transforming the architecture information from the previous phase into a standardized data format [5].

---

[6] https://oauth.net/2/.

3. The *View Fusion and Manipulation* phase combines the architecture information stored in the database to improve the accuracy of the reconstructed architecture design. The manipulation step in this phase aggregates and interprets the combined information to create a *hypothesis* on the software system's architecture [5].
4. *Architecture Analysis* is the final phase of the SAR process and is related to the analysis of the hypothesis about the software system's architecture of the previous stage. The thesis needs to be analyzed and tested to prove its correctness by a software architecture or analyzer tool- [5].

3   Case Study Introduction

This section introduces a case study to exemplify our model-driven approach to resolving security smells in MSA. The example software system is commonly used in the academic context for demonstration purposes and depicts a fictional restaurant software system [27]. The source code for the application is publicly available on Github[7] Figure 1 displays the architecture of the restaurant case study software system, including functional microservices, infrastructure components, and frontend service.

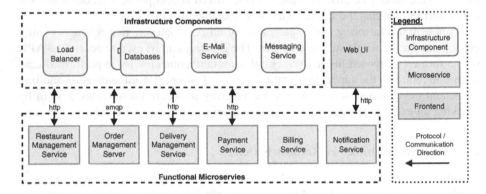

Fig. 1. Food to Go Restaurant application microservice architecture [27].

The software system's data management has a separate Database for each functional microservice to promote loose coupling between services and allow for the autonomous development of the microservices. The Load Balancer provides scalability functionalities, and the E-mail E-Mail and Messaging Service enables service-to-service communication and the messaging of emails to customers.

This case study software system does not represent a fully functional software system. It was developed to exemplify approaches in research and development of software systems, such as demonstrating architectural patterns or deployment technologies. Therefore, if we look at the design, technologies used, and security configuration, we can identify the following security smells in the software systems' architectural design:

---

[7] https://github.com/microservices-patterns/ftgo-application/.

- All functional microservices of the restaurant software system have publicly exposed APIs. This indicates the occurrence of the *Publicly Accessible Microservice* security smell, which increases the security risk by broadening the attack surface and decentralized authorization enforcement. Additionally, the individual APIs of the microservices also decrease maintainability and usability.
- The restaurant software system also indicates means of *Insufficient Access Control* on its API endpoints, which can be exploited for misuse, possibly leading to confidentiality violations and data leaks, to resolve the security issues, the suggested refactoring is the integration of an access delegation framework such as OAuth 2 to control the access at the API.

We contemplate the implementation of the Food to Go restaurant software system manually and suggest the integration of an API Gateway and the usage of an authorization framework as refactoring to resolve the security smells. Nevertheless, the analysis of a complex and expensive software system, the detection of smells, and the refactoring are currently done manually. It would be beneficial to have support for automating the detection of security smells and the reasoning on how to refactor them, which is the purpose of this paper.

4 Model-Driven Security Smell Resolution

This section examines our strategy for resolving microservice security smells using a model-based approach, based on the case study of Sect. 3 and the identified flaws in architecture design and security configuration. Therefore, the first part of our approach consists of the model construction process using LEMMA's *Software Architecture Reconstruction* [5] framework described in Sect. 4.1. The next part of the process includes modeling security configurations in LEMMAs TML (Sect. 4.2). In Sect. 4.3 provides insight into detecting security smells in the reconstructed LEMMA architecture and technology models. Additionally, refactoring strategies for resolving identified security smells are presented in Sect. 4.4 combined with the user-guided refactoring process utilizing LEMMA.

4.1 Model-Based Reconstruction of Microservice Architecture

The first step in our approach to detecting security smells in MSA starts with an automated process of architecture model construction utilizing SAR. Figure 2 shows the various components of our software reconstruction workbench in LEMMA to restore the architectural design of a technology heterogeneous software system.

The Reconstruction Frameworks orchestrates the first three phases of the SAR process described in Sect. 2.3. Therefore, the framework is responsible for extracting architecture information and the fusion and manipulation of reconstructed information using standardized data formats from the Reconstruction Database. The first phase of the SAR restores architecture information from, e.g., Source Code and Deployment Specifications. For this purpose, the framework analyzes the

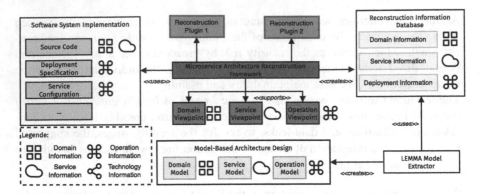

Fig. 2. Structure of LEMMAs Reconstruction Framework and Plugins to reconstruct a software system's architecture.

development artifacts and invokes the `Reconstruction Plugins` to extract architecture information such as domain concepts, service interfaces, and deployment information. The `Reconstruction Plugins` provide technology-specific functionalities for reconstructing architecture information regarding different viewpoints in MSA.

The second phase consists of constructing the database to store the recovered information about the software system's architecture. Therefore, we derived a standardized data format for each viewpoint in MSA (cf. Sect. 2). The data format consists of the specific concepts for each viewpoint to store the reconstructed architecture design, e.g., the framework and database address concept for microservice modeling of service interfaces and dependencies.

In the third phase of the SAR process, the framework aggregates all recovered architecture information recovered from the implementation, increasing the accuracy of the reconstructed architecture design. For this purpose, the framework transforms the viewpoint-specific architecture information into an architecture design for the software system and `stores` it into the `Reconstruction Database` in the standardized viewpoint-specific data format.

The fourth and last phase of the SAR process consists of the architectural analysis of the recovered architecture design. Our approach addresses this phase in two sequential steps. To provide the Software Architect with a readable representation of the reconstructed architecture design, the `LEMMA Model Extractor` [25] uses the information in the `Reconstruction Database` to derive viewpoint-specific LEMMA models from it. Particularly `Domain Data`, `Service`, and `Operation Models` utilizing the eponymous modeling languages. In the final step of our approach, a Software Architect or model validator analyzes the architecture design of the software system based on the LEMMA models.

4.2 Security Smell Modeling for Microservice Architecture

The use of LEMMA's TML *aspect* concept to incorporate meta-information into a LEMMA service- or operation model is employed to model microservice security configurations, as mentioned in Sect. 2.1. Figure 3 depicts modeling microservice security smells using LEMMA's TML. The first step involves selecting a security smell e.g., Publicly Accessible Microservices. After selecting the security smell, the `analysis` process starts to derive the necessary security information from the smell to detect it in a software system.

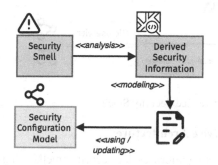

Fig. 3. Modeling Microservice Security Smell Process.

```
technology SecurityConfiguration {                              1
                                                                2
    service aspects{                                            3
        aspect usesApiGateway for microservices;                4
        aspect Authorization for microservices {                5
            string protocolName;                                6
        }                                                       7
                                                                8
        aspect Secured for interfaces, operations {             9
            string role;                                       10
        }                                                       11
                                                               12
    }                                                          13
                                                               14
    operation aspects {                                        15
        aspect ApiGateway for infrastructure;                  16
    }                                                          17
}                                                              18
```

Listing 1.1. LEMMA technology model with security configurations.

The root cause of the *Publicly* `Accessible Microservices` security smell is the decision not to use an API gateway to access all exposed microservices [27]. The API gateway architecture pattern includes a gateway component that handles API composition, routing of requests to the corresponding microservice, and the backend microservices API exposure.

The next step of the process consists of using or updating LEMMA's `security configuration model` with the derived security information. The functionalities of LEMMA provide a security configuration model Listing 1.1, which supports the security smells mentioned in Sect. 2, but it can be extended with additional security smell for microservices to address other security smells in MSA. The resulting model can be used for automated tests to identify security smells in LEMMA models. The model presented in Listing 1.1 includes the information about the modeled architecture derived from the security smells being considered, namely, *Publicly Accessible Microservices* and *Insufficient Access Control*.

Line 1 in Listing 1.1 specifies `SecurityConfiguration` as LEMMA's technology model name. The following Lines 3–13 contain `service aspects` that are used for the microservice concept of LEMMA's SML to include architecture or security information. The aspect `usesApiGateway` explicitly states that the microservices make their interface available through an API Gateway. (Line 4). The following Line (5) outlines the authorization protocol for granting access, while Line (9) provides a configuration for role-based access control for microservices API endpoints.

Additionally, Lines 15–17 of Listing 1.1 define an `operation aspect` called `ApiGateway` to recognize an infrastructure node in LEMMA's operation models as a node the implements the functionality of an API Gateway.

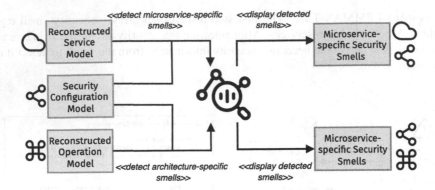

Fig. 4. Detection Process of Microservice Security Smells.

4.3 Security Smells Detection for Microservice Architecture

In this section, we describe the process of detecting microservice security smells using the automatically reconstructed LEMMA service and operation from Sect. 4.1 and the technology model from Sect. 4.2 to detect security smells in MSA. Figure 4 depicts the overall process of detecting microservice-specific and architecture-specific smells.

The process of detecting security smells in MSA is separated into two different detection steps. The first step consists of the analysis of the security configuration of the microservice itself, for example, the enforcement of proper access control by using an authorization protocol such as OAuth2[8] to avoid the security smell of *Insufficient Access Control*. Furthermore, to detect security smells in the architecture of the overall software system, the detection process includes a second analysis step to validate the system's general security. This consists of the detection of architecture-related security smells, e.g., *Publicly Exposed Microservices* by the absence of an API Gateway in the software systems architecture.

Listing Listing 1.2 lists a recovered LEMMA service model from the case study example containing the `Order Service` utilizing LEMMAs software architecture reconstruction framework (cf. Sect. 4.1).

Listing 1.2. LEMMA service model for the OrderService from the case study.

```
1   import datatypes from "../domain/Order.data" as Order
2   import technology from "../../technology/Spring.technology" as Spring
3
4   @technology(Spring)
5   public functional microservice net.chrisrichardson.ftgo.OrderService {
6       @endpoints({Spring::_protocols.rest:"order";})
7       interface OrderInterface {
8           @Spring::_aspects.Post
9           create( sync out createOrderResponse : ResponseEntity,  sync in createOrderRequest : RequestEntity);
10          @Spring::_aspects.Get
11          getOrder( sync out getOrderResponse : Order::Order.GetOrderResponse,  sync in orderId : long);
12          @Spring::_aspects.Put
13          makeGetOrderResponse( sync out getOrderResponse : Order::Order.GetOrderResponse,
14              sync in order : Order::Order.Order);
15          @Spring::_aspects.Delete
16          cancel( sync out getOrderResponse : Order::Order.GetOrderResponse,  sync in orderId : long);
17          @Spring::_aspects.Put
18          revise( sync out getOrderResponse : Order::Order.GetOrderResponse,  sync in orderId : long,
19              sync in reviseOrderRequest : RequestEntity);
20      }
21
```

---

[8] https://oauth.net/2/.

```
22   @endpoints({Spring::_protocols.rest:"restaurant";})
23   interface RestaurantInterface {
24       @Spring::_aspects.Get
25       getRestaurant( sync out getRestaurantResponse : Order::Order.GetRestaurantResponse, sync in restaurantId : long);
26   }
27 }
```

The first two lines of the listing show import states for LEMMA's domain and technology model. The `order` domain contains the reconstructed domain concepts from the source code used in the API specification of the `OrderService`. Additionally, the `spring` technology model is imported to enhance the service model with technology decisions, such as the HTTP-REST method for endpoints. The spring technology model is imported into the reconstructed service model due to the restaurant software systems implementation technology and the reconstruction process.

The following listing contains the definition of the `OrderService` as a functional microservice of the software system. The microservice consists of the `Order-` and `RestaurantInterface`, representing the microservices API. The `OrderInterface` contains the API endpoints for creating, receiving, making, and canceling an order, including the corresponding REST method and URI used in the process. Furthermore, the model specifies the `RestaurantInterface` of the `OrderService`. The interface has a separate URI defined via an interface-specific endpoint and access method.

The subsequent step in the detection process consists of analyzing architecture-specific security smells. For this purpose, we analyze LEMMA's operation model to identify the microservice security smells. Listing 1.3 describes the deployment specification for OrderService (cf. Listing 1.2) with deployment technologies and runtime dependencies on other components of software systems such as databases or service registries.

Listing 1.3. LEMMA operation model for the OrderService from the case study.

```
1  import microservices from "OrderService.services" as OrderService
2  import technology from "deploymentBase.technology" as deploymentBase
3  import technology from "protocol.technology" as protocol
4  import nodes from "infrastructure.operation" as infrastructure
5
6  @technology(deploymentBase)
7  @technology(protocol)
8  container OrderServiceContainer
9      deployment technology deploymentBase::_deployment.Docker
10     deploys OrderService::net.chrisrichardson.ftgo.OrderService
11     depends on nodes
12         infrastructure::ServiceDiscovery,
13         infrastructure::MySQLDatabase {
14         default values {
15             basic endpoints { protocolTechnology::_protocols.rest: "http://localhost:8110"; }
16         }
17 }
```

Listing 1.3 begins with an import statements for the `OrderService` to specific its deployment in the listed operation model. Moreover, the following three imports enable the use of a technology-specific deployment specification for the OrderService, including a `deploymentBase` technology for the operation environment of the microservice, a `protocol` technology for service communication, and `infrastructure` technology for runtime dependencies.

Lines 6 to 17 defining the `OrderServiceContainer` as a component that includes all the necessary specifications for the description of the deployment, including the `Docker` technology and the fully qualified name of the deployed microservice.

Additionally, the container contains specified dependencies to infrastructure components of the software system, e.g., the dependency to a `MySQLDatabase` for data persistency and a `ServiceRegistry` for load balancing purpose.

The final section of the listing specifies default values that apply to all microservices that are deployed in the `OrderServiceContainer`, in this specific case, the Order-Service. This listing specifies the `basic endpoint` for communication via HTTP. In this specification, the beginning of the URI extended by endpoint specification of the service model (cf. Listing 1.2).

The last step of the microservice and architecture-specific security smell detection process includes analyzing the service and operation model to detect and display the occurring microservice security smells. This functionality is provided by LEMMA's model validators that are included in the Eclipse modeling environment using the `Eclipse Modeling Framework` (EMF)[9]. We extended LEMMAs model validators for the presented approach to detect security smells in service and operation models. Suppose the validators detect a security smell in the models. In that case, they will show a warning in the model editor that includes the name of the security smell and potential resolving strategies.

4.4   Security Smell Resolving for Microservice Architecture

This section elaborates on resolving security smells in the LEMMA service and operation model. Additionally, it describes the user-guided process facilitated by the LEMMA modeling editor. The resolution process, which is illustrated in Fig. 5, begins with the selection of the security smell that should be resolved, e.g., the microservice or architecture-specific smell and the corresponding LEMMA model.

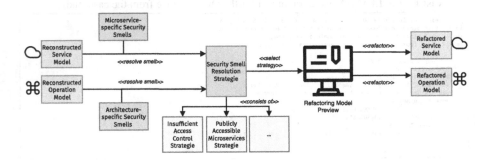

Fig. 5. Activities of resolving microservices' security aspects with LEMMA.

After selecting the security smell, which should be addressed in the resolution process, the next step is to choose a resolution strategy to resolve the smell. The strategy to resolve the security smell depends on the characteristics of the specific smell, e.g., to resolve the security smell of insufficient access control, an authorization protocol such

---

[9] https://projects.eclipse.org/projects/modeling.emf.emf.

as OAuth2 needs to be implemented in the microservices interface or mark the security smell as to be ignored, because it is an explicit design decision to leave the microservice unsecured. Moreover, in the case of publicly accessible microservices, a resolution strategy is the integration of an API Gateway to centralize microservice interface access or to avoid the microservice's public access by configuring it as internal.

Once the resolution strategy has been chosen, the next step is to preview the refactoring results specific to the selected strategy. LEMMA's modeling editor provides a workflow to help the user through this process. Finally, the last activity is to confirm the model changes and implement the resolution strategy on the models involved.

To demonstrate the results of solving the publicly accessible microservices security smell by including an API Gateway for public microservice exposure, a section of the refactored operation model of the `OrderService` is presented in Listing 1.4.

Listing 1.4. Refactored LEMMA operation model for the OrderService from the motivating example.

```
 1   ...
 2   import nodes from "infrastructure.operation" as infrastructure
 3
 4   @technology(deploymentBase)
 5   @technology(protocol)
 6   container OrderServiceContainer
 7       deployment technology deploymentBase::_deployment.Docker
 8       deploys OrderService::net.chrisrichardson.ftgo.OrderService
 9       depends on nodes
10           infrastructure::ServiceDiscovery,
11           infrastructure::APIGateway,
12           infrastructure::MySQLDatabase {
13           ...
14   }
```

The operation model remains the same in most parts, except for adding Line 11. This line indicates a dependency on the infrastructure component of an `API Gateway`. As a result of the API Gateway's inclusion by the resolution strategy, a corresponding operation model is also generated during the refactoring of the `OrderService` model.

Listing 1.5. LEMMA operation model for an API Gateway using the Zuul technology.

```
 1   import ...
 2   @technology(Zuul)
 3   APIGateway is Zuul::_infrastructure.Zuul
 4       depends on nodes ServiceRegistry
 5       used by services orderService::net.chrisrichardson.ftgo.OrderService,
 6       used by nodes coreContainer::OrderServiceContainer {
 7       default values {
 8           hostname = "APIGateway"
 9           port = 8080
10           apiUri = "eureka:8080"
11       }
12   }
13   ...
```

Listing 1.5 displays the deployment specification of the API Gateway infrastructure component using Netflix Zuul as a concrete technology stack. The lines 2–3 assign the Zuul technology to the corresponding specification of an `APIGateway`. The following line states that the API Gateway requires a `ServiceRegistry` to route the request to the microservices. Additionally, the `used by` specifications in Lines 5–6 indicate that the OrderService API is exposed through the Gateway. The remaining lines of the listing define `default values`, such as the hostname or operation port.

5 Case Study Validation

This section provides evidence of the practical feasibility of using MDE to resolve security smells with LEMMA in MSA-based software systems. We have outlined the process of resolving the security smells of publicly accessible microservices and insufficient access control in Sect. 2 and Sect. 4. This case study validation tests our approach to detecting security smells. It is the first step towards a complete and validated support for resolving security smells in microservice software systems with LEMMA.

Our implementation to resolve the security smells extends LEMMA's current functionalities with the capabilities to automatically reconstruct the software systems architecture, detect the security smell, and resolve the smell using a selected resolution strategy.

Figure 6 show the Eclipse-based editor of LEMMA's with the opened `OrderService` service and operation model presented in Listing 1.2 and Listing 1.3. The figure shows a warning in the Eclipse modeling editor, indicating that the security smells of publicly accessible microservices and insufficient access control are found in the corresponding models. Moreover, by hovering over the warning, LEMMA's security smell resolution functionality opens a dialog to select security smell-specific resolution dialog to choose a strategy by using the Eclipse Quickfix[10] function.

```
@technology(Spring)
public functional microservice net.chrisrichardson.ftgo.OrderService {
    @endpoints({Spring::_protoc   ⚠ Insufficient Access Control Security Smell detected
    interface OrderController {    1 quick fix available:
        @Spring::_aspects.Post         Select resolution strategy for Security Smell: Insufficient Access Control.
        create( sync out create...............................tOrderRes
        @Spring::_aspects.Get
        getOrder( sync out getOrderResponse : Order::Order.GetOrderResp
                                                                Press 'F2' for focus


@technology(Docker)
container OderServiceContainer
    deploy ⚠ Publicly Accessible Microservice Security Smell detected     t.Docker
    deploy  1 quick fix available:                                        n.ftgo.OrderService
    depend     Select resolution strategy for Security Smell: Publicly Accessible Microservices.  eRegistry {
    defaul.  ........ .                                Press 'F2' for focus
        basic endpoints {
```

Fig. 6. LEMMA Eclipse editor presenting the OrderService service and operation model with security smell publicly accessible microservices and insufficient access control.

The beginning of the resolution process is initiated by selecting the quick fix option. This provides the opportunity to pick a resolution strategy tailored to the security smell. Figure 7 shows the possibility of resolving publicly accessible microservices.

There are various ways to address the security smells, such as using an API Gateway. Another option is to mark the security smell as "ignored" as an explicit design

---

[10] https://www.eclipse.org/Xtext/documentation/310_eclipse_support.html#quick-fixes.

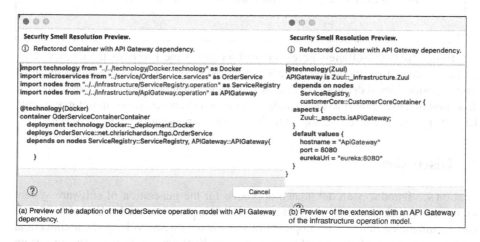

Fig. 7. Selection of the security smell-specific strategy for resolving publicly accessible microservices and insufficient access control.

decision. Alternatively, configuring the OrderService as "internal" can also resolve the security smell by preventing public exposure.

The next step of the security smell resolution process is to preview and confirm the proposed refactoring adaptation of the service and operation model. During the security smell resolution process, the LEMMA editor previews every modified model to guide the user and to inform him of every occurring change. In publicly accessible microservices, the aim is to integrate an API Gateway, which preview is depicted in Fig. 8. The preview shows the infrastructure node of an API Gateway that extends the software systems architecture (c.f. Fig. 8 (b.)) and the refactored OrderService operation model (c.f. Fig. 8 (a.))

Security Smell Resolution Preview.
ⓘ Refactored Container with API Gateway dependency.

```
import technology from "../../technology/Docker.technology" as Docker
import microservices from "../service/OrderService.services" as OrderService
import nodes from "../../infrastructure/ServiceRegistry.operation" as ServiceRegistry
import nodes from "../../infrastructure/ApiGateway.operation" as APIGateway

@technology(Docker)
container OderServiceContainerContainer
    deployment technology Docker::_deployment.Docker
    deploys OrderService::net.chrisrichardson.ftgo.OrderService
    depends on nodes ServiceRegistry::ServiceRegistry, APIGateway::APIGateway{

    }
```

Security Smell Resolution Preview.
ⓘ Refactored Container with API Gateway dependency.

```
@technology(Zuul)
APIGateway is Zuul::_infrastructure.Zuul
    depends on nodes
        ServiceRegistry,
        customerCore::CustomerCoreContainer {
    aspects {
        Zuul::_aspects.isAPIGateway;
    }
    default values {
        hostname = "ApiGateway"
        port = 8080
        eurekaUri = "eureka:8080"
    }
}
```

(a) Preview of the adaption of the OrderService operation model with API Gateway dependency.

(b) Preview of the extension with an API Gateway of the infrastructure operation model.

Fig. 8. Refactoring previews of the OrderService and API Gateway operation model for resolving publicly accessible microservices.

The last step of LEMMA's security smell resolution process consists of applying the preview changes to the actual service and operation models. Additionally, to the presented security smell resolution function, LEMMA enables means towards code generation, e.g., the generation of infrastructure nodes like API gateways, service registries, identity providers, and databases.

Resolving the security smell of insufficient access control in microservices involves similar steps as those described for the publicly available microservices security smell, except for the resolution strategy, which is tailored to the microservice-specific security smell. The resolution depends on the refactorings suggested for the relevant microservice security smell (cf. Sect. 2). A potential refactoring to address the problem of insufficient access control in microservices is to implement an authorization protocol like OAuth2 [21].

Listing 1.6 introduces the refactored OrderService as a LEMMA service model. Due to the lack of a specification of an authorization protocol for the microservice, the security of the service suffers from insufficient access control in the automated reconstructed model. In order to resolve the security smell the integration of OAuth2 as an authorization protocol resolves the security smell. Listing 1.6 specifies a LEMMA technology model with an `Authorization` and `Secured` aspect to specify a protocol for role-based access control of microservices.

Listing 1.6. LEMMA service model for the OrderService from the case study restaurant software system.

```
1   import technology from "securityAspects.technology" as securityAspects
2   @technology(spring)
3   @technology(securityAspects)
4   @securityAspects::_aspects.Authorization(^protocol="OAuth2")
5   public functional microservice net.chrisrichardson.ftgo.OrderService {
6       @endpoints({Spring::_protocols.rest:"order";})
7       interface OrderInterface {
8           @Spring::_aspects.Post
9           @securityAspects::_aspects.Secured("ROLE_GUEST")
10          create( sync out createOrderResponse : ResponseEntity,  sync in createOrderRequest : RequestEntity);
11          @Spring::_aspects.Get
12          @securityAspects::_aspects.Secured("ROLE_STUFF")
13          getOrder( sync out getOrderResponse : Order::Order.GetOrderResponse,  sync in orderId : long);
14          ...
15      }
16      ...
17  }
```

To resolve the insufficient access control security, Line 1 imports the `security-Aspcet` technology model and Line 3 applies the security technology to the specified microservice. Line 4 defines `OAuth2` as an authorization protocol to the OrderService. Additionally, to enable role-based authorization at a microservice endpoint granularity, Line 9 applies the `Secured` aspect to the `create` endpoint of the OrderService.

6   Discussion

Section 4.1 introduces an automated approach for the generation of software system architecture models using LEMMAs as a concrete approach towards MDE of MSA that can be integrated into the development of the whole systems to keep the architectural design consistent with the actual implementation. Furthermore, as the software system evolves, the models are updated to reflect the changes in the source code. This approach uses SAR for the automated model creation and, therefore, leverages the mentioned unaddressed challenge in our previous work [36].

Our current approach can detect two microservices' security smells identified in [22]. However, it is essential to note that these two smells are among the top three most occurring in MSA. Nevertheless, one of the limitations of our approach is that it does not cover all of the microservices' security smells yet. We believe that LEMMA's aspect-oriented modeling capabilities have promising potential to detect additional security smells, but also general *Anti-Pattern* [32] in Microservice Architecture, such as *Hard-Endpoints, Lack of Monitoring,* and *Cyclic Dependencies* [33].

Our current approach aims to enable the automated reconstruction of LEMMA's service and operation model and detect microservice security smells in the reconstructed models. Additionally, we aim to eliminate security smells in microservices and microservice architecture by identifying smells in LEMMA models and suggesting automated resolution strategies based on the security smell itself. However, at the current stage of our approach implementation, developers still need to manually intervene in the process of resolving security smells in the source code of the software system. However, this process can be supported by utilizing LEMMA's code generation features in conjunction with the refactored model that enables the resolution of selected security issues at the implementation level. Our approach provides developers with facilitated awareness of security smells and aids them in making their microservices more secure.

7 Related Work

The work presented in [22], Ponce et al. suggest a list of microservice security smells, along with the recommended refactoring techniques that can be applied to resolve the smell and corresponding security violation. However, the automatic detection of such smells in microservices and the subsequent application of refactoring strategies to address them remains an unresolved issue. To our knowledge, there is only one existing approach in this direction, presented in [21]. This approach assumes that the security smells have already been identified and proposes a trade-off analysis to decide whether applying a refactoring technique is worth it, taking into account how the smell and refactoring will impact the overall quality of the application.

There are other approaches available that allow for the detection and resolution of architectural smells in microservices. [20,29] suggest two solutions for identifying architectural smells in microservice-based software systems. Both approaches share the general idea of starting from smells identified within industry-driven reviews of software systems, with [20] selecting those from [32], while [29] picking those from [18]. [29] actually also shares the idea of using MDE to identify and refactor microservice security smells. The main difference between [20,29], and our proposal relies on the considered types of smells, with [20,29] focusing on architectural smells. We complement their results by enabling the identification and refactoring of microservice security smells from [22]. Moreover, the integration in LEMMA's modeling ecosystems allows the automated reconstruction of viewpoint-specific architecture models, which depict the up-to-date implementation of the source code of the software system.

There are already some methods and tools for analyzing microservices applications' security, which can also be used to detect other security smells. For instance, [26] proposes a static analysis technique to detect security smells in infrastructure-as-code [17] scripts. [26] however, differs from our proposal in its objectives, as it focuses on detecting security smells for infrastructure-as-code only, while we consider the detection and refactoring microservice security smells for different viewpoints, e.g., the service or operation viewpoint.

There exist several methods and tools that can be utilized to analyze the security of MSA-based software systems, which can also be employed to identify other potential security violations. For instance, [26] has proposed a static analysis technique that is able to detect security issues within *Infrastructure as Code* (IaC) [17] scripts. However, [26] differs from our proposal in terms of objectives, as it focuses solely on detecting security issues in IaC, whereas we aim to identify and refactor security issues in microservices from different perspectives such as the service or operation viewpoint. Additionally, the IoC approach only considers a specific set of technologies. In contrast, by leveraging LEMMAs modeling languages and the abstraction from specific technologies, our presented approach is able to cover a heterogeneous technology stack, that is quite common in MSA [6].

Tools that are ready for use in analyzing security, e.g., such as Kubesec.io,[11] Checkov,[12] OWASP Zed Application Proxy (ZAP),[13] and SonarQube.[14] offer reliable solutions for detecting security issues and conducting vulnerability assessments, which also apply to microservice-based software systems. Nevertheless, our proposal enhances the analysis provided by the tools mentioned earlier, as it not only detects security smells but also suggests refactorings for microservice security smells such as those described in [22].

The same considerations apply to [4, 12]. Both approaches organize information from industry-scale projects and derive guidelines that help to design microservices without common architectural issues. Our approach complements [4, 12] in their effort towards resolving smell in microservice-based software systems by enabling the detection of microservices' security smells and resolutions to resolve their possible effects.

Additionally, it is also worth relating our microservice-oriented proposal with existing solutions for detecting smells in classical services.

Additionally, if we compare our presented approach for security smell resolution for microservice-based software systems to the approach for security vulnerability detection on other software architectures, there are noticeable similarities. For instance, [1,9,28] present three MDE-based approaches to identify architectural smells in software systems, with [1,9] using on UML to model software services, and [28] relying on Archery. [2,35] can be used to analyze the source code of a service and detect any smells, while supporting refactoring to resolve them. Our proposal differs from the approaches mentioned earlier in [9], in a similar way as discussed above. [1,28], Our

---

[11] https://kubesec.io.

[12] https://www.checkov.io.

[13] https://owasp.org/www-project-zap/.

[14] http://sonarqube.org/.

proposal complements existing research by enabling detection and refactoring of security smells in microservice applications, building upon [2,35].

8   Conclusions

We have developed a new approach for resolving security smells in MSA, which is based on extending the LEMMA functionalities. Our approach enhances LEMMA with the functions to automatically detect the two most occurring security smells in microservices and provide recommendations for refactoring strategies to resolve their effects.

We have validated the practicality of our proposed approach and demonstrated it through a case study validation on a microservice-based software system, that is commonly used in MSA research. Additionally, we have assessed how the implementation can help detect and resolve microservice security smells in LEMMA models capturing the software systems architecture. Our approach represents the initial phase in the field of automated MDE-based resolution of security smells for MSA.

In our future work, we intend to expand the current implementation into a fully functional prototype that incorporates a model-driven approach to resolve security smells in MSA. Additionally, we plan to include code generation into our approach to automatically transfer the applied resolution strategies of the security smell to the implementation of the software system.

We plan to use the full-fledged prototype to validate and evaluate our method on real-world applications and test the feasibility on industry-level applications. Furthermore, our goal is to provide developers with guidance on how to address security smells detected in MSA. This will involve integrating our prototype with trade-off analyses and code generation functionalities that can automatically resolve security smell at the implementation level. We also plan to broaden our approach to include other microservice-related smells, such as architectural smells.

Acknowledgments. This work was partially supported by ANID under grant *PIA/APOYO AFB180002, Instituto de tecnología para la innovación en salud y bienestar, facultad de ingeniería* (Universidad Andrés Bello, Chile), and by the project *hOlistic Sustainable Management of distributed softWARE systems* (OSMWARE, UNIPI PRA_2022_64), funded by the University of Pisa, Italy.

References

1. Arcelli, D., Cortellessa, V., Pompeo, D.D.: Automating performance antipattern detection and software refactoring in UML models. In: Wang, X., Lo, D., Shihab, E. (eds.) 2019 International Conference on Software Analysis, Evolution and Reengineering, SANER 2019, pp. 639–643. IEEE Computer Society (2019)
2. Arcelli Fontana, F., et al.: Arcan: a tool for architectural smells detection. In: Malavolta, I., Capilla, R. (eds.) 2017 IEEE International Conference on Software Architecture Workshops, ICSA 2017 Workshops, pp. 282–285. IEEE Computer Society (2017)
3. Balalaie, A., Heydarnoori, A., Jamshidi, P.: Microservices architecture enables DevOps: migration to a cloud-native architecture. IEEE Softw. **33**(3), 42–52 (2016)

4. Balalaie, A., Heydarnoori, A., Jamshidi, P., Tamburri, D.A., Lynn, T.: Microservices migration patterns. Softw. Pract. Experience **48**(11), 2019–2042 (2018). https://doi.org/10.1002/spe.2608
5. Bass, L., Clements, P., Kazman, R.: Software Architecture in Practice, 3rd edn. Addison-Wesley Professional (2012)
6. Bogner, J., Fritzsch, J., Wagner, S., Zimmermann, A.: Microservices in industry: insights into technologies, characteristics, and software quality. In: 2019 IEEE International Conference on Software Architecture Companion (ICSA-C), pp. 187–195. IEEE (2019)
7. Combemale, B., France, R.B., Jézéquel, J.M., Rumpe, B., Steel, J., Vojtisek, D.: Engineering Modeling Languages: Turning Domain Knowledge into Tools, 1st edn. CRC Press (2017)
8. Di Francesco, P., Lago, P., Malavolta, I.: Migrating towards microservice architectures: an industrial survey. In: 2018 IEEE International Conference on Software Architecture (ICSA), pp. 29–38. IEEE (2018)
9. Garcia, J., Popescu, D., Edwards, G., Medvidovic, N.: Identifying architectural bad smells. In: Winter, A., Ferenc, R., Knodel, J. (eds.) Proceedings of the 2009 European Conference on Software Maintenance and Reengineering, CSMR 2009, pp. 255–258. IEEE Computer Society, USA (2009). https://doi.org/10.1109/CSMR.2009.59
10. Granchelli, G., Cardarelli, M., Francesco, P.D., Malavolta, I., Iovino, L., Salle, A.D.: Towards recovering the software architecture of microservice-based systems. In: 2017 IEEE International Conference on Software Architecture Workshops (ICSAW), pp. 46–53. IEEE (2017)
11. Hardy, N.: The confused deputy: (or why capabilities might have been invented). ACM SIGOPS Operating Syst. Rev. **22**(4), 36–38 (1988)
12. Haselböck, S., Weinreich, R., Buchgeher, G.: Decision models for microservices: design areas, stakeholders, use cases, and requirements. In: Lopes, A., de Lemos, R. (eds.) ECSA 2017. LNCS, vol. 10475, pp. 155–170. Springer, Cham (2017). https://doi.org/10.1007/978-3-319-65831-5_11
13. Hassan, S., Ali, N., Bahsoon, R.: Microservice ambients: an architectural meta-modelling approach for microservice granularity. In: 2017 IEEE International Conference on Software Architecture (ICSA), pp. 1–10. IEEE (2017)
14. JHipster: JHipster Domain Language (JDL) (2023). https://www.jhipster.tech/jdl/intro
15. Kapferer, S., Zimmermann, O.: Domain-driven service design. In: Dustdar, S. (ed.) SummerSOC 2020. CCIS, vol. 1310, pp. 189–208. Springer, Cham (2020). https://doi.org/10.1007/978-3-030-64846-6_11
16. Knoche, H., Hasselbring, W.: Drivers and barriers for microservice adoption – a survey among professionals in Germany. Enterp. Model. Inf. Syst. Archit. **14**(1), 1–35 (2019)
17. Morris, K.: Infrastructure as Code. O'Reilly Media (2020)
18. Neri, D., Soldani, J., Zimmermann, O., Brogi, A.: Design principles, architectural smells and refactorings for microservices: a multivocal review. SICS Softw.-Intensive Cyber-Phys. Syst. **35**(1), 3–15 (2020). https://doi.org/10.1007/s00450-019-00407-8
19. Newman, S.: Building Microservices: Designing Fine-Grained Systems. O'Reilly (2015)
20. Pigazzini, I., Fontana, F.A., Lenarduzzi, V., Taibi, D.: Towards microservice smells detection. In: Proceedings of the 3rd International Conference on Technical Debt, TechDebt 2020, pp. 92–97. Association for Computing Machinery, New York, NY, USA (2020). https://doi.org/10.1145/3387906.3388625
21. Ponce, F., Soldani, J., Astudillo, H., Brogi, A.: Should microservice security smells stay or be refactored? Towards a trade-off analysis. In: Gerostathopoulos, I., et al. (eds.) Software Architecture, ECSA 2022. LNCS, vol. 13444, pp. 131–139. Springer, Cham (2022). https://doi.org/10.1007/978-3-031-16697-6_9
22. Ponce, F., Soldani, J., Astudillo, H., Brogi, A.: Smells and refactorings for microservices security: a multivocal literature review. J. Syst. Softw. **192**, 111393 (2022). https://doi.org/10.1016/j.jss.2022.111393

23. Rademacher, F.: A Language Ecosystem for Modeling Microservice Architecture. Ph.D. thesis, University of Kassel (2022)
24. Rademacher, F., Sachweh, S., Zündorf, A.: Deriving microservice code from underspecified domain models using DevOps-enabled modeling languages and model transformations. In: 2020 46th Euromicro Conference on Software Engineering and Advanced Applications (SEAA), pp. 229–236. IEEE (2020).https://doi.org/10.1109/SEAA51224.2020.00047
25. Rademacher, F., Sachweh, S., Zündorf, A.: A modeling method for systematic architecture reconstruction of microservice-based software systems. In: Nurcan, S., Reinhartz-Berger, I., Soffer, P., Zdravkovic, J. (eds.) BPMDS/EMMSAD -2020. LNBIP, vol. 387, pp. 311–326. Springer, Cham (2020). https://doi.org/10.1007/978-3-030-49418-6_21
26. Rahman, A., Parnin, C., Williams, L.: The seven sins: security smells in infrastructure as code scripts. In: 2019 IEEE/ACM 41st International Conference on Software Engineering (ICSE), pp. 164–175 (2019). https://doi.org/10.1109/ICSE.2019.00033
27. Richardson, C.: Microservices Patterns. Manning Publications (2019)
28. Sanchez, A., Barbosa, L.S., Madeira, A.: Modelling and verifying smell-free architectures with the ARCHERY language. In: Canal, C., Idani, A. (eds.) SEFM 2014. LNCS, vol. 8938, pp. 147–163. Springer, Cham (2015). https://doi.org/10.1007/978-3-319-15201-1_10
29. Soldani, J., Muntoni, G., Neri, D., Brogi, A.: The μTOSCA toolchain: mining, analyzing, and refactoring microservice-based architectures. Softw. Pract. Experience **51**(7), 1591–1621 (2021). https://doi.org/10.1002/spe.2974
30. Soldani, J., Tamburri, D.A., Heuvel, W.J.V.D.: The pains and gains of microservices: a systematic grey literature review. J. Syst. Softw. **146**, 215–232 (2018)
31. Sorgalla, J., Wizenty, P., Rademacher, F., Sachweh, S., Zündorf, A.: Applying model-driven engineering to stimulate the adoption of DevOps processes in small and medium-sized development organizations: the case for microservice architecture. SN Comput. Sci. **2**(6), 459 (2021)
32. Taibi, D., Lenarduzzi, V.: On the definition of microservice bad smells. IEEE Softw. **35**(3), 56–62 (2018). https://doi.org/10.1109/MS.2018.2141031
33. Taibi, D., Lenarduzzi, V., Pahl, C.: Microservices anti-patterns: a taxonomy. Microserv. Sci. Eng., 111–128 (2020)
34. Terzić, B., Dimitrieski, V., Kordić, S., Milosavljević, G., Luković, I.: Development and evaluation of MicroBuilder: a model-driven tool for the specification of REST microservice software architectures. Enterp. Inf. Syst. **12**(8–9), 1034–1057 (2018)
35. Vidal, S., Vazquez, H., Diaz-Pace, J.A., Marcos, C., Garcia, A., Oizumi, W.: JSpIRIT: a flexible tool for the analysis of code smells. In: Marín, B., Soto, R. (eds.) 34th International Conference of the Chilean Computer Science Society, SCCC 2015, pp. 1–6. IEEE Computer Society (2015)
36. Wizenty., P., et al.: Towards resolving security smells in microservices, model-driven. In: Proceedings of the 18th International Conference on Software Technologies - ICSOFT, INSTICC, pp. 15–26. SciTePress (2023). https://doi.org/10.5220/0012049800003538

Indentation and Reading Time: A Controlled Experiment on the Differences Between Generated Indented and Non-indented JSON Objects

Stefan Hanenberg[1]([⊠]), Johannes Morzeck[2], Ole Werger[1], Stefan Gries[3], and Volker Gruhn[1]

[1] University of Duisburg-Essen, 45127 Essen, Germany
`stefan.hanenberg@uni-due.de`
[2] Augsburg, Germany
[3] codecentric AG, 42697 Solingen, Germany

Abstract. It is commonly accepted to indent source code to improve its readability, but the evidence for that is quite low. Up to 2022 only few experiments can be found that reveal a positive effect of indentation in terms of reported evidence and reported effect size – actually, the authors of the present paper are only aware of one single experiment up to 2022 that matches the previous statement. In other words, the often articulated positive effect of indentation was hardly backed up by experimental results reported in the literature. The situation changed in 2023, where an experiment suddenly revealed a strong ($p < .001$) and large (effect size = .832; ratio of means = 2.781) effect of indentation in code consisting of if-statements, i.e., a large effect of indentation on the readability of control flows was measured. However, taking the history of studies on indentation into account, it is reasonable to doubt the results: possibly, the effect was caused by hand-chosen examples, respectively by the kind of code used in the experiment (control flows). The here presented study is a follow-up study. First, instead of using hand-chosen examples, the experiment uses generated code. Next, instead of relying on an application's control flow, the present study focusses on data structures by using JSON objects. And finally, the study was designed as a replicated N-of-1 experiment executed on 40 professional developers, where each single subject receives multiple repetitions of all treatment combinations. The study showed a strong ($p < .001$) and large (effect size = .596; ratio of means = 6.44) effect of indentation. A further finding was that the indentation effect varies between participants. And finally, the study's results are comparable to the results achieved by running the experiment only on four of the present paper's authors.

Keywords: Programming · Readability · Indentation

J. Morzeck—Independent Reasearcher.

H.-G. Fill et al. (Eds.): ICSOFT 2023, CCIS 2104, pp. 50–75, 2024.
https://doi.org/10.1007/978-3-031-61753-9_4

1   Introduction

It is common sense to emphasize the need to indent code. Taking a look into well-known teaching books on programming, such as, for example, *"Structure and Interpretation of Computer Programs"* by Abelson and Suessman from 1985, one finds statements such as *"we can help ourselves by [...] following a formatting convention known as pretty-printing [...]. The resulting indentations display clearly the structure [...]"* [2, pp. 6–8]. The JavaScript edition of the book from 2022 contains the similar statement *"adding such whitespace characters to [...] a program text in order to make the text easier to read is called pretty-printing."* [1, p. 337]. Similar statements that argue that indentation improves readability can be found manyfold on the web as well (examples are *"indentation is used to format program source code to improve readability"*[1], or Wikipedia's statement that indentation *"helps better convey the structure of a program to human readers"*[2]). Due to this general acceptance of the benefit of indentation, a number of IDEs (Eclipse, Visual Studio, Visual Studio Code, IntelliJ, just to mention to a few) provide tool support to automatically indent code.[3]

From a scientific view it is necessary to ask, whether such general acceptance of the benefits of indentation is backed up by empirical evidence or whether such strong belief is rather the result of misinformation – and one should keep in mind that misinformation can have a strong effect and that *"misinformation can often continue to influence people's thinking even after they receive a correction and accept it as true"* [8, p. 15].

Taking a look into the scientific literature up to 2022, it turns out that the evidence for the benefit of indentation is far from being conclusive: between 1974 and 2022, the authors of the present paper found twelve experiments in nine publications that use indentation as a controlled factor. If one accepts evidence standards such as CONSORT [20] or APA JARS [4] as validity criteria for reported evidence (both standards consider reported effect sizes – among other things – as a minimum requirement for quantitative studies), only one single experiment remains where a positive effect was found and an effect size was reported – but the reported effect was quite small ($\eta^2=.047$, see [3, p. 3]). Among the other studies, there are seven that explicitly clearify that they did not find an effect of indentation, and among those seven studies, there is even one that explicitly states that *"indentation is indeed simply a matter of task and style, and do(es) not provide support for program comprehension"* [5, p. 163].

With these results in mind, the strong belief in the benefit of indentation is rather surprising. However, it is a well-studied phenomenon that empirical evidence for software technologies in general is rather scarce (see for example

---

[1] http://dev.to/sanjaysinghrajpoot/why-indentation-is-more-important-than-coding-4fn1.

[2] http://en.wikipedia.org/wiki/Indentation_style.

[3] While for some programming languages (such as Python) the use of indentation is part of the programming language semantics, the majority of languages (such as Java, C, or C++ among many others) leaves it up to the developer to decide whether or not (and how) the code should be indented.

[6, 13, 16, 29, 31] among others). Hence, the rather low evidence for the benefit of indentation could mean that current empirical studies were not yet able to reveal the existing benefit of indentation. But it could also mean that the strong, positive effect of indentation is simply a myth.

In 2023, a paper by Morzeck et al. appeared where a strong and large positive effect of indentation was measured (p < .001, $\eta_p^2 = .832$, [21]) – non-indented code took between 142% and 269% more time to read. Additionally, the study gives first indicators that the time benefit could be caused by the code that can be skipped while reading the indented code (but which still needs to be read in non-indented code). In contrast to the previous experiments in the literature, the experiment by Morzeck et al. used artificial code snippets consisting of nested if-statements where participants had to determine the result of the code.

Taking the large divergence between the study by Morzeck et al. with the other studies in literature into account, it is plausible to double-check, whether the measured differences by Morzeck et al. were really caused by indentation or whether they were caused by other effects. We see mainly two possible threats to the validity in Morzeck et al.'s study:

– First, the study used hand-picked code examples (which is quite usual in the literature) – and possibly these examples were (intentionally or accidentally) the main drivers for the difference. I.e., possibly the same kind of code in slightly different variations could reveal different results.
– Second, the focus on control flows was mainly responsible for the difference – and possibly the difference vanishes as soon as code structures would be the focus of the study.

In a (currently unpublished) follow-up study Hanenberg et al. double-checked the first question [10]. In that study, we generated code snippets from a formal model (again, consisting of nested if-statements) and formalized the idea of "skipping code". The strength and size of the measured effects were comparable to the original study (p < .001, $\eta_p^2 = .198$, $\frac{M_{Non-Indented}}{M_{Indented}} = 2.13$). Furthermore, the study gave strong evidence that the skipped code was indeed responsible for the differences in reading time. Hence, that study rejected the hypothesis that the original results by Morzeck et al. were caused by hand-picked code.

The present paper introduces a study that focusses on the second threat, i.e., the possible threat that the results were caused by code that focusses on control flow. In order to do so, an experiment was designed and executed that focussed purely on data structures in general, respectively JSON objects in particular. We gave 40 professional developers generated JSON objects (either represented as indented or non-indented code) to read and asked them the simple question, how many fields the shown object has. The length of the code shown to the participants was the same as in the study by Hanenberg et al. Additionally, the experiment was executed on four of the present authors. It turns out, that – again – there is a strong and large effect of indentation. And it turns out that the results achieved by the authors alone are comparable to the results achieved by 40 professional developers.

The rest of the paper is structured as follows. Section 2 gives a brief overview of indentation and discusses its possible effects. Next, related work will be discussed in Sect. 3. Section 4 describes the design and the results of the experiment. Afterwards, we introduce the study executed on only four authors of the present paper (see Sect. 5) and it turns out that the results are comparable to the results achieved by 40 professional developers. After describing the study's threats to validity in Sect. 6, we summarize and discuss the present study (Sect. 7). Finally, Sect. 8 concludes the paper.

2   Indentation and Its Possible Effects

When speaking about a technology and the effect that is assumed to be connected to that, it makes sense to distinguish both – the description of the technology and the description of the assumed effect. Hence, we start with a very brief description of indentation and then discuss the possible effects.

2.1   Indentation: A Brief Description

In text-based programming languages the term indentation decribes rules for source code elements that receive additional space in terms of white spaces or tabs in the beginning of some lines. In programming languages such as Java, such rules typically express (in addition to some other rules) that after each opening brace a new line follows and the following lines receive additional space in the beginning up to the line that contains the closing brace. Similar indentation rules exist for a number of data formats such as XML, JSON, YAML, etc.

Since we already described indentation in source code of programming languages already in the predecessor of the present study (see [21]), we focus here on data formats (more precisely on JSON objects) taking into account that the here presented study focusses on the possible effect of indentation on data structures.

```
1  {                                      1  {
2      "aField": "aValue",                2  "aField": "aValue",
3      "someOtherField": {                3  "someOtherField": {
4          "yetAnotherField": 42,         4  "yetAnotherField": 42,
5          "evenOneMore": {               5  "evenOneMore": {
6              "almostDone: true          6  "almostDone: true
7          }                              7  }
8      }                                  8  }
9  }                                      9  }
```

Fig. 1. JSON object visualized as indented, respectively non–indented text.

Figure 1 illustrates a simple JSON object consisting of 2 fields where the 2nd field's value is again a JSON object (with 2 fields). A field consists of a key (the left hand side of the colon), a colon, and a value, where the key is written using a string literal. Values can be literals as well or (again) JSON objects. Fields are separated using commas.

In the indented version of the code, additional two whitespaces appear in the beginning of each indentation level (i.e., each nested object), while the non-indented version only uses line breaks.

Different indentation styles have different indentation sizes. The example used two whitespaces at each indentation level. However, 4 whitespaces per level (as proposed in the OpenStack JSON conventions[4]) are also quite popular.

2.2   Possible Effects of Indentation on Reading

A closer look into Fig. 1 gives some first ideas why there are some strong beliefs in the positive effect of indentation.

The indented version of the JSON object seems to make the structure of the object obvious: just by vertically moving one's eyes, one can directly detect that the object has two fields and that the inner object (i.e., the value at the key "someOtherField") has two fields as well. Detecting the same fact from the non-indented version is much harder and requires from the reader a different kind of behavior. The reader of the non-indented code has to detect where opening brackets appear and the reader has to keep in mind (i.e., the reader has to count) for each line how many brackets are still open in order to determine how to interpret the current line of code. I.e., we assume that the reader has to keep in mind that in line three a new inner object begins, and in line five the reader has to keep in mind that an inner object of the (already opened) inner object appears. At line seven, the reader has remember that this is the end of the innermost object. In line eight the reader has to keep in mind that it is the end of the value of "someOtherField" and finally, he has to remember, that there were two values in the outermost object.

We think it is plausible from the previous description to assume that the indented JSON object is easier to read than the non-indented JSON object in case some questions about the structure of the object are asked. If, for example, one asks how many fields the shown object has, we think that this question can be easily answered for the indented code where one just has to count the elements on the first indentation level. For the non-indented code one has to read the whole object and follow the previously described approach of counting opening and closing brackets. Hence, one could quickly come to the conclusion that indentation has a positive effect on reading.

However, we should also emphasize that it probably depends on what information one has to gather from the document. If, for example, the task is to determine how long the object is (in terms of lines of code), it probably does not make any difference whether or not the document is indented. If someone has to determine how many field names appear in the whole object, it also probably does not matter whether or not the document is indented.

Hence, we think that the effect of indentation probably depends on the kind of task one has to fulfill – and we think the more a task requires to understand the structure of the object, the larger is the benefit of indentation.

---

[4] https://docs.openstack.org/doc-contrib-guide/json-conv.html.

3   Related Work

A list of experiments with the controlled factor indentation was already described by Morzeck et al. (see [21]) and based on that a more detailed description of those experiments in the literature was already given by Hanenberg et al. [10]. Due to this, we do not describe each experiment from the literature in detail, but refer to the work by Morzeck et al. for a more detailed description of each experiment (Table 1).

Table 1. Experiments (No) on indentation and publications where they were described (PNo). Kind=Kind of task used in the experiments, DP = Number of data points, Effect = whether a (significant) indentation effect was determined, RE = whether an effect size was reported (only considered, if an effect was shown). The last experiment describes the present experiment. Excerpts from the table were originally described by Morzeck et al. [21] and later on described in a slightly different form by Hanenberg et al. [10].

No	PNo	Experiment	Kind	DP	Effect	RE
1	1	Weissman '74 (1) [32]	self-rating	32	no	–
2	1	Weissman '74 (2) [32]	self-rating	96	no	–
3	1	Weissman '74 (3) [32]	self-rating	48	?	no
4	2	Shneiderman, McKay '76 [28]	bug finding	48	no	–
5	3	Love '77 [17]	recall	124	no	–
6	4	Norcio '82 (1) [22]	fill in the blank	420	yes	no
7	4	Norcio '82 (2) [22] (maybe replicated in No 8)	fill in the blank	360	yes	no
8	5	Norcio, Kerst '83 [23] (maybe replication of No 7)[a]	fill in the blank (maybe recall)	360	no	–
9	6	Miara et al. 1983 [19] (replicated by No 12 with different results)	quiz	86	yes	?
10	7	Kesler et al. 1984 [15]	quiz	72	no	–
11	8	Albayrak and Davenport 2010 [3]	bug finding	88	yes	yes
12	9	Bauer et al. 2019 [5] (replication of No 9 with different results)	output detection	88	no	–
13	10	Morzeck et al. 2023 [21]	output detection	240	yes	yes
14	11	Hanenberg et al. 2023 [10]	output detection	2430	yes	yes
15	12	*present paper*	question about code structure	1050	yes	yes

[a] We are not 100% sure whether the reported experiment in [23] is maybe the same experiment as reported in [22, p. 118] – The experiment setup looks similar (and maybe identical), but the reported results are different.

Altogether, we are aware of 15 experiments (including the one by Morzeck et al. [21], its successor by Hanenberg et al. [10], as well as the present one). If we concentrate on those up to 2022, we find 12 experiments with mixed results.

While the first four experiments by Weissmann [32] and Shneiderman and McKay [28] did not find an effect of indentation, two experiments by Norcio found such an effect [22]. However, the experiments by Norcio do not describe how large the effect is. I.e., following research standards such as CONSORT or APA JARS (that explicitly state that reporting effect sizes are a minimun requirement for quantitative studies) one should today rather not consider the experiments by Norcio as evidence for the benefit of indentation.[5]

The experiment by Miara et al. [19] also showed an effect of indentation – but it is unclear whether or not this experiment should be considered as evidence for the effect of indentation: the experiment does not report numbers on the differences between indented and non-indented code. But the corresponding publication contains a graphical representation of the measurements, which is a first step towards the reporting of effect sizes. However, the same experiment was (according to Bauer et al.) replicated by Bauer et al. [5] without finding an effect. Hence, our interpretation is that the experiment by Miara et al. should not be considered as evidence for the effect of indentation.[6]

What finally remains is the experiment by Albayrak and Davenport that measured an effect of indentation and reported the effect size [3]. In that study, participants where asked to detect a bug in some given code, whereby the authors hardly describe what the code was (except that it had approximately 100 LOC written in Java) and what errors were to be found. From our perspective, this could be definitively considered as evidence for the effectiveness of indentation and the authors reported that 25% less errors were found without indentation – however, the reported effect size was not extraordinary strong (p = .042) and quite small (η^2 = .047).

It is worth mentioning that all those experiments up to 2022 have a large variety of different code shown to participants (all except Albayrak and Davenport and Bauer et al. used code snippets from text books). Additionally, there is a large variety of different independent variables in the experiments (different questionnaires, time measurements, number of errors) as well as different kinds of tasks given to the participants (from self-ratings up to output detection). And finally, the number of data points differed quite drastically in those studies.

---

[5] The mentioned research standards appeared later than the mentioned studies. I.e., the statement that – today – one should not consider these experiments, should not be considered as a criticicm of the authors of the study or the study itself. It means, that today's interpretation of quantitative studies is different than decades ago.

[6] Actually, the problem is slightly more complicated. Here, we follow the argument by Bauer et al. [5] who explicitly state that their experiment is a replication of experiment by Miara et al. [19]. Actually, we have doubts whether the experiment by Bauer et al. should be considered as a replication – the differences to the original experiments are quite large (used programming language, used progams, used measurements and measurement techniques).

While, for example, the first study by Weissman just collected 32 data points, the first study by Norcia collected 420 data points.

The situation changed in 2023 when the predecessor of the present study waspublished by Morzeck et al. [21] where for the first time not only a strong (p < .001), but also large effect of indentation was measured ($\eta_p^2 = .832$, $\frac{M_{Non-Indented}}{M_{Indented}}$ = 2.79). In that study, (nested) if-statements were shown to participants and it was asked, what the result of the code is. The dependent variable was time to answer. It turned out that non-indented code required more time to answer the question in comparison to indented code. Additionally, the study revealed a first indicator that the difference in times could be caused by the code that can be skipped. However, although skipping was in principle a controlled factor, the source code for skippable and non-skippable code was hand-picked and it is not 100% clear how the distinction can be less subjectively done.

In a follow-up study, we focussed on the possibility to explain the differences in answer time between indented and non-indented code. From on a formal model that assumed to predict such differences, parameters were extracted and used as independent variables, where all code shown to the experiment's participants had the same length (29 LOC). The code itself was randomly generated from the formal model. Additionally – in order to make results between participants comparable – the experiment was a so-called N-of-1 following the principles as described by Hanenberg and Mehlhorn [9]: all participants received multiple repetitions of all treatment combinations in random order (i.e., the order was randomly chosen for the experiment, while each participant received the identical order). Again, the study shows a strong (p < .001) and large positive effect of indentation ($\eta_p^2 = .198$, $\frac{M_{Non-Indented}}{M_{Indented}}$ = 2.13). The experiment confirmed that code that can be skipped influences the difference between indented and non-indented code (p = .001, $\eta_p^2 = .072$).

As already stated, the here presented experiment – although it no longer concentrates on control flows – is in line with its two predecessors. Again, strong and large positive effects of indentation were detected (details will be described in the following sections).

4   Experiment

The goal of the present study is to study the possible effect of indentation on structures instead of control flows. Before introducing the formal layout, its execution, and the results, we first discuss some initial considerations that finally led to the experiment design.

4.1   Initial Considerations

The goal is to design a controlled experiment where data objects are shown to participants. For the code to be shown, we took different possibilities into account. One alternative could be (to be in line with previous studies) to use the syntax of a programming language and then ask questions about the code. However, we also see the possibility to use an often used data format.

Data Format. Examples of such formats could be XML, YAML, or JSON. We decided to use JSON objects, because it seems that XML is less often used in the more recent past and it is not yet clear whether data formats such as YAML will become similarly popular as JSON currently already is.

Measurements. As practiced in multiple previous experiments (see for example [9,18,21,27]) we measure reaction time, i.e., the time a participant requires to answer a question. We did that by starting a time measurement when a task is shown to the participant and by stopping the time when an answer was given.

Task. We discussed in Sect. 2.2 that the effect of indentation possibly depends on the given task. We do not think that for tasks such as "count the lines of code" indentation has any effect – but considering that the goal of indentation is to highlight code structures, we see no reason for giving participants such a task. Instead, we want to ask people a question that is related to an object's structure. We decided to ask participants the single question *"how many fields has the outermost object?"*.[7]

Code Generation (1). Our goal was not to use hand-picked examples, but generated examples – an approach we already applied multiple times (see for example [9–11,27]). There are different reasons why we used generated code. First, generated code potentially even permits the authors to participate in an experiment, which makes it easier to pilot a study. Next, generating code increases the replicability of a study, because one has to define precisely how the code was generated. Additionally, the same generation principle can be applied in order to generate a test phase for participants. We generated code according to the following principle. First, in order to make the results somehow comparable to the study by Hanenberg et al. [10], we used the same lines of code (29 LOC) as in the previous experiment. In order to make the code snippets within the experiment comparable, we furthermore required a generated statement to contain seven fields with atomic values. The field names were randomly chosen from the list of words we already used in previous experiments (see [9]). Keys and values were string literals (including quotation marks).

Code Generation (2). Since we asked participants for the number of fields in the outermost object, there is the need to vary this. It is to a certain extent plausible to us that a different number of fields influences the answer time - but we do not know (and actually doubt) that the number of fields has any interaction effect with the main variable indentation. In other words, although there is a

---

[7] It has some practical benefits to ask one single question for all tasks: participants do not need to read and understand different questions for different tasks which potentially influences the measurements. A more detailed argumentation for asking a single question can be found for example in [9].

need to vary the number of elements in a controlled way (since it potentially influences the measurements), this variable would only be of interest, if there are interaction effects with the main variable indentation. When deciding for the number of different treatments for the variable number of fields, one has to keep in mind that N-of-1 experiments need to contain repetitions for each treatment combination. Hence, a larger number of treatment combination also increases the effort for participants in the experiment. Because of this, we decided to only have three treatments for the number of fields: 1, 3, and 5.

4.2   Experiment Layout

Following the previous discussion, the experiment was designed as an N-of-1 experiment. The experiment layout consists of the following parameters:

- **Dependent variables:**
  - **reaction time:** The time until the participant responds to the question.
  - **correctness:** Whether or not the response was correct.
- **Independent variables:**
  - **indentation:** The representation of the code with the two treatments indented and non-indented code. Indented code has four whitespaces for each level of indentation.
  - **number of fields:** The number of children of the outermost object with the treatments 1, 3, and 5.
- **Fixed variables:**
  - **given code:** JSON objects consisting of 29 lines of code, containing exactly seven atomic fields. Field names were string literals (i.e., with quotations marks), the only atomic values were string literals as well.
  - **randomization:** The JSON objects were randomly generated. All strings were randomly chosen from a list of nouns.
  - **repetitions:** Each participant received 5 repetitions per treatment combination, i.e., altogether 30 code snippets.
  - **ordering:** The code snippets where randomly ordered before the experiment. All participants received the same snippets in the same order.
- **Task:** *"How many fields has the outermost JSON object?"*

The independent variable *number of fields* is a technical variable that plays from our perspective a rather minor role. It would only become relevant, if it interacts with the main variable indentation.

4.3   Protocol

The experiment was implemented via a web application[8] that guided participants thoughout the experiment.[9] After the experiment is executed, a csv file

---

[8] The application is public available and executable via the link: https://htmlpreview. github.io/?https://raw.githubusercontent.com/shanenbe/Experiments/main/ 2023_Indentation_JSON/index.html.

[9] The experiment has an IRB approval (No 2303001) of the ethics board of the University of Duisburg–Essen, Faculty of Economy.

is generated and the participant is asked to send the csv file in addition to an information sheet to one of the authors of the present paper.[10] The experiment was not supervised. I.e., it is not possible to determine for the authors whether data sent to them can be considered as serious experiment participation.

The application generates a test-phase where a number of indented and non-indented code snippets are shown to the participant. The participants are explicitly asked to practice the experiment – and they are told that it is up to them to decide whether or not they consider the training as sufficient. Furthermore, the participants were told that it is possible to take a break between two tasks, i.e., when an answer was given. The app does not log whether and how long such breaks were taken.

4.4   Execution

The participants where chosen based on purposive sampling [25]: the authors asked colleagues working in the industry (i.e., professional developers) to participate. The participants were told that participation takes between 5 to 10 min (depending on the training phase).

Altogether, we received 40 responses. 26 participants answered to the question how many years of working experience as a software developer they have. The arithmetic mean of working experience (on those participants who answered the question) was 5.9 (median 5).

4.5   Possible Outliers

Before analyzing, we manually inspected the data in order to detect possible outliers. Actually, we think it is problematic in general to exclude data from a sample, because it too easily leads to a possible confirmation bias of authors. Furthermore, we are aware – although there are multiple technical ways to handle outliers (see for example [26]) – that there is no non-subjective way to identify data sets that actually are outliers. Before going into detail we want to point out that we are aware of the potential risk to remove data from the data set. Because of that potential risk, we decided to report in the analysis section not only the results of the corrected sample (removed outliers) but also the raw sample (where it turns out that the main result of the experiment is the same). Still, considering that the data collection was not supervised, we think there is a need to identify possibly outliers.

Manually inspecting the sample revealed the following phenomena:

First, a number of participants had a substantial large number or errors. We think it is plausible to consider only participants who "seriously tried to solve the tasks" – and we assume that if someone has 10 or more errors (in 30 tasks), that probably the tasks have not been appropriately solved. Hence, we think

---

[10] On the information sheet, the participant signs that they agree that they permit the authors to use the data in a scientific analysis and a possible publication.

it is valid to categorize participants with 10 or more errors as outliers. Eight participants had ten or more errors.

There is one participant (no 24) who required extraordinary long to do tasks for the indented code (while most participants required only few seconds to solve an indented task, all times of that participant were higher than 10 s). We asked the participant after receiving the data set how it comes the the whole experiment took him much longer than expected (we did not tell him that he required much longer than all other participants) and he told us that he assumed there there would be errors in the indented code. He told us that he inspected the indented code as careful as he inspected the non-indented code (despite the fact that no task in the training set contained any errors). Because of that, we think that this participant can be considered as a outlier as well. We identified another data set comparable to participant 24 (participant 16, this time, there was no single answer for indented code less than 10 s). We contacted the participant later on, but did not get a response. We believe, that something comparable to participant 24 happened here and we believe that for the same reason the participant should be considered as an outlier.

There is one single data point for one participant (no 19) that is extraordinary larger than all other data points: for participant 19, the very first task (which was an indented task) took him more than 180 s. We believe that the participant must have misunderstood the information when a break can be taken. We think that this alone could be reason enough to identify that participant as outlier – actually, the same participant made 10 errors, hence, he was already classified as outlier using the previous outlier criterion.

Again, in the following the sample was analyzed with and without outliers to make clear that – even in case our identification of outliers is rather a form of confirmation bias of the authors – the main results of the study are comparable – independent of the question whether or not outliers were removed.

4.6 Analysis

The data was analyzed using an ANOVA for the dependent variable reaction time. The dependent variable number of errors was analyzed using a χ^2 test (each using Jamovi 2.3.19.0 [12]). In addition to the variables indentation and number of fields, the variable participant was considered (in order to check, whether there are differences between different participants).[11]

The results for the raw sample (including outliers) are shown in Table 2, the results of the sample where outliers were removed are shown in Table 3.

Although the numbers slightly differ in detail between the analysis with and without outliers, it turns out that in both cases (for the dependent variable reaction time) the identical variables are significant, respectively non-significant: the main variable indentation is significant, the helper variable number of fields is

---

[11] Again, we need to point out that this it is a characteristic of N-of-1 trials. Multiple repetitions per treatment combination are given to participants which permit to use the participant as an independent variable on its own.

Table 2. Raw experimental results (without removing outliers). Confidence intervals (CI) and means (M) are given in seconds (with only two decimals); Treatments (TRT) are abbreviated to ease the readability of the table (indented=i, Non-Indented=ni). The variable number of fields is abbreviated by num (n).

ANOVA on Reaction Time

Variable	df	F	p	η_p^2	TRT	$CI_{95\%}$	M
indent. (i)	1	636.725	<.001***	.399	i	4,48; 6.22	5.355
					ni	19.64; 21.31	20.47
num (n)	2	8.717	<.001***	.018	1	9.80; 12.69	11.25
					3	11.14; 14.46	12.80
					5	12.82; 15.67	14.25
part. (p)	39	19.334	<.001***	.440	*see Section 4.7*		
p*i	39	7.161	<.001***	.225	*see Section 4.7*		
p*n	78	.671	.987	.052	*omitted due to non-significant effect*		
i*n	2	.316	.729	.001	*omitted due to non-significant effect*		
p*i*n	76	.698	.977	.054	*omitted due to non-significant effect*		

χ^2-Test on Errors

Variable	df	χ^2	p	N	Treatment	Errors
indentation	1	237	<.001***	600	i	10
				600	ni	220

Table 3. Experimental results (outliers removed). Confidence intervals (CI) and means (M) are given in seconds (with only two decimals); Treatments (TRT) are abbreviated to ease the readability of the table (indented=i, Non-Indented=ni). The variable number of fields is abbreviated by num (n).

ANOVA on Reaction Time

Variable	df	F	p	η_p^2	TRT	$CI_{95\%}$	M
indent. (i)	1	1064.073	<.001***	.596	i	2.85;3.50	3.17
					ni	19.08; 21.73	20.41
num (n)	2	13.195	<.001***	.029	1	8.87; 11.84	10.35
					3	9.88; 13.07	11.48
					5	12.03; 15.06	13.55
part. (p)	29	14.471	<.001***	.368	*see Section 4.7*		
p*i	35	9.946	<.001***	.286	*see Section 4.7*		
p*n	70	.918	.649	.069	*omitted due to non-significant effect*		
i*n	2	1.013	.364	.003	*omitted due to non-significant effect*		
p*i*n	72	.785	.876	.059	*omitted due to non-significant effect*		

χ^2-Test on Errors

Variable	df	χ^2	p	N	Treatment	Errors
indentation	1	144	<.001***	450	i	3
				450	ni	131

significant and the variable participant is significant as well.[12] Furthermore, the variable participant interacts with the variable indentation. No other interactions were detected. With respect to the dependent variable number of errors, indentation is in both cases significant.

While it is interesting that certain variables are significant, one should not forget to take a look at the effect sizes. No matter whether or not outliers were considered, the effect of indentation is large ($\eta_p^2 = .399$, $\frac{M_{Non-Indented}}{M_{Indented}} = 3.82$ including outliers, $\eta_p^2 = .596$, $\frac{M_{Non-Indented}}{M_{Indented}} = 6.44$ excluding outliers). However, the difference in the ratios is worth mentioning, because including outliers reading the indented code requires "just" factor 2.82 more time, while without outliers the indented code requires factor 5.44 more time to read in comparison to the non-indented code.

With respect to the number of errors, the ratios $\frac{Number\,of\,errors_{Non-Indented}}{Number\,of\,errors_{Indented}}$ $= 22$ (including outliers) and $\frac{Number\,of\,errors_{Non-Indented}}{Number\,of\,errors_{Indented}} = 43.67$ (with removed outliers) also differ substantially. However, in both cases, the differences are still large.

4.7 Analysis per Participant

The experiment was designed as an N-of-1 trial. In such kind of experiments all participants received all treatment combinations with multiple repetitions. As a consequence, it is possible to analyse each participant in separation.

Table 4 summarizes the results for each participant. In order to improve the readability, we only describe for each participant whether the p-value for the independent variable indentation was significant. Additionally, we describe the means for the indented and the non-indented JSON objects as well as the number of errors each participant had in the experiment. Furthermore, we describe for each participant the ratio of means for non-indented and indented reaction times ($\frac{M_{Non-Indented}}{M_{Indented}}$, abbreviated as $\frac{M_{NI}}{M_I}$).

If we ignore whether or not a participant can be considered as an outlier, 34/40 participants (i.e., 85%) revealed a positive effect of indentation (with p < .001 for 33/40 participants). By just focussing on the ratios, it turns out that two participants had a negative effect of indentation.

As soon as we remove the ten outliers, the situation is slighty different: 28/30 participants (i.e., 93.3%) revealed a positive effect of indentation while two (No 9 and 17) did not reveal a signficant effect of the variable indentation. Still, both participants show a ratio $\frac{M_{Non-Indented}}{M_{Indented}}$ considerably larger than 1: in both cases the non-indented JSON objects required more than twice the time the indented JSON objects required.

---

[12] For the analysis of the corrected sample (removed outliers) the degrees of freedom for the variable participant as well as the degrees of freedom for the corresponding interactions are different, because we removed participants (outliers).

Table 4. Results per participant: p = p-value for the variable indentation; E = number of errors. Outlier describes whether the participant was considered as an outlier (no value = no outlier, errors = outlier because of the number of errors, behavior = outlier because of the behavior, see Sect. 4.5).

ANOVA on Reaction Time

No	p	E	M_I; M_{NI}	$\frac{M_{NI}}{M_I}$	outlier?	No	p	E	M_I; M_{NI}	$\frac{M_{NI}}{M_I}$	outlier?
1	< .001	3	1.8; 11.0	6.1		21	< .001	8	8.1; 40.4	4.99	
2	< .001	8	2.7; 13.0	4.81		22	.041	13	3.6; 16.5	4.58	errors
3	< .001	0	2.7; 22.0	8.15		23	.001	12	2.3; 7.9	3.43	errors
4	< .001	5	3.5; 15.0	4.29		24	< .001	10	3.4; 28.1	7.39	errors
5	< .001	1	2.2; 25.5	11.60		25	< .001	4	3.1; 37.6	11.06	
6	< .001	2	2.7; 29.4	10.89		26	< .001	1	1.5; 13.7	9,13	
7	< .001	3	2.3; 14.4	6.26		27	< .001	10	9.0; 22.1	2.45	errors
8	< .001	7	3.9; 30.0	7.69		28	< .001	9	1.1; 3.3	3.00	
9	.438	1	10.2; 28.2	2.76		29	< .001	7	2.7; 8.7	3.22	
10	< .001	16	2.1; 4.9	2.33	errors	30	< .001	7	3.0; 17.2	5.73	
11	< .001	1	2.3; 25.1	10.91		31	< .001	5	8.0; 21.9	2.74	
12	< .001	6	3.3; 21.1	6.39		32	< .001	10	4.9; 11.2	2.29	errors
13	< .001	6	2.9; 25.9	8.93		33	< .001	3	3.6; 18.1	5.03	
14	< .001	5	2.5; 12.1	4.84		34	.147	11	3.3; 4.9	1.48	errors
15	.087	0	38.8; 55.0	1.41	behavior	35	< .001	9	2.8; 9.1	3.25	
16	.532	4	27.5; 25.4	0.92	behavior	36	< .001	1	4.1; 29.1	7.07	
17	.106	8	3.11; 18.2	5.85		37	< .001	2	1.9; 21.5	11.20	
18	< .001	5	1.6; 10.1	6.31		38	< .001	9	1.9; 20.2	10.63	
19	.687	10	23.9; 19.0	0.79	errors	39	< .001	4	2.5; 44.6	17.84	
20	.001	5	2.4; 17.0	7.08		40	< .001	0	1.2; 8.3	6.92	

It is noteworthy how large the difference in the ratios $\frac{M_{Non-Indented}}{M_{Indented}}$ are. While there are seven participants where the mean for the non-indented JSON objects was more than 10 times of the mean for the non-indented JSON object, there are (beyond the already mentioned outliers) participants where the ratio is below 3 (such as participant 31 or participant 9). I.e., there is a large variation in the ratios. A plausible idea could be that participants who did less errors probably spent more time in general and especially more time on the non-indented JSON objects. However, testing this via a linear regression (number of errors as predictor for the ratio) gives only a first impression that this could be the case (p = .057).

4.8 Discussion So Far

So far, we received a clear answer to the possible effect of indentation on the readability of JSON objects. No matter whether or not we exclude participants (because they are possibly outliers), the effect of indentation is strong (p < .001) and large (at least $\eta_p^2 = .399$, $\frac{M_{Non-Indented}}{M_{Indented}} = 3.82$). I.e., reading non-indented JSON objects required the participants on average factor 2.82 more time. Additionally, the number of errors for non-indented JSON objects were much higher than for indented JSON objects (220/10 errors including data sets that we considered as outliers, respectively 131/3 errors).

It might be slightly surprising that participants even did errors for the indented JSON objects. However, we need to take into account that there is always the chance of a typo (i.e. a participant pressed accidenally a button although he intended to press a different one). But we also need to consider that participants could possibly give a correct answer although the response was just guessed. We also need to include the possibility that participants are not aware of the complexity of the given tasks: possibly some participants just guess the number of fields in a non-indented JSON object instead of counting.

When concentrating on each individual participant, we see that there is a large variation between them: while for a substantial number of participant the ratio $\frac{M_{Non-Indented}}{M_{Indented}}$ is larger than 10 (and there is even one participant with a ratio of almost 18), there are even participants who do not reveal a significant effect of the variable indentation: this statement holds true for 6 participants – where four or them were identified as outliers. This emphasizes once more that outlier identification possibly influences the interpretation of the experiment. However, this also possibly reveals something else: the potential risk of running N-of-1 studies only on a single participant. Following the approach, six of fourty participants would not have shown an effect of indentation. Again, this argumentation does not mean that the study revealed any indicator that there could not be a difference in readability of indented and non-indented code: the effect of indentation is clearly shown by the study.

We should point out that the experiment follows the principle of its predecessors [10,21]: the experiment is highly controlled (by using artificial code snippets) and the question is the same for all shown code snippets. As already discussed in Sect. 2.2 we do not think that indentation is helpful in all cases and under all conditions – and probably the most trivial task could be "count the number of lines of code" where indentation has (probably) no effect. One could argue that this approach is mainly responsible for showing an effect – and it explains why in literature most experiments do not reveal a difference. However, our interpretation is different. First, we use artificial code snippets in order to reduce the deviation caused by other effects of natural code (such as difficulty of the code caused by the underlying algorithms). Second, we use one single question in order to have comparable results between the different code snippets. From our perspective, this is rather a characteristic of highly controlled experiments – which permits to reveal the studied effect without having the measurements polluted too much by confounding factors that are not in the focus of the study.

5 Exploratory Analyses: The Authors' Results

However, one question remains – and this kind of question is something that we frequently ask ourselves when running (repeated) N-of-1 studies: How many participants should have been used in the study? Actually, the question to us is often, whether it is enough to run a study only on the experimenters themselves (see for example the discussion in [9]).

Before giving an experiment to participants, one usually runs a pilot study. Such pilot study is not only necessary to test whether the experiment is understandable and correct. Such pilot is also necessary to estimate the time required by participants in an experiment (in order to give participants a fair estimation what effort is required by the experiment). Four of the authors of the present study ran the present study before it was delivered to participants. Table 5 shows the results of these four authors.

Table 5. Results of the pilot (four authors of the present study). Confidence intervals (CI) and means (M) are given in seconds (with only two decimals); Treatments (TRT) are abbreviated to ease the readability of the table (indented=i, Non-Indented=ni). The variable number of children is abbreviated by num (n).

ANOVA on Reaction Time							
Variable	df	F	p	η_p^2	TRT	$CI_{95\%}$	M
indent. (i)	1	193.195	<.001***	.668	i	2.53;3.41	2.97
					ni	15.56; 22.21	18.89
num (n)	2	2.347	.101	.047	omitted due to non-significant effect		
part. (p)	3	24.90	<.001***	.438	see Table 6		
p*i	3	22.404	<.001***	.412	see Table 6		
p*n	6	.840	.542	.050	omitted due to non-significant effect		
i*n	2	.249	.780	.005	omitted due to non-significant effect		
p*i*n	6	.764	.600	.046	omitted due to non-significant effect		

χ^2-Test on Errors						
Variable	df	χ^2	p	N	Treatment	Errors
indentation	1	26.9	<.001***	60	i	0
				60	ni	22

It turns out that the main variable indentation is significant for the authors, while the variable number of children is not significant (p = .101). The authors themselves had significantly different response times and while there is a significant interaction between variable participant (i.e., authors in the present analysis) and the variable indentation, there are no other significant interactions. The authors did not do any error in the non-indented code, but altogether, they did 22 errors for non-indented JSON objects. The ratio $\frac{M_{Non-Indented}}{M_{Indented}}$ is 6.36 (Table 6).

Table 6. Results per author: p = p-value for the variable indentation; E = number of errors.

ANOVA on Reaction Time									
No	p	E	M_I; M_{NI}	$\frac{M_{NI}}{M_I}$	No	p	E	M_I; M_{NI}	$\frac{M_{NI}}{M_I}$
1	< .001	7	3.0; 26.2	8.73	3	< .001	8	2.6; 7.7	2.96
2	< .001	5	2.9; 11.2	3.86	4	.041	2	3.4; 30.5	8.97

A closer look into the individual results of the authors reveals a large deviation between the authors (all of them have a significant effect of the variable indentation). While two authors have a ratio $\frac{M_{Non-Indented}}{M_{Indented}}$ above 9, one has a ratio close to 3, another one a ratio close to 4.

If we compare the authors' results with the sample consisting of professional developers, there is one noteworthy difference: none of the authors would have been classified as an outlier. The second difference is, that in the whole sample of all authors the technical variable number of fields was not significant. With respect to the number of errors, the authors did not make any error in the indented code (but also have 2–8 errors each in the non-indented code).

But it turns out that the main results of the study are comparable to the results that would have been achieved with the data from the authors: the variable indentation is strong (p < .001 for both, the whole sample and a sample consisting only of the authors) and large (without the outliers the results were $\eta_p^2 = .596$, $\frac{M_{Non-Indented}}{M_{Indented}} = 0.44$, the results of the authors are $\eta_p^2 = .668$, $\frac{M_{Non-Indented}}{M_{Indented}} = 6.36$): not only the effect sizes are quite similar, even the ratios are comparable.

In other words, the present study was executed on 40 professional participants. But if the study would have been executed only on the authors, the main results would have been the same. Even the concrete numbers would have been comparable.

6 Threats to Validity

We see a number of possible threats to validity in the present study.

Non-supervised Experiment Execution (1). The experiment execution was not supervised. Consequently, it is not possible to judge whether or not a participant followed the experiment protocol or whether the execution was disturbed by some external factors. As described in Sect. 4.5 we think that some data sets indicate that some other factors played a role. One could argue that this should rather be an argument for running only supervised experiments. The alternative is to remove data sets from the analysis that are suspicious. In the present study we reported the results including and excluding potential outliers. Although the consequence was that the size of the effect differed, it turned out that in both cases the effect of indentation was strong and large.

Non-supervised Experiment Execution (2). The experiment requires that participants do seriously try to solve the given tasks. We got a number of comments from the participants (when they submitted the data to us) that they considered the non-indented code as extraordinary hard and that they sometimes rather guessed what the answer was for the non-indented code (instead of double-checking whether the answer was correct). The potential threat is caused by participants who give up too quickly and "just press a button". In that case one receives fast response times that do not indicate that the task was quickly solved, but rather that the task was not seriously answered. As a consequence, one also receives a higher number of errors. We handled the situation by removing participants with a high number of errors (where at least a third of the responses was wrong), but also analyzed and reported the data including the outliers.

Intention of Participants. Another threat is, that participants could intentionally adapt their behavior because they want to enforce certain experimental results. I.e., the main difference to the previously mentioned threats is the possible intent of participants. While there are techniques in other disciplines to handle such situation (such as blinded experiments or placebo experiments, see Kaptchuk [14] for a historical description in medicine, respectively Stefik et al. [30] as a trial to run placebo studies in programming language studies), we are not aware how such techniques could be applied to software science experiments in general, respectively in the present study in particular.

Removing Outliers. All the previously mentioned threats address the problem that potentially the received data does not represent the "real data" and we argued in the present paper that removing outliers reduces this problem. However, we need to point out that removing outliers from the sample could also express a confirmation bias of the experimenters: instead of trying to find out clear exclusion criteria, experimenters might be attempted to remove those data sets that do not match the expected outcome. Such behavior (which could be intentional or accidental) of experimenters could contradict the whole idea of running controlled experiments that potentially show different results than expected by the experimenters. In order to overcome this potential threat, we reported the analysis including and excluding outliers and it turned out that the general result (strong and large positive effect of indentation) is the same.

Training. We left it to the participants to decide whether the training was enough for them. This probably caused that some participants were better trained than others. In principle, one could argue that this is a potential problem, because there are probably some participants who practice the experiment more than others. However, we are not yet aware how this could be handled better. One could argue that there should be a clearly defined training phase (either in terms of number of tasks to be done before the experiment, or in terms of the time someone should spend on the training phase), but one should keep in mind that training might be an individual activity: even testing participants after a training session (by defining some inclusion criterion such as number of correct answers, etc.) does not automatically mean that the participants' capabilities with respect to the studied item are comparable (because some might still be better than others).

Generated Source Code – Carry Over Effects. We think that the approach to generate tasks for an experiment is rather a strength of this kind of experiment. However, the experimental environment also randomly generated source code for the training sessions. As a consequence, it is possible that some identical or comparable code snippets are shown to participants in the training session. Although we cannot exclude that there are some carry-over effects from the training session to the experiment sessions, we actually doubt that participants remember possible similarities between JSON objects in the training and in the experiment session: again, the training session was randomly generated.

Generated Source Code – Generalizability. The here presented experiment intentionally used artificial code snippets (comparable to the experiment's predecessors). Obviously, the code does not represent arbitrary industrial code. This implies that we cannot generalize the measured differences to arbitrary industrial code – but we want to emphasize that this is not an accidental problem of the present study, but an intended feature: our goal was (similar to this experiment's predecessors) to remove potential confounding factors such as algorithmic complexity, etc. But removing such confounding factors automatically implies that the resulting code used in a study does no longer represents industrial code.

Given Task – Generalizability. Finally, the given task is a threat on its own. The experiment just asks for the number of fields of the outermost object. Obviously, this is not the only question one could ask, and possible it takes longer (even for the indented code) to identify the number of fields of some inner objects. One could (and should) say that the task itself is only an indicator whether the given structure is better understood. However, giving participants just one single task has from an experimental perspective the benefit that participants do not need to understand different tasks. Still, obviously the measurements are not generalizable with respect to that they represent the time one requires to understand a given structure.

7 Summary and Discussion

The original study by Morzeck et al. [21] was motivated by the fact that indentation – although massively taught and applied – has hardly any evidence in the literature and that even a suprising number of published experiments did not show any effect of indentation at all. The study by Morzeck et al. executed a randomized control trial on 20 participants. The participants had to detect the outcome of given source code, whereby the source code consisted of (nested) if-statements. Morzeck et al. found a strong (p < .001) and large effect ($\eta_p^2 = .832$, $\frac{M_{Non-Indented}}{M_{Indented}} = 2.781$): on average, non-indented code required 178% more time to read than indented code. Because of the surprising difference to the existing literature, we first executed a follow-up study that confirmed the results of the original study – again, if-statements were used and again the effects were strong and large ($\eta_p^2 = .198$, $\frac{M_{Non-Indented}}{M_{Indented}} = 2.13$ on average). That study also revealed that non-indented code caused a higher number of errors in the responses.

The present study is another follow-up study with the focus on data objects (instead of if-statements). Thereto, JSON objects were shown to 40 professional developers and they were asked, how many fields the shown JSON object has. The present study showed again a strong and large effect of indentation (p < .001; $\eta_p^2 = .596$; $\frac{M_{Non-Indented}}{M_{Indented}} = 6.44$). Additionally, the study showed that non-indented JSON objects caused a higher number of errors.

Comparing the results of these three experiments (i.e., our original experiment [21] and its two follow-up studies) with the previously reported experiments in the literature, it is noteworthy how large the differences are: these three experiments revealed not even an indicator that non-indented code could lead to comparable numbers as non-indented code (although the majority of experiments in the literature did not detect such as difference).

We believe that the reason for this phenomenon is caused by three factors.

First, our experiments are highly controlled experiments, where not only the experimental environment is controlled but the code given to participants is controlled as well: all code snippets were chosen with strong constraints. For example, the original experiment by Morzeck et al. already restricted the lines of code, so did its two successors. Furthermore, the language constructs were highly controlled (either nested if-statements or generated JSON objects) instead of using code snippets from industrial code, i.e., any algorithmic complexity was removed from the code snippets.

Second, we collected a high number of data points in all experiments (240, 2430, respectively 1050). While the first experiment did not collect an extraordinary high number of data points (the experiments by Norcio [22] and Norcio and Kerst [23] already collected 420 respectivly 360 data points), they are still much higher than the majority of experiments. It is a known fact that the higher the number of data points, the higher the chance to detect an effect in an experiment (*"[...] if the null hypothesis is not rejected, it usually is because the N is too small."* [24, p. 643]). Hence, we think that a larger N contributed to the results of the present study (and its predecessors).

Third, the dependent variables (reaction time, respectively number of errors) probably have a larger effect on the results. In literature, a number of different dependent variables (and measurement techniques) were applied. In the beginning, self-ratings were applied (see [32]) as well as so-called quizzes (such as [15,19]). We believe that such approaches are rather problematic because it (probably) depends largely on the kinds of questions being asked and such approaches (probably) cause a larger deviation between participants.

We believe that the combination of the previously mentioned factors has an additive effect, which permits more easily to reveal the effect of indentation.

Finally, we want to point out that we believe that the application of a N-of-1 trial has some other effects that should not be underestimated. We know from literature that developers have the tendency to believe in the effect of a technology based on their personal experience and not based on reading literature: the study by Devambu et al. [7] revealed that the vast majority of developers stated that their knowledge about software technology is mainly driven by their own personal experience instead of reading scientific reports. N-of-1 studies could be a chance to combine both: developers can (by participating in such an experiment) experience the potential effect of technology. At the same time, it is possible to evaluate their results using the scientific method. Hence, we believe that N-of-1 experiments could potentially help to bring scientific results into industry.

Nevertheless, we should also point out potential problems of non-supervised N-of-1 trials (and possibly non-supervised experiments in general): it is possible that participants do not follow the experimental procedure. As a consequence, it is possible that results do not reveal the "actual results of the study" but results that are caused by participants who somehow adapted their behavior within or throughout the experiment. We think that we detected some of such outliers in the experiment. But we should point out that the results of the present experiment do not change in their interpretation whether or not outliers were removed. However, we are also aware of the potential problem of removing outliers (which could express a confirmation bias of the experimenters) and intentionally analyzed the results with and without outliers.

In general, we think that the problem of possible (or not possible) outliers reflects on a general problem we find today in software science experiments: the problem that participants today have a strong effect on an experiment's results. In other disciplines such as medicine such problem is known since centuries – and different techniques such as blinded experiments were invented and applied (see [14] for an history of blinded experimentation in medicine). However, it is up to our knowledge unclear how similar techniques could be applied in software science in general, respectively in readability experiments in particular: participants can obviously see a treatment. I.e., it is unclear to us how a placebo could be given to participants in a sense that participants "think" that they are somehow treated (although they are not). One might argue that not telling participants the focus of the study would reduce the problem,[13] however, it is up to our knowledge not clear whether or not this would lead to the desired

---

[13] We should point out that not telling participants the goal of a study is a practical problem: some IRBs explicitly require from experimenters to tell possible participants the goal of experiments. For example, the ethics board that approved the present study explicitly requires from us to make the goal of experiments explicit. Hence – in order to get an IRB approval – not telling participants what is studied in an experiment is not an option.

effect: in the end, participants can still just do something different than what is expected and it is hard to find non-subjective criteria that distinguish between participants who follow an experimental protocol and those who don't.

In addition to the previously said, we think it is desirable in the future not only to determine whether or not an effect of indentation exists, but to find the reasons for the difference between indented and non-indented code. Such reasons could help to identify readability models that give evidence for different coding styles, etc. We were able to identify such a readability model (at least to a certain extent) in a previous study on control flows (see [10]), but so far we are not aware how this could be applied to the indentation effect on code structures.

And finally, the present study reveals something that we also experienced in a previous study (see [9]): the experiment only applied to the authors revealed results comparable to the same experiment applied to different participants. We are aware that experimental results just based on authors themselves should be handled with much care. But on the other hand, it raises the question how large experiments (in terms of number of participants) should be in order to be accepted by the scientific community as a form of documented evidence. Taking into account that it is documented that the currently reported evidence in the scientific literature is rather low (see [6,13,16,29,31] among others), N-of-1 experiments could help to reduce the effort to run experiments – and they could help that way to increase the number of reported experiments in the literature. Hence, we even think that N-of-1 experiments with a small number of participants provide acceptable evidence – if it turns out that the given evidence is comparable to the evidence gathered from a different sample (which might be the authors themselves).

8   Conclusion

The here presented experiment gives strong evidence that indentation not only has a positive effect on the readability of control flows (which was already detected by the experiment's predecessors) but also a strong ($p < .001$) and large effect on the readability of data structures. On average, the 40 professional developers who participated in the experiment required 282% more time to read non-indented JSON objects in comparison to indented JSON objects. When outliers were removed from the sample, the remaining 30 participants required 544% more time to read non-indented JSON objects.

Acknowledgement. The authors would like to thank the volunteers who participated in the here presented experiment. Without their contribution, experiments such as the present one could not be executed.

Conflict of Interest. The authors declare that they have no conflict of interest.

Data Availability Statement. A replication package of the experiment, the experiment's raw data and the analysis files are public accessible under the following link: https://github.com/shanenbe/Experiments/tree/main/2023_Indentation_JSON. The experiment can be executed via the public accessible link: https://htmlpreview.gi thub.io/?https://raw.githubusercontent.com/shanenbe/Experiments/main/2023_Inde ntation_JSON/index.html.

References

1. Abelson, H., Sussman, G.J., Henz, M., Wrigstad, T., Sussman, J.: Structure and Interpretation of Computer Programs, JavaScript Edition. MIT Electrical Engineering and Computer Science, MIT Press (2022)
2. Abelson, H., Sussman, G.J., Sussman, J.: Structure and Interpretation of Computer Programs. MIT Press, Cambridge (1985)
3. Albayrak, Ö., Davenport, D.: Impact of maintainability defects on code inspections. In: Proceedings of the 2010 ACM-IEEE International Symposium on Empirical Software Engineering and Measurement, ESEM 2010, New York, NY, USA. Association for Computing Machinery (2010)
4. Appelbaum, M., Cooper, H., Kline, R., Mayo-Wilson, E., Nezu, A., Rao, S.: Journal article reporting standards for quantitative research in psychology: the apa publications and communications board task force report. Am. Psychol. **73**, 3–25 (2018)
5. Bauer, J., Siegmund, J., Peitek, N., Hofmeister, J.C., Apel, S.: Indentation: simply a matter of style or support for program comprehension? In: Proceedings of the 27th International Conference on Program Comprehension, ICPC 2019, pp. 154–164. IEEE Press (2019)
6. Buse, R.P.L., Sadowski, C., Weimer, W.: Benefits and barriers of user evaluation in software engineering research. In: Proceedings of the 2011 ACM International Conference on Object Oriented Programming Systems Languages and Applications, OOPSLA 2011, pp. 643–656. Association for Computing Machinery, New York (2011)
7. Devanbu, P.T., Zimmermann, T., Bird, C.: Belief & evidence in empirical software engineering. In: Proceedings of the 38th International Conference on Software Engineering, ICSE 2016, Austin, TX, USA, 14–22 May 2016, pp. 108–119 (2016)
8. Ecker, U.K.H., et al.: The psychological drivers of misinformation belief and its resistance to correction. Nat. Rev. Psychol. **1**(1), 13–29 (2022)
9. Hanenberg, S., Mehlhorn, N.: Two n-of-1 self-trials on readability differences between anonymous inner classes (aics) and lambda expressions (les) on java code snippets. Empir. Softw. Eng. **27**(2), 33 (2021)
10. Hanenberg, S., Morzeck, J., Gruhn, V.: Indentation and reading time: a randomized control trial on the differences between generated indented and non-indented if-statements. Currently under review (2023)
11. Hollmann, N., Hanenberg, S.: An empirical study on the readability of regular expressions: textual versus graphical. In: IEEE Working Conference on Software Visualization, VISSOFT 2017, Shanghai, China, 18–19 September 2017, pp. 74–84. IEEE (2017)
12. The jamovi project. [Computer Software] (2022). https://www.jamovi.org

13. Kaijanaho, A.J.: Evidence-based programming language design: a philosophical and methodological exploration. University of Jyväskylä, Finnland (2015)
14. Kaptchuk, T.J.: Intentional ignorance: a history of blind assessment and placebo controls in medicine. Bull. Hist. Med. **72**(3), 389–433 (1998)
15. Kesler, T.E., Uram, R.B., Magareh-Abed, F., Fritzsche, A., Amport, C., Dunsmore, H.E.: The effect of indentation on program comprehension. Int. J. Man-Mach. Stud. **21**(5), 415–428 (1984)
16. Ko, A.J., Latoza, T.D., Burnett, M.M.: A practical guide to controlled experiments of software engineering tools with human participants. Empir. Softw. Engg. **20**(1), 110–141 (2015)
17. Love, L.T.: Relating individual differences in computer programming performance to human information processing abilities. PhD thesis (1977)
18. Mehlhorn, N., Hanenberg, S.: Imperative versus declarative collection processing: an RCT on the understandability of traditional loops versus the stream API in java. In: 44th IEEE/ACM 44th International Conference on Software Engineering, ICSE 2022, Pittsburgh, PA, USA, 25–27 May 2022, pp. 1157–1168. ACM (2022)
19. Miara, R.J., Musselman, J.A., Navarro, J.A., Shneiderman, B.: Program indentation and comprehensibility. Commun. ACM **26**(11), 861–867 (1983)
20. Moher, D., et al.: Consort: explanation and elaboration: updated guidelines for reporting parallel group randomised trials. BMJ **340**, 2010 (2010)
21. Morzeck, J., Hanenberg, S., Werger, O., Gruhn, V.: Indentation in source code: a randomized control trial on the readability of control flows in java code with large effects. In: Proceedings of the 18th International Conference on Software Technologies (ICSOFT 2023). SITEPRESS (2023)
22. Norcio, A.F.: Indentation, documentation and programmer comprehension. In: Proceedings of the 1982 Conference on Human Factors in Computing Systems, CHI 1982, pp. 118–120. Association for Computing Machinery, New York (1982)
23. Norcio, A.F., Kerst, S.M.: Human memory organization for computer programs. J. Am. Soc. Inf. Sci. **34**(2), 109–114 (1983)
24. Nunnally, J.: The place of statistics in psychology. Educ. Psychol. Measur. **20**(4), 641–650 (1960)
25. Patton, M.Q.: Qualitative Research & Evaluation Methods: Integrating Theory and Practice. SAGE Publications, Thousand Oaks (2014)
26. Prechelt, L.: Kontrollierte Experimente in der Softwaretechnik: Potenzial und Methodik. Springer, Heidelberg (2001)
27. Reichl, J., Hanenberg, S., Gruhn, V.: Does the stream API benefit from special debugging facilities? a controlled experiment on loops and streams with specific debuggers. In: 45th IEEE/ACM International Conference on Software Engineering, ICSE 2023, Melbourne, Australia, 14–20 May 2023, pp. 576–588. IEEE (2023)
28. Shneiderman, B., McKay, D.: Experimental investigations of computer program debugging and modification. Proc. Hum. Fact. Soc. Ann. Meet. **20**(24), 557–563 (1976)
29. Stefik, A., Hanenberg, S., McKenney, M., Andrews, A., Yellanki, S.K., Siebert, S.: What is the foundation of evidence of human factors decisions in language design? an empirical study on programming language workshops. In: Proceedings of the 22nd International Conference on Program Comprehension, ICPC 2014, pp. 223–231. Association for Computing Machinery, New York (2014)

30. Stefik, A., Siebert, S., Stefik, M., Slattery, K.: An empirical comparison of the accuracy rates of novices using the quorum, perl, and randomo programming languages. In: Proceedings of the 3rd ACM SIGPLAN Workshop on Evaluation and Usability of Programming Languages and Tools, PLATEAU 2011, pp. 3–8. Association for Computing Machinery, New York (2011)
31. Tichy, W.F., Lukowicz, P., Prechelt, L., Heinz, E.A.: Experimental evaluation in computer science: a quantitative study. J. Syst. Softw. **28**(1), 9–18 (1995)
32. Weissman, L.M.: A Methodology for Studying the Psychological Complexity of Computer Programs. PhD thesis. AAI0510378 (1974)

The Sustainable User Experiences Enabled Human-Centered Framework for Systems Design

Urooj Fatima(✉) [ID] and Katrien De Moor [ID]

Department of Information Security and Communication Technology, Norwegian University of Science and Technology (NTNU), 7491 Trondheim, Norway
{urooj,katrien.demoor}@ntnu.no
http://www.ntnu.edu

Abstract. The research lacks the evidence that our software systems technology has made us psychologically healthier. The ubiquitous software systems have been eminently impacting our well-being which is our fundamental goal in life as human beings. Studies have shown that the human well-being (a primary user experience outcome) is dependent on the satisfaction of certain psychological needs. However, normally, the software system development processes neglect the psychological requirements of humans who use and interact with these systems, focusing primarily on the purpose of the system itself. In order to address this challenge, this paper contributes a framework: Sustainable User eXperiences Enabled Human-centered (SUXEH) framework that promotes to actively support human psychological needs by providing guidelines on how to model the fundamental psychological needs as explicit system functionalities in the early stages of the software systems development process. The framework does so in a way that eases the integration of sustainable user experience aspects (mediated by the human needs) in the systems design phase of the overall development process. The SUXEH framework guidelines are demonstrated using a case study, the Taxi System.

Keywords: Software systems design · Human-centered design · User experience · Sustainability · Human needs

1 Introduction

There is a large emerging public concern of potential influence of ubiquitous software systems present in almost all aspects of our daily life. Hence, it has the immense capacity to affect our quality of life and hence the human well-being. Well-being is referred as "a positive state", encompassing e.g., a good quality of life, by the World Health Organization [57]. Recent studies from the more human-centered perspective (see e.g., [20,37,41]) have proven that the everyday technology we use has nuanced impacts on our psychological well-being. The design and development of technology to support psychological well-being and human potential is referred as "positive computing" in [6]. More concretely, in late 2010s, it has been proposed in the Human-Computer Interaction (HCI) and User Experience (UX) domain that certain human psychological needs are mediators of long-term sustainable user experience outcomes like that of human well-being, engagement, and motivation [43]. The term "user experience" is defined as *"user's perceptions and responses that result from the use and/or antici- pated use of a system, product or service"* [30]. In order to improve user experience and well-being, the authors in [43] emphasize on supporting certain psychological needs via technology designs using a model named METUX (Motivation, Engagement and Thriving in User Experience), which we elaborate further on in this work.

However, in the software engineering domain, the focus of software engineering design methods has remained on guidelines and/or rules on how to specify a system from the perspective of its functionality, that is, what and how the system performs its functions, i.e., focusing on purpose of the system itself. Whereas, the psychologi- cal needs of the people who use these socio-technical systems and interact with them, have traditionally not been taken into account during the main software system develop- ment activities. On the one hand, and partly due to the demand of short time-to-market and prevalent fuzziness in understanding human-psychological needs, the focus in soft- ware systems engineering and the user satisfaction of a system has always remained connected to the fulfilment of the system-centered requirements and not the human- centered ones [5,46]. On the other hand, software developers lack guidelines on how to cater and analyse human psychological needs during the development process. In this paper, we argue that the identification of human psychological needs at an early stage of software development can play an important role in making design decisions. Inclusion of these needs at later stages, in particular once the system has been developed, may be difficult, insufficient and expensive. In this work, we therefore address these problems by answering the following research questions:

1. What human psychological needs may be taken care of while acquiring the require- ments?
2. How can the requirements acquired in (1) be represented in requirements specifica- tions?
3. Can the satisfaction of a human psychological need prevent other requirement goals from being satisfied and in what ways? How can such conflicts be identified and represented?
4. In what way can these human-centered requirements specifications provide valuable input to the design phase of the system development?

Whether it is in the HCI or software engineering domain, normally, the user- centered requirements are limited to the details of the direct interaction of the user with the system, rarely taking into account how they contribute to the overall sustain- able human well-being (see Sect. 2 for details). One of the distinct properties of the METUX model is that it allows to analyse not only the direct impact of technology use on momentary human psychological experience, i.e., hedonic experiences (e.g., plea- sure and comfort), but also the broader long term impact on other aspects of human life, i.e., eudaimonic experiences (or true flourishing) that are strongly linked to the concept of well-being [23]. In this article, and inspired by the METUX model, we therefore present a framework, referred to as *Sustainable User eXperiences Enabled Human-centered (SUXEH)* framework proposed earlier in [14], that addresses the for- mulated research questions (1, 2 and 4) for inclusion of human psychological require- ments essential to human well-being (and other long-term sustainable user experience

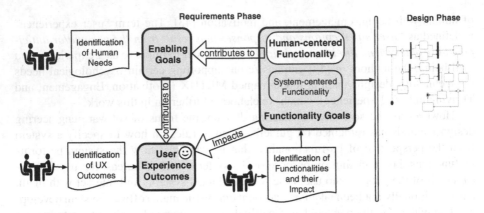

Fig. 1. An Overview of the SUXEH Framework [14].

outcomes) in the early stages of the software development process. The research question no. 3 is exclusively addressed in this very article. More concretely, in this article, the framework guidelines are extended on the identification of certain designs that may be avoided because they: (1) may satisfy human psychological needs on the interaction level but frustrates the human psychological needs of overall sustainable well-being by explicitly considering eudaimonic experiences; (2) may satisfy psychological need of one type of user interacting with the system and frustrate the needs of other types of users that interact with the system; (3) may negatively impact other sustainability goals of the system (explained in Sect. 4.5). The framework guidelines are explained by applying them on a more complete demonstration case study (the Taxi System) than earlier presented (partially) in [14].

In terms of software engineering goals, the proposed framework aims to assist software engineers from the requirements acquisition phase to the early design phase. During the requirements acquisition phase, the framework helps in identification of the basic human needs that are required to be satisfied for better user experience. Our framework provides the constructs to represent these requirements as the goals of a system, that is, in a form acceptable by the requirements specification phase or early design phase. For this, the framework uses the goals-oriented requirements language (GRL) that offers a graphical means of describing and structuring various types of concepts that appear during the requirement process. The GRL, like other goal modelling languages, is a valuable tool for discussions with stakeholders involved in defining requirements. It provides the constructs needed for our primary concerns of (1) reasoning of human-centered requirements, (2) modelling human needs that are fuzzy in nature, and (3) describing impact (positive or negative) of system functionalities (satisfying specific needs) on overall human well-being and other system goals.

Figure 1 serves to illustrate the overview of our proposed (SUXEH) framework and its components. The main contribution of the framework is the provision of guidelines on:

- The identification of basic human psychological needs relevant to the system to be specified

- The representation of these needs in requirements models
- How and to what extent the system can support these basic needs through its functionality
- Avoidance of designs that can hinder these needs by their negative influence on overall human well-being
- Identification and representation of possible conflicts between human-centered functionality goals and other goals of a system under consideration

The rest of the paper is organized as follows. Related work is discussed in Sect. 2. Overview of the SUXEH framework is provided in Sect. 3 in terms of its components and the relationship between them. Section 4 describes the details of the framework guidelines that are proposed to be followed to model basic human needs for requirements specifications. In Sect. 5, we describe how to use the framework by applying the guidelines on a case study, the Taxi System. We discuss our research contributions in Sect. 6, and the conclusion and future work is presented in Sect. 7.

2 Related Work

The human factors in software engineering and HCI have been studied for multiple decades for the desire to design for human needs. However, the rapid rate of technology change outpaces the advances in its design and as a result challenges are ever present [40].

In software engineering, several approaches are proposed in the past [8, 12, 27, 34] that can be embraced under the term "human-centered design (HCD)" by ISO [31]. One of the first approaches was soft system methodology (SSM) [8], which was also applied to capture the impacts on people involved (e.g. stakeholder, actors, and clients) and considered different views of interactive systems during development. The SSM, work done in [1], and earlier HCD approaches overviewed in [36] aim to merge HCI and user experience methods and practises in software development process in order to achieve usability goals in terms of user satisfaction. This requires extra resources and expertise along with other limitations listed in [36].

Efforts in value-sensitive design (VSD) have been made by HCI and software engineering community [18,53]. It is a technology design approach that accounts for human values as the primary goal during the design process, however these values are moral values that deal with ethical issues.

In the recent past, there has been an increased focus on exploring different human aspects (e.g., human diversity, human emotions, user involvement) and supporting them during software development. One of the recent works [21], takes into account end-user human diversity in terms of software user age, accessibility challenges, ethnicity, language or gender in the digital health requirement models for which they use Domain Specific Visual Language (DSVL). The authors propose to incorporate these human aspects in one of the main stream software systems development methodologies, i.e., the Model-Driven Software Engineering (MDSE). The work is extended in [22] where the authors presented a preliminary taxonomy of some of the end-user human diversity aspects for software developers guidance by dividing human characteristics in groups.

In another work [9], the authors propose a requirements engineering approach to take into account emotional aspects of software usage in smart home technology for the elderly. Their definition of emotional goals refer to how users perceive the end product and hence it is product specific. This approach emphasizes on linking emotional goals with functional or quality goals. Another perspective of addressing human aspects in software engineering in the past is to consider user involvement during the software development life cycle to generate more usable solutions (see e.g. [29,32]. Human aspects in software engineering have also been studied from the perspective of targeting software practitioners and tasks associated with team processes in terms of favouring team efficiency and performance highlighting motivation and personality as important aspects [26,44].

Over the past decade, HCI has gained momentum among the contributions in the areas of positive technologies [19,45], positive design [11], and positive computing [6]. These approaches deal with deeper considerations to design for human flourishing and some of them shows psychological factors affecting human well-being.

While relevant and bridging more towards the user and human perspective, the approaches discussed above do not explicitly consider and address the characteristics of user experience. None of the approaches provide design guidelines to support more than just immediate hedonic experiences. Their investigation mostly focuses on the ease-of-use and usability of the systems and hence lacks a more holistic or realistic picture in terms of the system's broader impact on long-term eudaimonic experiences that contribute to sustainable human well-being. Further, the relationship between user experience outcomes and human psychological needs, and differentiation of unhealthy experiences from healthy ones, as proposed in the model based approach METUX [43], have not been taken into account. Moreover, the recent approaches proposed in [9,21] are MDSE and product-specific respectively. To the best of our knowledge, none of the work mentioned above provide guidelines on how to identify and represent *conflicting* human psychological needs in software models. Based on the METUX model, the framework we propose would allow design strategies to be identified that address these research gaps.

3   Overview of the SUXEH Framework and Its Components

In the requirements engineering process, goals have been considered as the basic driving forces for the identification of requirements and providing the rationale for them, i.e., they are primarily concerned with elaborating on "why" certain system functionalities are needed and introduced [54]. The SUXEH framework focuses on the identification of these goals as basic human needs and propose to introduce system functionalities that accommodate these needs, hence, following the basic principle of human-centered design [40]. The SUXEH framework does so by defining three components distinguishing human-centered needs goals (the enabling goals component), user experience outcomes (The user experience outcomes component), and the human-centered functionality goals (the functionality goals component). The SUXEH framework depicted in Fig. 2 illustrates the framework given in Fig. 1 with emphasis on the types of relationship between these components and how they support each other. Hence, these components do not exist in isolation. They belong to domains that traditionally do not negotiate or interact with each other. The framework we propose identifies the links between these components that represent different domains, hence allowing these domains to interact and exploit the links between them for better system modelling in terms of improved and sustainable user experiences. These components are different views of the same system enabling us to design holistically for better human well-being. The decomposition into components helps in reducing the complexity of the modelling effort for these different domains. The framework components and the relationships between them are defined in the following subsections.

3.1 The Enabling Goals Component

This component represents the fundamental human psychological needs set as explicit goals to be taken into account during the requirements acquisition phase. This enables software engineers and key stakeholders to focus on the appropriate set of needs for a given system and justify the system requirements accordingly. As depicted in Fig. 2, the whole framework is driven by this component and it acts as a glue to connect all framework components. On the one hand, these fundamental human psychological needs are actually the enablers of sustainable user experience outcomes (represented the user experience outcomes component), hence defined as *enabling* goals. On the other hand, it is actually these high-level enabling goals that are refined in a way that the functionality goals component is able to define explicit functions for each of them.

3.2 The User Experience Outcomes Component

The user experience outcomes are represented by a specific component of the SUXEH framework. These outcomes are enabled by the satisfaction of the identified basic human needs in the "enabling goals" component. The framework depicted in Fig. 2 represents the relationship of user experience outcomes component with the enabling goals component via the GRL contribution links. For the sake of comprehension of the framework, this paper focuses on the following primary user experience outcomes: motivation, engagement and well-being proposed in [43]. However, the framework is not restricted to these outcomes and can include other outcomes as per requirements. Various other models linking UX to user/human goals have been proposed in the literature. An influential other view in this respect, is Hassenzahl's model of pragmatic and hedonic quality perceptions [24]. It differentiates user experience from usability as UX anticipates outcomes beyond purely instrumental ones (e.g., efficiency, effectiveness) and is associated with the fulfillment of what Hassenzahl calls "be goals" (e.g., relatedness, stimulation, identification) [24,25].

Eudaimonic and Hedonic Aspects of User Experiences. Studies have confirmed that elements of human experiences like that of engagement and enjoyment do not always contribute positively to sustainable well-being. For instance too much engagement in video games (see e.g., [51] and media consumption (see e.g., [16] can increase the user engagement to the extent that leads to health issues and impact overall well-being negatively. It is because the technology design is usually focused on the direct impact of

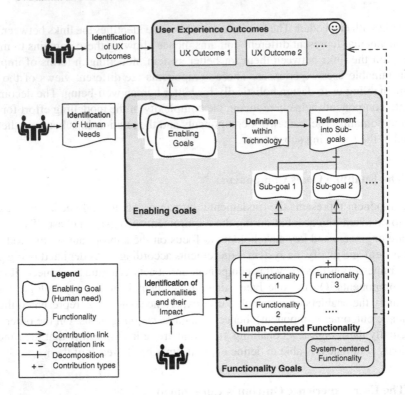

Fig. 2. The details of the SUXEH framework shown in Fig. 1 illustrating the framework guidelines and relationship between its sub-components [14].

the system's use on humans and not the wider impact on other aspects of a human's life. However, experiences can be either eudaimonic or hedonic or both (see e.g., [23] for a classification). Therefore, when we talk about *sustainable* user experience outcomes in this context, it is important to differentiate between the immediate "hedonic experience" and the long-term "eudaimonic experience" as recommended in the research conducted by [49].

More specifically, eudaimonic experiences are more about pursuing personal goals whereas hedonic experiences are largely about "momentary pleasures" like relaxing and with little lasting personal impact. Eudaimonic experiences have long-term importance and are often considered strongly related to the experience of *meaningfulness* and well-being than hedonia. Further, eudaimonic experiences were also found to be linked to positive affect in [23,35]. The distinguishing concepts of eudaimonic and hedonic aspects of a user's experience that result from the use/anticipated use of a system facilitate the discussions on avoiding certain functionalities/design decisions (discussed later in Sect. 4.5) that have long term negative impact on human well-being.

3.3 The Functionality Goals Component

Once the enabling goals are obtained, other goals can be identified by their refinement. As enabling goals are refined, system functions emerge which are represented by the functionality goals component. Hence, enabling goals are achieved through the system functions identified in the functionality goals component. In other words, we propose to upgrade the traditional functional model of a system that normally neglect basic human needs and contains mainly those functions that are essential to make the system work and explains what the system does (system-centered functionality). In the SUXEH Framework, the human-centered functionality goals are defined explicitly to support the fundamental human needs.

The functionalities defined in the functionality goals component not only contributes to the enabling goals component (represented via the GRL contribution links between the components in Fig. 2) but this helps towards fulfilling user experience outcomes. Such side-effects are called *correlations* in GRL that are represented using dashed arrows between the functionality goals component and the user experience outcomes component in Fig. 2.

4 The Framework Guidelines Towards Requirements Specifications

This section describes in detail the framework guidelines for software systems development team and the stakeholders involved in defining the system requirements. The process starts with a focus on identifying the enabling goals first and then defining functionality goals that contribute towards achievement of these enabling goals. For this, the identified high-level enabling goals are first defined within technology domain and then further refined into sub-goals to derive specific system functionalities that are based on human needs. Once the functionality goals are defined, they are analysed to investigate if they impact or contribute positively or negatively towards other system goals. The process is described in detail in the following subsections.

4.1 Identification of Human Needs

Good design starts with an understanding of human psychology and their needs that the design is intended to support [40]. One of the challenges at this stage is that users are not necessarily aware of their true fundamental psychological needs and how these latent needs may drive their choices and the quality of their experiences. To this end, methods such as laddering [47] and experience interviews (see e.g., [15] have been proposed in the literature.

Psychologists have made attempts to determine which needs are *truly* fundamental for humans and proposed variety of theories. Among such attempts is the work of Sheldon et. al in [52] who identified a set of the 10 most fundamental needs for humans: autonomy, competence, relatedness, self-esteem, physical thriving, security, self-actualization, pleasure-stimulation, money luxury, and popularity-influence. Out of these 10 needs, Sheldon et. al. claim that the four needs, i.e., autonomy, competence, relatedness and self-esteem, are the most important ones. Deci and Ryan [10] claim that autonomy, competence and relatedness are universal psychological needs that can be found within every member of the human species and are important within every sphere of life. Although, the set of 10 needs is not claimed by the authors to have captured all potential psychological needs, the chosen set has a considerable range and represents prominent theories including Self-Determination Theory (SDT) [48,49] within the literature. The SDT, an empirically validated approach, examines factors that promote sustainable well-being and identifies autonomy, competence and relatedness as the basic needs essential to people's motivation and psychological well-being. The SUXEH framework is based on the METUX model that uses SDT to define core elements to design for well-being and proposes autonomy, competence and relatedness as the most critical needs within HCI contexts. Their absence is linked with ill-being and distress. The authors of the METUX model support their claim by referring to empirical research carried out by the authors in [49,56], whose work revealed that the three basic needs are the most rigorously shown to be essential, predictive and reliable mediators of primary user experience outcomes: motivation, engagement and well-being.

Some of these needs may be more relevant for specific types of systems than others and not all of these basic needs may be relevant for all types of systems. Therefore, we propose to include all 10 needs identified in [52] for a better representative set of needs that is applicable to a considerable range of systems. The selection of basic psychological needs that are most relevant for the system is an important step towards modelling of the needs. Like all requirement engineering processes, the discussions between software development team and stakeholders are important at this stage. They are mainly facilitated by the designers in order to guide the overall process from the perspective of realizability of the selected needs.

In the following sections, we further describe how to model a basic psychological need in a way that it facilitates the system's design phase. For this, the modelling process is illustrated for *autonomy* as the example human need. The motivation behind choosing autonomy mainly comes from the work of Peters et al. in [43]. Also some aspects of human autonomy are listed in [22] among the keys areas of human aspects that need careful consideration in software engineering life cycle.

4.2   Defining Human Needs (Enabling Goals) Within Technology

The main challenge to model a human psychological need is to deal with the fuzziness of its requirements in technology domain. In order to address this challenge, we propose to first define the human need within technology domain to be clear on its meaning with the stakeholders during requirements phase.

Consider the example of *autonomy*. Autonomy is more controversial and an easily misunderstood concept [52]. As mentioned in [43], autonomy does not merely mean doing things independently, but has a deeper meaning of acting with *"high willingness and in accordance with personal goals and values"*. Autonomous experience results in higher quality of an individual's behaviour and performance and they experience greater wellness. It is important to mention here that the focus of our framework is on human-centered requirements of autonomy which differs from system-centered requirements of autonomous systems like that of robots and driver-less cars. Human-centered requirements of autonomy explores human autonomy as part of overall psychological needs satisfaction.

4.3 Refining Enabling Goals into Sub-Goals

Once the meaning of an enabling goal is clearly defined within technology domain and the consensus is reached between stakeholders and the software development team, it is refined into sub-goals in a way that potential design solutions in the form of functions can be driven out of it. This can be done by following the steps below:

- Look into how the enabling goal is studied in the technology domain.
- Use Jakob Nielsen's usability heuristics [39] of the user experience domain in order to explore usability design requirements to support human autonomy.

We follow the guidelines mentioned above by starting with studying how the autonomy is studied in the past in the technology domain.

Studying the Enabling Goal *(autonomy)* **in the Technology Domain.** The findings in [43] provide a good summary on how technology can help users develop a better sense of autonomy for example. The objective is to assist system designers to support human autonomy in technology design. Various aspects of software systems have been identified in the past [17] that can support or hinder user autonomy, i.e., system capability and complexity, misrepresentation and fluidity. These aspects are more focused on the direct impact of the system's use (referred as the *Interface* and *Task* levels of user experience in Sect. 4.5) and not the broader impact on other aspects of a user's life (i.e., on the levels beyond the *Interface* and *Task*). Personalization has been mentioned among the factors that improve sense of autonomy [50]. People want to feel that the activities they perform are self-chosen and endorsed, hence having the experience of choice. Studies in [49, 50] have identified that offering "options" and "customization" in the context of system usage, helps in the creation of a sense of autonomy and ownership. This type of autonomy design is familiar to game designers and can have a broader impact on human's life. We take these aspects (offering "options" and "customization") as guidelines for our first criterion to identify autonomy-enhancing system functions in the functionality goals of our framework.

Using Jakob Nielsen's Usability Heuristics. The authors in [43] highlighted the fact that *all usability heuristics can be explained by the needs of competence and autonomy*. Following their direction, we propose to choose Jakob Nielsen's 10 heuristics of usability design [39] in software systems design as valuable guidelines to improve user experience. The guidelines given in the Nielsen's heuristics are normally used as an evaluation method of user interfaces. However, we here emphasize that we are not applying the heuristics for evaluation of user interfaces. Instead they are used as a valuable tool to refine basic human needs (enabling goals) into sub-goals that are more precise in terms of their required system functionality.

The Nielsen's heuristics follow the principles of cognitive psychology that put emphasis on human needs as a basic foundation for usability design. Nielsen's heuristics are widely accepted and well-supported in the user experience domain. In addition, these guidelines are relatively limited and easy-to-use, and hence can be equally used by non-user experience designers and stakeholders. Following are Nielsen's 10 heuristics, further explained in [39]:

1. Visibility of system status
2. Match between system and real world
3. User control and freedom
4. Consistency and standards
5. Error prevention
6. Recognition rather than recall
7. Flexibility and efficiency of use
8. Aesthetic and minimalist design
9. Help users recognize, diagnose, and recover from errors
10. Help and documentation

All these heuristics can enhance a user's sense of autonomy (and competence) and can serve as important sub-goals to drive specific system functionalities that contribute towards achievement of human autonomy and are equally important for the psychological need of competence [43].

4.4 Deriving Functionality Goals from Sub-Goals

The enabling sub-goals, resulting from refinement of human need (as explained for autonomy in Sect. 4.3), provide the required input for the functions in human-centered functionality goal component. Now we need to introduce and define autonomy-supportive system functions that offer more options and customization choices to the user. For the sake of brevity, we summarize specific system functionalities that manifests some of the Nielsen's guidelines given in Sect. 4.3) as follows: clarity on feedback and available actions; provision of consistent and standard order of operations and language; clearly marked emergency exits without extended dialogues; provision of constraints and confirmation of risky actions. Clearly, these factors can be satisfied with provision of system specific functions and hence must be addressed in requirements models.

The functionality goals component manifests through its functions that how the goals identified in the enabling goals component can be achieved. It is important to mention here that we do not say that a goal is accomplished or satisfied in a clear-cut sense. But it can be said that certain functions (design decisions) may contribute positively or negatively towards accomplishment of a certain goal. In this way, the framework can generate advance warnings to signal negative (and positive) impacts of a certain human-centered requirement to the next phases of the development process.

4.5 Analysing Functionality Goals for Their Impact on Other System Goals

The introduction of human-centered functionality goals may prevent satisfaction of other goals of the systems from different perspectives and system views. In requirements engineering, such interference, interdependency or inconsistency between requirements is termed as *conflict* [33]. In the SUXEH framework, we propose to analyse conflicts by looking into the details of human-centered functionality goals and to investigate if they contribute positively or negatively towards: (1) enabling goals on the same interface/view of the system; (2) enabling/functionality goals of other interfaces/views of the system; (3) other sustainability dimensions defined in the Karlskrona Manifesto for Software Sustainability Design by Becker et. al in [4], i.e., environmental, economical, social, and technical. Identification of such conflicts is beneficial for system requirements allowing further elicitation of information that would have been missed otherwise, and hence they are desirable [55].

(1) Conflict of a Functionality Goal with the Enabling Goal on the Same System Interface/View. It is discussed earlier in Sects. 2 and 3.2 that technology design concentrates on the direct impact of the system's use on human and not the broader long-term impact of human well-being. Interaction designers are working for decades to make the products and systems enjoyable and engaging, and to enhance the hedonic experiences of users. However, this engagement can increase to an extent that may introduce negative impacts on human health and other eudaimonic aspects of user experiences. In order to provide guidance on how to detach unhealthy positive experiences from healthy ones that contribute to sustainable user experience outcomes, the authors in [7] have emphasized the importance of differentiating various levels of user experience within which human needs can be influenced by technology. Four different levels or spheres of experience are identified in the METUX model within which human need satisfaction can take place: *(1) As part of interacting with the technology via its interface (interface level); (2) As part of engaging with technology-enabled tasks (e.g. self tracking) (task level); (3) In relation to the over-arching technology-enabled behaviour (e.g. exercise) (behaviour level); (4) As part of an individual's overall life (life level).* Hence, on the same system interface/view, a functionality goal can be need-satisfying (i.e., healthy) at one level of user experience and need-frustrating (i.e., unhealthy or addictive), and thus in conflict, at another, and hence affect the user experience outcome of well-being negatively. Consideration of these different levels of user experience facilitates the discussions between the stakeholders and designers on the calculation of positive or negative impact of a certain design decision (a specific function) on the experience levels, beyond the mere interface. It can also help to avoid the creation of designs that are in conflict with higher levels of long term sustainable user experience outcomes.

In the light of the above discussion, after defining the functions satisfying certain enabling goals/sub-goals, there is a dire need to check whether the defined functionality goals frustrate human needs on the levels beyond the *Interface* and *Task* spheres of user experience. In order to represent the relationship of how functions defined in the functionality goal component contribute (positively or negatively) towards achievement of enabling goals, we use the GRL *contribution links* that connect the framework components with each other with explicit notations of "+" and "-" on the links representing their positive and negative impacts respectively (see Fig. 2). The GRL contribution links can have various degrees of impact[1] but we only include links with some-positive and

---

[1] The details of various degrees of impact on GRL contribution links can be found in [3].

some-negative impacts in our framework. Some-positive and some-negative contributions are positive and negative contributions respectively, but the extent of the contribution is unknown. The SUXEH framework does not restrict the usage of only some-positive and some-negative contribution links. The other degrees of impact can be used if the system specification requires them. In this paper, we explain the two contribution types only to keep it simple enough for the sake of understanding the framework guidelines.

(2) Conflict of a Functionality Goal with the Enabling Goal on the Other Interface/View of a System. There is a possibility of a conflict if a functionality that contributes positively towards a human psychological need on one interface/view, contributes negatively towards the human psychological need on another interface. Hence, the functionality is in conflict with respect to its overall contribution towards a specific (enabling) goal of a system that impacts user experience outcomes. To understand this, consider an example of a tele-medicine system where the patients are given the option of an autonomy-supportive function of "choosing preferred doctors" to book appointments. This autonomy-supportive functionality goal supports patient's autonomy positively on the patient interface/view but may affect doctor's autonomy negatively on the doctor interface/view of the system. Therefore, such conflicts of functionality goals across interfaces/views of a system need to be identified and represented explicitly for cautious system modelling.

(3) Conflict of a Functionality with Other Sustainability Dimensions. The SUXEH framework directly supports *individual* sustainability by providing guidelines on designing for better human well-being. Individual sustainability is one of the five sustainability dimensions mentioned in Karlskrona manifesto for sustainability design [4] proposed for the software engineering community. The other four dimensions mentioned in the manifesto are: environmental, economical, social and technical dimensions. These dimensions are interdependent and can affect each other. Therefore, the human-centered functionality goals that directly support individual sustainability can have negative impacts on other dimensions of sustainability, and hence must be investigated for such conflicts.

5   The Taxi System: A Demonstration Case Study

This section explains a case study, a Taxi System, that is here understood as a specific system example used to explain the framework (also referred as a demonstration case in [28]). The case study is based on similar types of real systems but simplified in order to investigate and illustrate the proposed framework more precisely. The Taxi System was proposed in [13] for illustration of a systems modelling approach. It is an example of distributed communicating systems. These systems maintain ongoing interaction with their environment. These are complex systems difficult to be designed because of the concurrency involved in their interactions with the system environment and different parts that communicate with each other within the system.

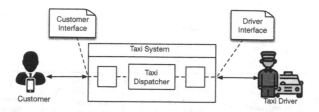

Fig. 3. The Taxi system overview showing its different interfaces with which it interacts with two examples of humans (customer and taxi driver) [13].

In the Taxi System shown in Fig. 3, a customer can book a taxi via an online booking system. A taxi dispatcher keeps an overview of the taxis and assigns an available taxi to the requesting user. If no taxi is available, the customer is asked to wait. Once available, the taxi is assigned and contacts the waiting customer.

In the following, the framework guidelines given in Sect. 4 are applied to the case study to demonstrate: how human psychological needs can be modelled as functionality goals of a system; and how their conflicts with other system goals can be identified.

5.1 Deriving the Taxi System Functionality Goals from Sub-Goals

In this section we demonstrate how the sub-goals, resulting from the decomposition of the enabling goals in Sect. 4.4, can be refined into precise functions of the Taxi System that have the potential to satisfy the fundamental human needs. The process is illustrated by working around one basic human need (i.e. the autonomy) to exhibit how a human psychological need can be translated into system functions that are required to generate sustainable user experiences of well-being for example.

We assume that the system-centered functional requirements of the Taxi System have already been identified and their functions are modelled. Here, we are focusing on human-centered functionality component that defines functions to support human autonomy in the Taxi System. The sub-goals refined for autonomy in Sect. 4.4 (i.e., offering "options" and "customization"; visualization of system status, user control and freedom (and other Nielsen's heuristics are not explained in this section)) are generic enough for HCI contexts. In the following, against these generic sub-goals, the functionality goals are defined separately for each interface (customer and taxi driver) of the Taxi System to differentiate *autonomy* modelling requirements for different types of system users (customer and taxi driver) interacting with the system.

Functionality Goals for the Customer Interface. The customer autonomy needs can be translated into system functions as follows:
Generic sub-goal 1: Alternatives and/or offering options
System-Specific Functions: A customer can choose

- different types of taxis based on their price, size, time-to-reach, distance from pickup point.
- to change destination at run-time.

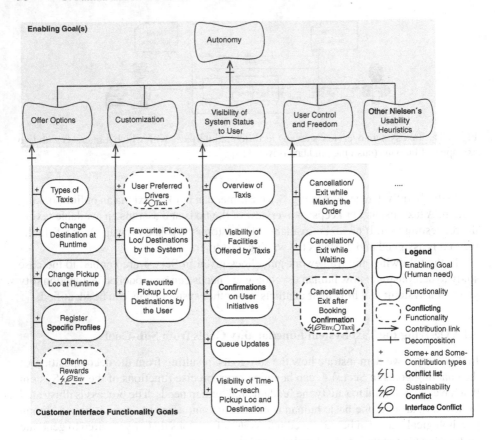

Fig. 4. The SUXEH framework applied to the Taxi System illustrating modelling of *autonomy* as an example human psychological need on the customer interface [14].

- to change pickup location at run-time.
- to register with specific profiles.
- to register for rewards that are offered depending upon how often they use the service.

Generic sub-goal 2: Customization (Flexibility and efficiency of use)
System-Specific Functions: A customer can

- choose a taxi from preferred driver options (can also improve relatedness).
- choose from favourite pickup/destination locations based on their past orders.
- create favourite list of destinations/pickup locations.

Generic sub-goal 3: Visibility of system status:
System-Specific Functions:

- Overview of taxis on a map with all the alternatives specified in the sub-goal 1 above.
- Taxis display other facilities they have like that of a baby seat.

- Clarity on "Taxi booked" and "Taxi cancelled" confirmations and other initiatives taken by the customer.
- Customer is updated about their queue position.
- Customer is shown the taxi remaining time-to-reach at pickup location and destination.

Generic sub-goal 4: User control and freedom
System-Specific Functions: A customer can

- cancel/exit the taxi ordering activity at all steps while making the order.
- cancel/exit the taxi order while in waiting queue.
- cancel taxi order after it is booked.

Functionality Goals for the Taxi Driver Interface. The taxi driver autonomy needs can be translated into system functions in the similar way as done for the customer interface. In the following some of the functionality goals contributing towards achievement of the taxi driver autonomy are described:
Generic sub-goal 1: Alternatives and/or offering options
System-Specific Functions: A taxi driver can choose

- to sign-up for advance taxi bookings to make sure of having confirmed trips during the day.
- to select their shift timings.
- to choose their break times during the day.
- to register with specific profiles mentioning for example extra facilities.
- to register for rewards that are offered depending upon how often they choose: weekends or night-time shifts to offer their services; long-distance trips; to take customers waiting for long in the queue.

Generic sub-goal 2: Customization (Flexibility and efficiency of use)
System-Specific Functions: A taxi driver can

- choose customers from preferred customer options (can also improve relatedness).
- choose their preferred area/region to pick customers.

Generic sub-goal 3: Visibility of system status:
System-Specific Functions:

- Overview of nearby taxis of the system on a map to have visibility on their trip chances.
- Visibility of all functions specified under sub-goal 1.

Generic sub-goal 4: User control and freedom
System-Specific Functions: A taxi driver can

- cancel/exit the taxi ordering activity at all steps while accepting a customer ride.
- cancel/exit while in waiting queue for orders.
- cancel customer order after it is accepted.

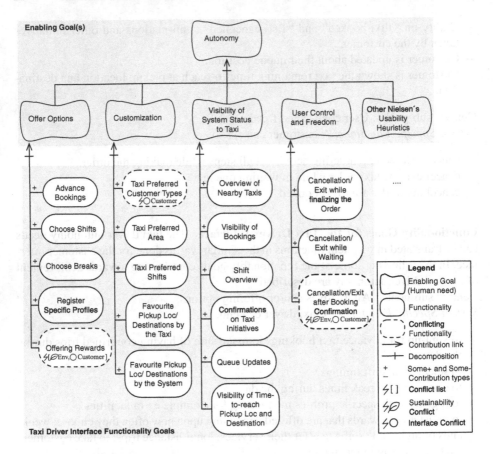

Fig. 5. The SUXEH framework applied to the Taxi System illustrating modelling of *autonomy* as an example human psychological need on the taxi driver interface.

The above mentioned goals are not the complete set of Taxi System functionality goals but are examples of how autonomy (an enabling goal) can be modelled in terms of less fuzzy and more refined functions on the customer and the taxi driver interfaces of the Taxi System. Figure 4 and Fig. 5 illustrate graphically the customer and the taxi driver interfaces functionality goals of the Taxi System respectively. We utilize the GRL decomposition links to denote decomposition of goals into sub-goals and functions. It can be clearly seen that the above functions of the Taxi System that contribute to the human psychological needs of a customer and a taxi driver are the functional requirements of the system and hence must be addressed at this early phase of system's development.

5.2 Analysing the Taxi System Functionality Goals for Conflicts

The next step is to analyse the defined functionality goals of the Taxi System for the conflicts classified earlier in Sect. 4.5. For this we consider functionalities on one interface at a time. Lets take the example of the customer interface of the Taxi System. We investigate if functionality goals of the customer interface are in conflict with:

1. *The Customer Autonomy on the Higher-Levels of User Experience Beyond the interface and task Levels.* For this we investigate whether the overall well-being of a customer is influenced positively or negatively by *increased* engagement in using the Taxi service via each of the specified functionality goals? For instance, consider the example of the function named "offering rewards" that contributes to the "offer options" sub-goal required to be designed for the satisfaction of customer autonomy. Apparently, this function increases engagement and motivation user experience outcomes mediated by increased autonomy and competence human needs (see Sect. 4.1). However, this happens only at the interface and task levels of the user experience exhibiting the direct impact of the system's use. Because the criterion of "offering rewards" is how often a customer uses the Taxi System, it can increase engagement to an extent where this function has negative impact on the customer's overall well-being. Hence, this "offering rewards" function "can" contribute negatively towards achievement of autonomy via "offer options" sub-goal and therefore its contribution is marked with "-" (some-negative) sign. In order to avoid need-frustrations at higher levels of user experiences that impact overall human well-being, such functions need to be designed carefully (e.g., with additional constraints for positive impacts). For instance, the function of "offering rewards" may be constrained only for long distances, and/or health warnings and saving money type of incentives may be given to the customer for avoiding the taxi service for shorter distances.

2. *The Taxi Driver's Autonomy on the Taxi Driver Interface.* We analyse whether any of the customer functionality goals supporting customer autonomy for their negative impacts on the taxi driver's autonomy. For example, consider the function "Cancellation/Exit after Booking Confirmation". This supports customer autonomy via "User Control and Freedom" sub-goal but can frustrate the taxi driver autonomy (and hence the driver's overall well-being) in general and specifically in the case when the taxi driver has covered a considerable distance right before the trip cancellation by the customer. This type of conflict across system interfaces is proposed to be represented by a zig-zag symbol followed by a *circle* and the *interface name* with which the conflict is identified, as depicted in Fig. 4. These symbols are placed inside the functionality goal having the conflict.

3. *Other Sustainability Dimensions.* This type of conflict is investigated on customer interface for each of its functionality goal to detect their negative interference with other sustainability dimensions, for example environmental sustainability. Lets take again the example of "offering rewards" on the customer interface. The criterion of "offering rewards" is how often the customer uses a taxi. This encourages increase in taxi usage that impact environmental sustainability negatively. We propose to represent this type of conflict with sustainability dimensions by a zig-zag symbol followed by a *leaf* and the *sustainability dimension name* with which the conflict is identified, as depicted for environmental sustainability, *Env*, on "offering rewards" in Fig. 4. The identification of this conflict requires change in the design considerations of "offering rewards". For instance, it can be changed to how often the user

uses a *shared* taxi to put less emphasis on individual taxi usage and more on the rides that are more beneficial for the environment and are less expensive.

A similar exercise of identifying conflicts, as described above, is executed on the taxi interface and the results are shown in Fig. 5. The SUXEH framework, hence, provides guidelines on how to identify such conflicts at an early stage of requirements specifications. These guidelines allow to signal the possible negative impact of a functionality to the later stages of system development that involves major design decisions. Hence, this indication helps designers to avoid such designs right from the beginning of requirements engineering process. In the case where certain functionalities are decided to be dropped due to their negative impact, still the information encompassing the reasoning can be made part of documentation to avoid repeating the discussions in the future.

6 Discussion

In this paper, we emphasize the importance of addressing humanistic needs and values during the early phases of software systems development process. The software systems design decisions affect positively and/or negatively particular human psychological needs that contribute to sustainable user experience outcomes. These needs are not taken into account during the requirements acquisition, which primarily focuses on the system's purpose. This problem is addressed by our framework, which enables software designers to capture and represent human psychological needs early in the software development process, when the requirements are elicited and specified, and design decisions are justified. This is referred to as the process-oriented approach in [38], as opposed to the product-oriented approach when the final product is evaluated.

In order to deal with the complexities of human psychological well-being, multidisciplinary partnerships with psychologists and sociologists are already common within branches of HCI. However, this is less common in the software engineering community. The SUXEH framework we propose includes the notion of human aspects from the HCI/UX discipline that help in building a more complete understanding of human psychological needs. This more holistic perspective also allows to focus beyond those traditionally considered as users ("user-centered design") and adopts a broader, human-centered view on those the system is designed for or who may be affected by its use [31]. Human-centered design directly supports *individual* sustainability [31], with sustainability being a central objective for system's development [42]. Therefore, it can be clearly argued that the SUXEH framework may have an impact on how software developers perform requirements engineering for one of the dimensions of sustainability.

As explained in Sect. 4.1, the human needs we emphasize leverage mainly the Self-Determination Theory (SDT). We choose *autonomy* to present guidelines on how to model a fundamental human psychological need. Autonomy (along with competence and relatedness) has a deep and clear link to more commonly verbalized concepts like meaning or happiness [49]. Hence the human emotions being modelled as target human aspects in software requirements (for instance in [9]), discussed earlier in the related work, are actually the desired outcomes of basic psychological needs satisfaction that our framework emphasizes on.

Unlike the approaches proposed in [1, 8, 12, 27, 34], and due to the limitations listed in [36], the framework we propose does not integrate HCI or the user experience design process as a whole in the software systems development process. However, we have used HCI and user experience domain knowledge in two ways: (1) In order to understand core elements of human psychological needs we have taken guidelines from a model [43] that explains these needs and their relationship with sustainable user experience outcomes in the context of HCI; (2) We utilize Nielsen's usability heuristics (along with other criteria that are driven by human psychology) not as an user interface evaluation method, but as an important input towards modelling the human psychological needs. These HCI and UX simple tools assist in formalizing simplistic yet effective guidelines that help in easy incorporation of basic human psychological needs requirements in the software systems development.

Since the human psychological needs are explicitly modelled in terms of system functions, the SUXEH framework support early analysis of human-centered functional requirements in terms of their conflicts with satisfaction of other human-centered system goals. Identification and resolution of requirements conflicts has been studied since long (e.g., studies referred in [2, 55]). However, to the best of our knowledge, the SUXEH framework is the first to provide guidelines on identifying and representing conflicts among *human-centered* requirements using the GRL. Our framework promotes user involvement in terms of negotiations with stakeholders mainly facilitated by the designers. The conflicts can be resolved via these negotiations in order to gather more information. This will also help in reconciliation of designers' and stakeholders' point of views on those human-centered requirements that are not realizable from a resource or technical point of view (for instance, requirements that may interfere with the system's basic functionality). Adding priorities as goal attributes has been used in the past for resolving conflicts among goals [54]. However, the resolution of the conflicts is not detailed in this paper.

While the framework aims to support the design of sustainable user experiences, we acknowledge that human-centeredness in system design may also trigger behavior that is unsustainable from e.g., an environmental point of view. Accordingly, the framework guidelines are provided to identify and represent such situations.

Further, we believe that the SUXEH framework has a potential to address human diversity. The SUXEH framework takes into consideration the differences in human needs of different categories of users that interact with the system. For instance, in the Taxi system, human needs of customers and taxi drivers are separately modelled and analysed for their impacts on each other. Similarly, the SUXEH framework allows to represent the users with special profiles. For instance, in the Taxi system, the "Register with Specific Profiles" functionality goal helps stakeholders and development team to explore the complexities of human diversity and can help towards understanding the connected challenges on a higher-level. Further possibilities of human diversity modelling in this context however, need to be explored in future work.

7 Conclusion and Future Work

In this paper, we have presented a framework, we refer to as SUXEH (Sustainable User eXperiences Enabled Human-centered) framework, which emphasizes that in order to support human psychological well-being, there is a dire need to consider it in the design cycle of software systems. For this, the framework provides guidelines on identifying and representing the fundamental human psychological needs (that are based on mature psychological theories) explicitly as systems functions in early stages of software development. Particularly in this paper, the guidelines are detailed to avoid designing those human-centered system functionalities that are in conflict with: long-term eudaimonic aspects of user experiences; sustainability goals; and human-centered goals across other interfaces of a system. With the help of a case study, the Taxi System, these guidelines are demonstrated by modelling autonomy as the detailed example need. This application of the framework on the demonstration case study shows that our framework is generic in a way that it is neither system specific nor end-user specific (e.g., not only targeting elderly people in welfare technologies). It deals with human diversity to some extent and applies to different types of human users and equally to all types of software systems. We also believe that the requirements models that result from application of our framework can be used by all software systems design methodologies. We look forward to conduct empirical case studies/user studies that allow to further refine and validate the framework.

We do not claim that our framework provides complete guidelines on integration of human psychological needs in the early stages of requirement specifications, but we believe that our framework provides initial directions that guides beyond GUI design and usability, and provides more holistic and realistic picture of integration to address broader impacts on human well-being and other long term eudaimonic aspects of sustainable user experience outcomes. We emphasize that provision of this information in requirements specifications acts as a significant input in making design decisions during software systems development.

Our research presented in this paper can form a useful starting point to further investigate generic models of human psychological needs in the software development process. More efforts for interdisciplinary research that may help in creation of new design methods, or investigation of most appropriate design methods that can be improved to incorporate human-centered requirements are required. Methods on how to resolve conflict among human-centered goals and their evaluation need to be explored. These are open research questions and we are looking forward to address these questions in our future publications.

References

1. Acuña, S.T., Castro, J.W., Juristo, N.: A hci technique for improving requirements elicitation. Inform. Softw. Technol. **54**(12), 1357–1375 (2012). https://doi.org/10.1016/j.infsof.2012.07.011, https://www.sciencedirect.com/science/article/pii/S0950584912001371, special Section on Software Reliability and Security
2. Aldekhail, M., Chikh, A., Ziani, D.: Software requirements conflict identification: review and recommendations. Int. J. Adv. Comput. Sci. Appl. (IJACSA) **7**(10), 326 (2016)
3. Amyot, D., Mussbacher, G.: Development of telecommunications standards and services with the user requirements notation. In: Workshop on ITU System Design Languages, vol. 2008, pp. 15–16 (2008)

4. Becker, C., et al.: Sustainability design and software: the karlskrona manifesto. In: 2015 IEEE/ACM 37th IEEE International Conference on Software Engineering, vol. 2, pp. 467–476 (2015). https://doi.org/10.1109/ICSE.2015.179
5. Brown, J.: Hci and requirements engineering-exploring human-computer interaction and software engineering methodologies for the creation of interactive software. SIGCHI Bull. **29**(1), 32–35 (1997)
6. Calvo, R.A., Peters, D.: Positive computing: technology for wellbeing and human potential. MIT press (2014)
7. Calvo, R.A., Peters, D., Johnson, D., Rogers, Y.: Autonomy in technology design. In: CHI 2014 Extended Abstracts on Human Factors in Computing Systems, pp. 37–40 (2014)
8. Checkland, P.: Systems thinking, systems practice john wiley & sons. New York (1981)
9. Curumsing, M.K., Fernando, N., Abdelrazek, M., Vasa, R., Mouzakis, K., Grundy, J.: Emotion-oriented requirements engineering: a case study in developing a smart home system for the elderly. J. Syst. Softw. **147**, 215–229 (2019)
10. Deci, E.L., Ryan, R.M.: The "what" and "why" of goal pursuits: Human needs and the self-determination of behaviour. Psychol. Inq. **11**(4), 227–268 (2000)
11. Desmet, P.M., Pohlmeyer, A.E.: Positive design: an introduction to design for subjective well-being. Intern. J. Design **7**(3) (2013)
12. Farooqui, T., Rana, T., Jafari, F.: Impact of human-centered design process (hcdp) on software development process. In: 2019 2nd International Conference on Communication, Computing and Digital systems (C-CODE), pp. 110–114 (2019). https://doi.org/10.1109/C-CODE.2019.8680978
13. Fatima, U., Bræk, R.: Modular solutions to common design problems using activities and the interface-modular method. In: Grabowski, J., Herbold, S. (eds.) SAM 2016. LNCS, vol. 9959, pp. 226–241. Springer, Cham (2016). https://doi.org/10.1007/978-3-319-46613-2_15
14. Fatima, U., Moor, K.D.: Towards integration of sustainable user experience aspects in systems design: A human-centered framework. In: Fill, H., Mayo, F.J.D., van Sinderen, M., Maciaszek, L.A. (eds.) Proceedings of the 18th International Conference on Software Technologies, ICSOFT 2023, Rome, Italy, 10-12 July 2023, pp. 129–140. SCITEPRESS (2023). https://doi.org/10.5220/0012091800003538
15. Fink, V., Zeiner, K.M., Ritter, M., Burmester, M., Eibl, M.: Design for positive ux: From experience categories to psychological needs. In: HCI International 2022–Late Breaking Posters: 24th International Conference on Human-Computer Interaction, HCII 2022, Virtual Event, 26 June –1 July 2022, Proceedings, Part I. pp. 148–155. Springer (2022). https://doi.org/10.1007/978-3-031-19679-9_19
16. Flayelle, M., Maurage, P., Di Lorenzo, K.R., Vögele, C., Gainsbury, S.M., Billieux, J.: Binge-watching: What do we know so far? a first systematic review of the evidence. Curr. Addict. Rep. **7**, 44–60 (2020)
17. Friedman, B.: Value-sensitive design. Interactions **3**(6), 16–23 (1996)
18. Friedman, B., Hendry, D.G., Borning, A., et al.: A survey of value sensitive design methods. Foundat. Trends Human–Comput. Interact. **11**(2), 63–125 (2017)
19. Gaggioli, A., Villani, D., Serino, S., Banos, R., Botella, C.: Positive technology: Designing e-experiences for positive change (2019)
20. Granow, V.C., Reinecke, L., Ziegele, M.: Binge-watching and psychological well-being: media use between lack of control and perceived autonomy. Commun. Res. Rep. **35**(5), 392–401 (2018)
21. Grundy, J., Khalajzadeh, H., McIntosh, J., Kanij, T., Mueller, I.: HumaniSE: approaches to achieve more human-centric software engineering. In: Ali, R., Kaindl, H., Maciaszek, L.A. (eds.) ENASE 2020. CCIS, vol. 1375, pp. 444–468. Springer, Cham (2021). https://doi.org/10.1007/978-3-030-70006-5_18

22. Grundy, J., Mueller, I., Madugalla, A., Khalajzadeh, H., Obie, H.O., McIntosh, J., Kanij, T.: Addressing the influence of end user human aspects on software engineering. In: Evaluation of Novel Approaches to Software Engineering: 16th International Conference, ENASE 2021, Virtual Event, 26-27 April 2021, Revised Selected Papers, pp. 241–264. Springer (2022). https://doi.org/10.1007/978-3-030-96648-5_11

23. Hammer, F., Egger-Lampl, S., Möller, S.: Quality-of-user-experience: a position paper. Qual. User Exper. **3**, 1–15 (2018)

24. Hassenzahl, M.: The thing and I: Understanding the relationship between user and product. Funology 2: from usability to enjoyment, pp. 301–313 (2018)

25. Hassenzahl, M., Roto, V.: Being and doing: a perspective on user experience and its measurement. Interfaces **72**(1), 10–12 (2007)

26. Hidellaarachchi, D., Grundy, J., Hoda, R., Mueller, I.: The influence of human aspects on requirements engineering-related activities: Software practitioners perspective. ACM Trans. Softw. Eng. Methodol. **32**(5), 1–37 (2023)

27. Hix, D., Hartson, H.: Iterative, evaluation-centered user interaction development. Developing User Interfaces: Ensuring Usability Through Product & Process, pp. 95–116, John Wiley & Sons, New York (1993)

28. Host, M., Rainer, A., Runeson, P., Regnell, B.: Case study research in software engineering: guidelines and examples. John Wiley & Sons (2012)

29. Iivari, J., Isomäki, H., Pekkola, S.: The user–the great unknown of systems development: reasons, forms, challenges, experiences and intellectual contributions of user involvement (2010)

30. Ergonomics of human-system interaction - Part 11: Usability: Definitions and concepts. Standard, International Organization for Standardization (2018). https://www.iso.org/obp/ui/#iso:std:iso:9241:-11:ed-2:v1:en

31. Ergonomics of human-system interaction - Part 210: Human-centred design for interactive systems. Standard, International Organization for Standardization (2019). https://www.iso.org/obp/ui/#iso:std:iso:9241:-210:ed-2:v1:en

32. Klemets, J., Storholmen, T.C.B.: Towards super user-centred continuous delivery: a case study. In: Bernhaupt, R., Ardito, C., Sauer, S. (eds.) HCSE 2020. LNCS, vol. 12481, pp. 152–165. Springer, Cham (2020). https://doi.org/10.1007/978-3-030-64266-2_9

33. Mairiza, D., Zowghi, D., Nurmuliani, N.: Managing conflicts among non-functional requirements. In: Australian Workshop on Requirements Engineering. University of Technology, Sydney (2009)

34. Mayhew, D.: The usability engineering lifecycle: a practitioner's handbook for user interface design (1999)

35. Mekler, E.D., Hornbæk, K.: Momentary pleasure or lasting meaning? distinguishing eudaimonic and hedonic user experiences. In: Proceedings of the 2016 CHI Conference on Human Factors in Computing Systems, pp. 4509–4520 (2016)

36. Metzker, E., Reiterer, H.: Use and Reuse of HCI Knowledge in the Software Development Lifecycle, pp. 39–55. Springer US, Boston, MA (2002). https://doi.org/10.1007/978-0-387-35610-5_3

37. Monge Roffarello, A., De Russis, L.: The Race Towards Digital Wellbeing: Issues and Opportunities, p. 1–14. Association for Computing Machinery, New York (2019). https://doi.org/10.1145/3290605.3300616

38. Mylopoulos, J., Chung, L., Nixon, B.: Representing and using nonfunctional requirements: a process-oriented approach. IEEE Trans. Software Eng. **18**(6), 483–497 (1992)

39. Nielsen, J.: Heuristic evaluation. John Wiley&Sons (1994)

40. Norman, D.A.: The Design of Everyday Things, 2nd edn. Basic Books, New York (2013)

41. Orben, A., Przybylski, A.K.: The association between adolescent well-being and digital technology use. Nat. Hum. Behav. **3**(2), 173–182 (2019)

42. Penzenstadler, B., Venters, C.: Software engineering for sustainability: Tools for sustainability analysis, pp. 103–121. Routledge Studies in Sustainability, Routledge, United Kingdom, 1st edn. (2017). https://doi.org/10.9774/gleaf.9781315465975_13
43. Peters, D., Calvo, R.A., Ryan, R.M.: Designing for motivation, engagement and wellbeing in digital experience. Front. Psychol., 797 (2018)
44. Restrepo-Tamayo, L.M., Gasca-Hurtado, G.P.: Human aspects in software development: a systematic mapping study. In: International Conference on Collaboration Technologies and Social Computing, pp. 1–22. Springer (2022). https://doi.org/10.1007/978-3-031-20218-6_1
45. Riva, G., Baños, R.M., Botella, C., Wiederhold, B.K., Gaggioli, A.: Positive technology: using interactive technologies to promote positive functioning. Cyberpsychol. Behav. Soc. Netw. 15(2), 69–77 (2012)
46. Rosenbaum, S., Bloomer, S., Rinehart, D., Rohn, J., Dye, K., Humburg, J., Nielsen, J., Wixon, D.: What makes strategic usability fail? lessons learned from the field. In: CHI 1999 extended abstracts on Human Factors in Computing Systems, pp. 93–94 (1999)
47. Rugg, G., McGeorge, P.: Laddering. Expert Syst. 12(4), 339–346 (1995). https://onlinelibrary.wiley.com/doi/abs/10.1111/j.1468-0394.1995.tb00271.x
48. Ryan, R.M., Deci, E.L.: Self-determination theory and the facilitation of intrinsic motivation, social development, and well-being. Am. Psychol. 55(1), 68 (2000)
49. Ryan, R.M., Deci, E.L.: Self-determination theory: basic psychological needs in motivation, development, and wellness. Guilford Publications (2017)
50. Ryan, R., Rigby, C.: MIT handbook of gamification. The MIT Press, Boston, MA (2018)
51. Sarda, E., Bègue, L., Bry, C., Gentile, D.: Internet gaming disorder and well-being: a scale validation. Cyberpsychol. Behav. Soc. Netw. 19(11), 674–679 (2016)
52. Sheldon, K.M., Elliot, A.J., Kim, Y., Kasser, T.: What is satisfying about satisfying events? testing 10 candidate psychological needs. J. Pers. Soc. Psychol. 80(2), 325 (2001)
53. Van Der Hoven, J., Manders-Huits, N.: Value sensitive design In: The Ethics of Information Technologies, pp. 329–332. Routledge (2020)
54. Van Lamsweerde, A.: Goal-oriented requirements engineering: a guided tour. In: Proceedings Fifth IEEE International Symposium on Requirements Engineering, pp. 249–262. IEEE (2001)
55. Van Lamsweerde, A., Darimont, R., Letier, E.: Managing conflicts in goal-driven requirements engineering. IEEE Trans. Software Eng. 24(11), 908–926 (1998)
56. Vansteenkiste, M., Ryan, R.M.: On psychological growth and vulnerability: basic psychological need satisfaction and need frustration as a unifying principle. J. Psychother. Integr. 23(3), 263 (2013)
57. World Health Organization: Promoting Well-being. https://www.who.int/activities/promoting-well-being (2023), ch1 WHO, retrieved October 28, 2023

DeepPull: Deep Learning-Based Approach for Predicting Reopening, Decision, and Lifetime of Pull Requests on GitHub Open-Source Projects

Peerachai Banyongrakkul$^{(\boxtimes)}$ and Suronapee Phoomvuthisarn

Department of Statistics, Chulalongkorn University, Bangkok, Thailand
{6480460026,suronapee}@cbs.chula.ac.th

Abstract. This paper introduces DeepPull, a novel multi-output deep learning-based classification approach designed to predict pull request outcomes in GitHub's pull-based software development model. The primary goal of Deep-Pull is to provide decision-making support for integrators in open-source software projects, with a particular focus on mitigating the challenges associated with managing high request volumes. DeepPull anticipates the reopening, decision, and lifetime of pull requests at the time of submission. Our method effectively leverages diverse data sources, including tabular and textual data, and incorporates a combination of SMOTE and VAE techniques to handle imbalances in reopening predictions. The evaluation of DeepPull on six well-known programming languages, along with 83 open-source projects, demonstrates significant performance improvements over both a randomized baseline and the existing approach. The approach greatly enhances balanced accuracy by 6.25%, AUC by 7.19%, and TPR by 16.78% in reopening prediction, improves accuracy by 7.71%, precision by 0.56%, recall by 10.96%, and F-measure by 6.27% in decision prediction, and reduces MMAE by 5.73% in lifetime prediction compared to an existing approach.

Keywords: Pull request · GitHub · Deep learning · Classification

1 Introduction

The *pull request*, a pivotal element in the pull-based development model, has revolutionized the way software projects are managed. It allows developers to make contributions (e.g., software changes) flexibly and efficiently [10]. GitHub[1] is the most popular choice that allows open-source projects to employ the pull-based model [3]. GitHub's pull-based model enables developers (i.e., *contributors*) to propose a set of changes through pull requests to the main repository of the project. Subsequently, developers of the project's core team (i.e., *integrators*) shoulder the responsibility of inspecting and assessing the quality of these contributions. The role of integrators is crucial [6], as evaluating pull requests is a very challenging task, especially in popular projects

---

[1] https://github.com/.

© The Author(s), under exclusive license to Springer Nature Switzerland AG 2024
H.-G. Fill et al. (Eds.): ICSOFT 2023, CCIS 2104, pp. 100–123, 2024.
https://doi.org/10.1007/978-3-031-61753-9_6

[22]. With an influx of incoming pull requests, integrators face the critical responsibility of promptly deciding whether to accept or reject requests, a decision that significantly impacts project growth and quality standards. [24]. Surveys have shown that while the pull-based paradigm lowers the barrier to entry for potential contributors, it also increases the burden on already-busy integrators [11] and many contributors are suffering from the delayed feedback of their pull requests [10].

In this context, a prediction could support the integrator's decision for their pull request management. Specifically, the integrators can identify which pull requests are likely to be rejected and those necessitating prolonged evaluation; therefore, they can prioritize their work and allocate their resources efficiently. Consequently, several studies have proposed a predictive model to address this circumstance. Currently, there are two primary predictive outputs of pull requests which are decision [5,9,13,19] and lifetime [7,9,23]. However, the standard decision and lifetime metrics may not fully capture pull request outcomes. Occasionally, a closed pull request needs to be reopened for further review, referred to as a *reopened pull request*. [17]. While these instances are relatively rare [12], they can have several negative impacts. [14,17]. A limited group of researchers [16,17] has developed models for predicting reopened pull requests, but they make predictions after the first decision point, which might be too late. Integrators could benefit from earlier predictions to identify potentially reopened pull requests and devise timely solutions. Nonetheless, early prediction is challenging due to limited information. Relying solely on common tabular features, like existing approaches, might not suffice for accurate predictions in this situation.

In our paper, we introduce DeepPull, a novel deep learning-based approach for predicting pull request reopening, decision, and lifetime at the time of submission, building upon the work originated from [2]. To be specific, these predictions offer immediate feedback to integrators after the pull request is created. Our approach incorporates textual data to address the limited information challenge. We employ pre-trained models for textual feature extraction. Moreover, we utilize a combination of SMOTE and VAE techniques to tackle the imbalance in reopened pull requests. Furthermore, our approach makes predictions by taking advantage of the relationship between pull request outcomes through shared learning.

We extend our experimentation to evaluate DeepPull's predictive performance across six programming languages. This evaluation encompasses four original languages (e.g., Python, R, Java, and Ruby) and expands to include PHP and C++, with 144,235 pull requests spanning 29 new projects adhering to the pull-based development model on GitHub. An additional valuable contribution is the publication of the dataset on Zenodo to facilitate future research[2]. By performance metrics, DeepPull outperforms the randomized baseline and the existing approach, achieving impressive results on average. DeepPull obtains 0.632 in balanced accuracy, 0.693 in AUC, and 0.685 in TPR for the reopening prediction, whereas DeepPull gains 0.767 in accuracy, 0.879 in precision, 0.797 in recall, and 0.833 in F-measure for the decision prediction and achieves 1.149 in MMAE for the lifetime prediction. These results offer compelling proof that DeepPull significantly enhances predictive performance within the realms of pull request reopening, decision, and lifetime. Apart from evaluation using performance measures, we also add further analysis to highlight the advantage of employing over-

---

[2] https://doi.org/10.5281/zenodo.10054035.

sampling with a combination of SMOTE and VAE and underscore the vital role played by textual features and the architectural design of DeepPull in making these predictions.

The structure of this paper is as follows: in Sect. 2, we present background information on the pull-based development model, while Sect. 3 offers a comprehensive literature review. In Sect. 4, we outline the formulation of predictive problems, and Sect. 5 delves into the specifics of our research design. Next, Sect. 6 introduces DeepPull, followed by Sect. 7 presenting our dataset, evaluation results, further findings, and threats to validity. Finally, Sect. 8 summarizes our conclusions and outlines future research directions.

2   Background

In this section, we provide the necessary background information, particularly focusing on the GitHub pull-based development model and the current challenges associated with it.

2.1   GitHub Pull-Based Development Model

The emergence of Git revolutionized distributed software development (DSD), introducing the pull-based development model [9]. Git is the preferred choice of developers, with 93.9% support in 2022[3], enabling services like GitHub, which boasts 94 million developers and 227 million merged pull requests in 2022[4]. In the GitHub pull-based model, there are two primary roles and two corresponding strategies:

- **Integrator.** A developer in the main team of the project.
- **Contributor.** A developer or a user that would like to contribute to the project from the outside.
- **Shared Repository.** A project repository that shares read and write permissions with the contributors.
- **Pull Request.** An event that allows a contributor to propose changes to a main project repository.

With these elements in place, contributors can fetch software changes from other repositories and integrate them into their local copies. This stands in contrast to the traditional distributed development approach, where changes are submitted and accepted via mailing lists or systems like Bugzilla, instead of directly pushing them to the project's main repository [24]. GitHub's pull-based development process is designed to enable *contributors* to modify open-source projects without requiring direct access to the *shared repository*. The workflow involves contributors creating their own forks of the repository and implementing changes locally. When they are ready to contribute their changes to the main repository, they initiate a *pull request*, which serves as a formal request for review and approval by a designated *integrator*. The integrator assumes the responsibility of examining the proposed alterations and offering feedback. The

---

[3] https://survey.stackoverflow.co/2022/.

[4] https://octoverse.github.com/developer-community/.

contributor can make additional commits to address feedback before approval. Once a pull request is approved, the changes submitted by the contributor are merged into the main project.

In GitHub, there are three states of pull requests, as shown in Fig. 1 including:

- **Open.** The pull request has been proposed by the contributor and is being discussed or is waiting for the integrator's decision on whether it will be accepted or rejected.
- **Merged.** The integrator satisfies the changes in the pull request. The integrator, thus, approves closing it by merging the changes with the main branch.
- **Closed.** The integrator is not satisfied with the changes. The integrator, thus, closes it by rejecting the pull request.

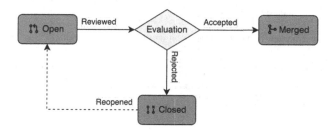

Fig. 1. GitHub pull request lifecycle, sourced from [2].

2.2 Current Challenges

In the pull-based model, it is essential to highlight that the ultimate decision to accept or reject these incoming pull requests lies with the integrators, and their experience can significantly influence the outcome. Moreover, although this pull request mechanism enhances software development efficiency and flexibility, it can also impose an increased workload on integrators, especially in the context of highly popular projects. Aside from the perspective of integrators, many contributors are suffering from the delayed feedback on their pull requests.

Figure 1 shows that the pull requests can also be reopened after their close when the decision is changed or further code review is required. The contributor or the integrator can attempt further discussion to reopen the reviewing process; this will lead to a new decision from the integrator. These pull requests are called *reopened pull requests*, as exemplified in Fig. 2. For this demonstration, the figure has been modified to focus on essential aspects of the pull request. The title and body of the pull request indicate that Mr.A, the contributor, has proposed changes to address a load error issue. Initially, Mr.B, the integrator, rejected the pull request, suspecting that it was unrelated to Ruby. However, he later decided to reopen it, recognizing that certain parts of the request appeared reasonable. Subsequently, the pull request underwent a review by another integrator, Mr.C, who ultimately accepted it. This example serves as a noteworthy illustration of the potential risks associated with reopening pull requests when an integrator's initial decision may be influenced by various factors.

The reopened pull requests can place additional demands on the integrator [14], potentially increasing software maintenance costs and adding to their workload [17].

Additionally, they may also cause conflicts with newly submitted pull requests if pull requests are reopened a long time after their closure. Therefore, early identification of such risks can assist integrators in making more effective and informed decisions. Consequently, there is a pressing demand for tools and strategies to support integrators in handling these challenges.

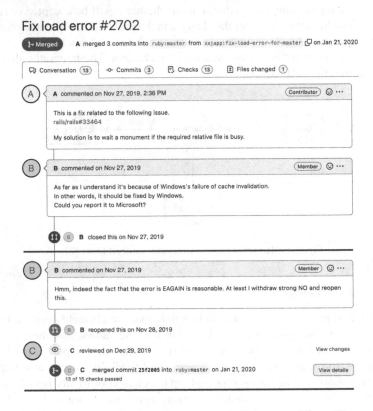

Fig. 2. An example of a pull request on GitHub, sourced from [2].

3   Related Work

As our study involves developing a predictive approach to address three aspects of pull request outcomes, the related work of this paper is mainly divided into three parts: pull request reopening, pull request decision, and pull request lifetime.

3.1   Pull Request Reopening

To the best of our knowledge, there is limited prior research concerning the prediction of reopened pull requests. Mohamed et al. [17] introduced an approach named DTPre, specifically designed to predict reopened pull requests after the initial merging decision. Their experimental results indicated that Decision Tree, in combination with oversampling, yielded the most effective predictive performance. Furthermore, the same research team, Mohamed et al. [16], extended their work to conduct additional cross-project experiments, utilizing the same dataset. Their objective was to address the cold-start problem commonly encountered in new software projects with a limited number of pull requests. Additionally, a study conducted by Jiang et al. [12] delved into the impact of reopened pull requests on the code review process, revealing that reopened pull requests exhibited lower acceptance rates, longer evaluation times, and a higher frequency of comments compared to non-reopened pull requests.

3.2 Pull Request Decision

Prior studies have examined factors influencing integrators' pull request acceptance decisions. Gousios et al. [9] found that pull request acceptance depends on recent code modifications, using Random Forest. Soares et al. [21] used multidimensional association rules to identify factors like programming languages that affect merging likelihood. Other studies have explored social and technical factors, such as the impact of comments on metrics [22] and the contributor's experience and politeness [20], using the logistic regression model. The work in [25] conducted a comprehensive analysis of the factors obtained from a systematic literature review using statistical methods. Aside from these research efforts focusing on the influencing factors, some studies aimed at building predictive models. Khadke et al. [19] and Jiang et al. [13] employed machine learning, using Random Forest and XGBoost effectively. Jiang et al. claimed outperformance over the method by Gousios et al. Moreover, Chen et al. [5] developed new features via crowdsourcing for their predictive model.

3.3 Pull Request Lifetime

Researchers focusing on pull request lifetime explored the factors influencing the lifetime and developed predictive models for estimating this duration. In addition to investigating pull request merging, Gousios et al. [9] investigated latency using logistic regression, random forest, and naive bayes, comparing different feature sets. In [23], variants of logistic regression were utilized to model pull request lifetime on GitHub opensource projects. They highlighted the new features' superior performance compared to Gousios et al.'s. Moreover, Zhang et al. [26] employed mixed-effect linear regression, finding varying factor importance across scenarios. Lastly, De Lima Júnior et al. [7] addressed pull request lifetime with regression and classification techniques and found that the linear model performed the best in the regression task, while random forest featured the best in the classification task.

3.4 Gaps in Literature and Motivations

The existing literature has primarily focused on pull request decision and pull request lifetime. Most of these studies have employed statistical methods and traditional machine learning techniques to investigate the tabular factors influencing the decision and the lifetime. Some have also developed predictive models. However, there is limited research on the topic of pull request reopening, which can have a negative impact on both productivity and quality of software development. Predicting reopening outcomes is an extremely challenging task due to the highly imbalanced nature of the problem. For instance, in the Rails project, only 2.43% of pull requests have been reopened [17].

Apart from the matter of reopening, the textual descriptions within pull requests serve as a valuable source of information, offering insights into the nature of the request. This includes details about the review process and the complexity of the proposed changes. Surprisingly, many previous approaches did not take into account the textual description of pull requests. Some considered it but overlooked its inherent character-istics, such as sequential properties and word dependencies, which can be challenging to analyze without advanced feature extraction techniques. Another motivation for our work is that the studies conducted by [21] and [12] found that there are relationships between reopening, decision, and lifetime. For instance, an increase in the evaluation time for a pull request reduces the chances of its acceptance, and reopened pull requests have lower acceptance rates and a longer evaluation time than non-reopened ones. The existing literature did not take advantage of these relationships in building predictive models.

Moreover, there is a notable absence of models that offer prompt predictions for integrators right after a pull request is initiated. Furthermore, previous research on pull request prediction has predominantly assessed models either at the project or all-in-one level, potentially leading to issues like the cold-start problem for new projects or exces-sively generalized models. Consequently, a literature gap exists in terms of employing a programming language-specific experimental framework to strike a balance between specificity and generalization, thereby enhancing the practicality and relevance of these models in real-world software development scenarios.

Hence, our prior work [2] leveraged deep learning to comprehensively address these gaps and motivations. Deep learning, in particular, offered the flexibility to design model architectures capable of capturing intricate relationships among outputs. Another aspect was that it provided a well-defined advanced architecture conducive to effective oversampling for highly imbalanced data for the reopening task. Finally, deep learn-ing empowered us with feature learning capabilities, including automatic feature engi-neering and textual feature extraction. Nonetheless, our prior work had certain limi-tations, as it only covered four programming languages and lacked further interpreta-tion and discussion of the results. Thus, as an extension of our previous research [2], we have conducted more extensive experiments across six popular programming lan-guages, including a larger dataset with over 100% more samples. This expansion aims to confirm the predictive performance of our approach in a broader context. We have also made the dataset available on Zenodo to support future research endeavors. Fur-thermore, we have performed additional analyses to assess the effectiveness of our pro-posed components, including our oversampling method, our textual features extracted from pre-trained models, and our deep learning-based architecture.

4   Predictive Problem Formulation

To formulate our predictive problem, we establish t_{pred} as the reference point repre-senting the time when a prediction is made for a pull request. This point refers to the submission time of the pull request. Our goal is to develop a classification approach that leverages the pull request information to predict the three following tasks for a given pull request at time t_{pred}: Reopening, Decision, and Lifetime, as stated in our previous study [2].

To formally describe our predictive problem using mathematical notations, let $X = \mathbb{R}^d$ denote the d-dimensional input space representing pull requests and $Y = Y^1 \times Y^2 \times Y^3$ denotes the pull request output space, which contains three class variables (i.e., reopening, decision, and lifetime). Here, Y^1 represents the reopening output, Y^2 represents the decision output, and Y^3 represents the lifetime output. Y^1 has two classes: C_1^1 (Non-Reopened) and C_2^1 (Reopened); Y^2 has two classes: C_1^2 (Rejected) and C_2^2 (Accepted); and Y^3 has five classes: C_1^3 (Hour), C_2^3 (Day), C_3^3 (Week), C_4^3 (Month), and C_5^3 (GTMonth). Given a training dataset, $D = \{x_j, y_j\}_{j=1}^M$ where $x_j = [x_1^j, x_2^j, ..., x_d^j] \in X$ and $y_j = [y_1^j, y_2^j, ..., y_d^j] \in Y$, our predictive task is to learn a mapping function, $f : X \rightarrow Y$, from the dataset D that can predict a proper output vector, $f(x) \in Y$, for an unseen pull request x.

It is crucial to note that these prediction outcomes will be generated solely based on the information available at the specific time t_{pred}. To illustrate this with an example, consider pull request ID 2702 (as shown in Fig. 2). At the specific time t_{pred}, which is 2:36 PM on November 27, 2019, we utilize the information available up to that moment to make predictions for this pull request. The predicted outcomes are as follows: *Reopened* (C_2^1) for the reopening output, *Accepted* (C_2^2) for the decision output, and *GTMonth* (C_5^3) for the lifetime output.

5 Research Design

The main focus of this study is to measure the performance of DeepPull in early-predicting pull request outcomes, which are reopening, decision, and lifetime. To achieve this goal, we intend to address two key research questions through our empirical evaluation, aiming to gain valuable insights into its effectiveness.

5.1 Research Questions

RQ1: Is DeepPull Appropriate for the Early Prediction of Reopening, Decision, and Lifetime of Pull Requests?
The objective here is to conduct a sanity check to assess the suitability of our approach in predicting pull request reopening, pull request decision, and pull request lifetime at the time of submission. It is crucial for our approach to outperform this baseline, which relies on random guessing, to establish its suitability for early-predicting reopening, decision, and lifetime of pull requests.

RQ2: Can DeepPull Outperform the Existing Approach?
This research question aims to compare how well DeepPull performs in prediction when contrasted with the existing methods. To establish the superiority of DeepPull, we expect that its performance surpasses that of the existing methods. This outcome would demonstrate that deep learning-based methods can effectively improve the accuracy of prediction for pull request reopening, decision, and lifetime compared to the existing approaches, as well as address the challenges posed by the limited data available at the time of submission and highly imbalanced data.

5.2 Experimental Procedure and Metrics

To evaluate the predictive performance of the approaches, we employed various standard binary classification metrics for the decision task, including accuracy, precision, recall, F-measure, and AUC. However, for the lifetime task, we utilized the Macro-Averaged Absolute Error (MMAE), as it is well-suited to measuring the distance between actual and predicted classes for ordinal classification. Additionally, for the reopening task, we employed metrics that can effectively handle highly imbalanced data and facilitate accurate anomaly detection. These metrics include balanced accuracy, AUC, True Positive Rate (TPR), and False Negative Rate (FNR). It is worth noting that in both the MMAE and FNR metrics, lower values indicate superior performance.

For a fair performance comparison, all approaches undergo training and validation in the same experimental environment using an identical dataset and data splitting. The dataset is described in Sect. 7.1. In the matter of building the baseline, we repeat the random guessing process 5,000 times and calculate the average performance to ensure statistical significance. In the case of the existing approach, due to the fact that no existing approach predicts in the same manner as our proposed approach, we utilize an alternative approach. This alternative method involves the use of tabular features, feature selection techniques, and conventional single-output machine learning classifiers, such as *Decision Tree*, *Random Forest*, and *XGBoost*, which have been recognized as the best performers in previous studies, to represent the existing approaches. The set of tabular features is consistent across both the existing approach and our approach. The tabular features are discussed in Sect. 6.2. Additionally, they employ the same hyperparameter tuning technique, utilizing a randomized algorithm with 30 iterations. Furthermore, they used the same performance metrics for model tuning. Specifically, AUC was used for the reopening and decision tasks, and MMAE was used for the lifetime task.

6 DeepPull

6.1 Overview Framework

DeepPull is a deep learning-based classification approach for predicting the reopening, decision, and lifetime of pull requests. During the training phase, historical pull request data is used to build predictive models with features extracted from tabular and textual data. Moreover, oversampling is employed to address data imbalances in the reopening task. In the execution phase, these models are used to predict reopening, decision, and lifetime for new pull requests. Due to the fact that reopening always occurs before the rest of the outcomes and may have an impact on them, DeepPull predicts the reopening output first. This predicted reopening output is then used as a feature along with the other input features to predict the decision and lifetime of the pull request. This section will further delve into feature extraction, oversampling methods, and model architecture.

6.2 Feature Extraction

Our approach incorporates two types of features: *tabular features* and *textual features*. These features play a crucial role in capturing relevant information from pull requests and facilitating accurate predictions.

Tabular Features. For characterizing pull requests, both project repositories, contributors, and the pull requests themselves offer numerous attributes that can be extracted and used as features. To facilitate feature extraction, we define three key aspects that describe a pull request: the pull request itself, the project it's associated with, and the contributor. Our tabular features draw inspiration from a set of features frequently used in prior research on prediction. It is important to note that the features we extract for our analysis are derived from the time of pull request submission (t_{pred}). In Table 1, a comprehensive list of 30 extracted tabular features and their descriptions is shown. We apply common feature extraction techniques such as counting, summation, subtraction, and ratio calculations based on the attributes of the pull request.

Table 1. List of the tabular features.

Feature	Source	Description
# of commits	Pull request	Number of commits in the pull request
# of modified files	Pull request	Number of files modified in the pull request
# of added files	Pull request	Number of files added by the pull request
# of deleted files	Pull request	Number of files deleted in the pull request
# of changed files	Pull request	Number of files changed by the pull request
# of changed src files	Pull request	Number of source files changed by the pull request
# of changed test files	Pull request	Number of test files changed by the pull request
# of changed doc files	Pull request	Number of document files changed by the pull request
# of changed other files	Pull request	Number of other files changed by the pull request
# of changed lines	Pull request	Number of lines changed by the pull request
# of added lines	Pull request	Number of lines added by the pull request
# of deleted lines	Pull request	Number of lines deleted by the pull request
has test	Pull request	If the pull request contains any test file
# of changes test lines	Pull request	Number of test lines changed by the pull request
has pr link	Pull request	If the description of the pull request has any pull request link
# of previous pr in project	Project	Number of previous pull requests received by the project
% of commits made by pr	Project	Percent of commits made by pull requests in last month
# of commits files touched	Project	Number of total commits on files changed by the pull request 3 months before
file rejected proportion	Project	Percent of previously rejected pull requests in files changed by the pull request
# of merged pr	Project	Number of merged pull requests in the latest 10 pull requests
# of rejected pr	Project	Number of rejected pull requests in the latest 10 pull requests
is recent pr rejected	Project	If the latest pull request is rejected
reputation	Contributor	Percent of the contributor's previous accepted pull requests
is first pr	Contributor	If the contributor has no experience in submitting pull request
contributor age	Contributor	Time, in minutes, since the contributor became a GitHub user
# of events in pr	Contributor	Number of interactions of the contributor in pull requests
# of comments in pr	Contributor	Number of comments of the contributor in pull requests
# of commits prev pr	Contributor	Number of commits of the contributor
# of previous pr created	Contributor	Number of pull requests submitted by the contributor
is core team	Contributor	If the contributor is a core team member for the project

Textual Features. A pull request usually contains two pieces of textual information: the title and the body. Contributors use these to summarize and describe the proposed changes. For instance, considering pull request ID 2702, the title is "Fix load error" and the body is "This is a fix related to the following issue. rails/rails#33464 My solution is to wait a monument if the required relative file is busy." The title and body can reflect the nature of a pull request, such as the details of a review task and the complexity of the task. Therefore, a well-crafted title and body can reduce the integrator's effort in executing the review task. Surprisingly, in the past, these textual aspects have not received the attention they deserve as predictors for pull requests. Therefore, we incorporate the text from the title and body as one of our features to better characterize our pull requests.

To utilize text data in machine learning, it's essential to convert it into numerical vectors. Traditional methods (e.g., Bag of Words, N-Gram, and Term Frequency-Inverse Document Frequency) suffer from sparsity and lose the sequential nature of text [2]. Advanced deep learning techniques, such as pre-trained word embeddings, excel at handling sequential data with intricate dependencies. To address this task, we consider three cutting-edge pre-trained word embeddings: *ch1Word2Vec* [15], *FastText* [4], and *BERT* [8] in this study. For the input to these pre-trained models, we aggregate two titles and one body, assigning higher importance to the titles (i.e., text = title + title + body). The text inputs undergo preprocessing steps like converting to lowercase, removing punctuation, and tokenization. During the embedding process, a fixed-length vector representation is generated for each token. Finally, we utilize the average pooling technique to obtain the final vector representation for the entire text.

6.3 Oversampling Approach

Figure 3 illustrates the oversampling process that combines SMOTE with VAE to address the substantial data imbalance in the reopening task. In this scenario, the non-reopening cases significantly outnumber the reopening cases. We primarily employ the *Variational Autoencoder (VAE)*, a generative model that approximates the probability distribution of input data. VAE achieves this by encoding the data into a lower-dimensional latent space and subsequently decoding it back into the original data space. Through sampling from this learned latent space, VAE can produce new data points that closely resemble the original data, effectively expanding the dataset.

However, to ensure an adequate number of reopening samples for VAE training, we initially employ *SMOTE* to upsample the positive class (i.e., the Reopened class). Following this, we exclusively train the VAE using pull requests from the Reopened class. The decoder component of the trained VAE is then utilized to generate reopening samples by introducing random noise derived from a normal distribution. Then, these generated samples are combined with the original ones.

6.4 Model Training

To mimic the real situation and address the relationship between pull request reopening, decision, and lifetime. We separate modeling into two main stages: the reopening stage and the evaluation stage. More precisely, the reopening output is predicted first, and it

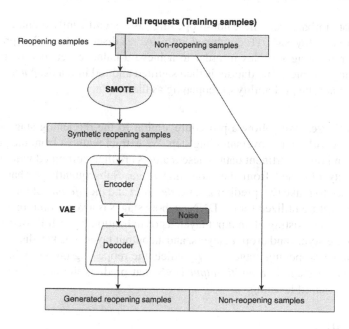

Fig. 3. An oversampling process through SMOTE and VAE for the reopening samples.

is used as one of the features to predict the pull request decision and lifetime, refer to Fig. 4.

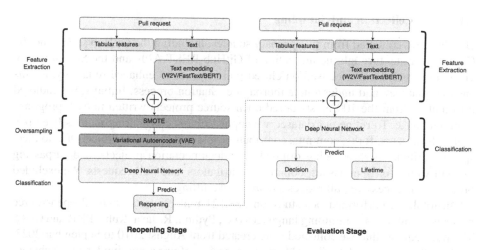

Fig. 4. A model architecture of DeepPull, adapted from [2].

Reopening Stage. We adopt a structured three-step approach encompassing feature extraction, oversampling, and classification. It starts by combining tabular and textual features extracted by pre-trained word embedding, as detailed in the preceding section.

Given the data imbalance, where non-reopening cases significantly outnumber reopening cases, we employ SMOTE combined with VAE as discussed in 6.3 to produce supplementary reopening samples in order to achieve a balance between reopening and non-reopening samples. The dataset is then shuffled and fed into a *deep neural network (DNN)* to predict the probability of reopening as the output.

Evaluation Stage. We follow a procedure similar to the reopening stage for feature extraction, but without the oversampling step. We extract features from the pull request description and other pertinent data. These features are then combined with the reopening probability obtained from the reopening stage. Subsequently, a shared-learning DNN is trained to make two predictions: the *decision* and the *lifetime* of the pull request.

The architecture utilized for the DNNs in both stages is a very common feedforward neural network, consisting of an input layer, a normalization layer, followed by multiple blocks of dense layers and dropout layers, and an output layer. The key distinction is that the DNN in the reopening stage solely predicts the reopening output, while the DNN in the evaluation stage is a *multi-output* DNN that predicts the decision and lifetime outputs using shared learning.

7 Evaluation

This section provides a comprehensive evaluation that we conducted for our approach[2]. We outline the data collection and processing methods used in our study, report our results, and highlight additional findings.

7.1 Data Collection and Sampling

Our data was collected from two primary sources, including the GitHub server and the GitHub website, through the utilization of GitHub REST APIs and the Selenium tool via Python scripts. We focused on closed pull requests to enhance reliability, as this ensured that they had undergone a thorough evaluation process. Initially, we gathered information from the 100 most-starred open-source projects written in each programming language. To refine our dataset, we applied filters, considering metrics like open issues, fork status, forks, commits, contributors, and pull requests. Projects had to meet specific criteria, such as being original, non-documentation projects, and surpassing median values for open issues, commits, contributors, and pull requests. We excluded projects with excessive pull requests to avoid overfitting.

In total, we performed our study on 288,121 pull requests from 83 open-source projects across six programming languages (i.e., Python, R, Java, Ruby, PHP, and C++). The pull requests that we collected were created from August 2010 to September 2023. Table 2 illustrates our dataset, including an overview of programming language characteristics, and summarizes the statistical characteristics of the dataset for each language in terms of the number of pull requests per project in values of median, mean, and standard deviation.

---

[2] All experimentation was conducted on a Macbook Pro equipped with macOS Monterey Version 12.4, an Apple M1 Pro chip, and 16GB of RAM

Table 2. Descriptive statistical information of our pull request dataset.

Language	Overview		# Pull Requests/Project		
	# Projects	# Pull Requests	Med	Mean	SD
Python	11	9,773	764.00	888.45	693.12
R	12	8,310	456.00	755.45	557.19
Java	12	29,202	1,247.00	2,433.50	2,055.49
Ruby	19	96,601	3,760.00	5,084.26	3,864.15
PHP	18	94,275	2,685.00	5,237.50	6,836.47
C++	11	49,960	3,214.00	4,541.82	3,685.75
TOTAL	83	288,121			

7.2 Data Splitting

We employed a *hold-out technique* to partition our data into three sets: training, validation, and testing. This separation allowed us to ensure that the model learned exclusively
from historical data available at the time of training. To achieve this, we sorted the pull
requests based on their close dates. Specifically, the pull requests in the training and
validation sets were closed before those in the testing set. Moreover, the pull requests
in the training set preceded the ones in the validation set. In our experiment, where the
focus was on different programming languages, we tailored a distinct approach for each
group of languages. For smaller community programming languages (e.g., Python and
R), a 60/20/20 split is used, while the large ones (e.g., Java, Ruby, PHP, and C++) use
an 80/10/10 split. This approach allowed us to utilize the training dataset for model
training and employ the validation dataset for both model selection and hyperparameter
tuning. Finally, we assessed our model's performance using the testing dataset.

7.3 Experimental Results

In this section, we present the results of the evaluation, addressing the research questions. In Table 3, the results of the performance comparison between the randomized
baseline, the existing approach, and DeepPull for reopening prediction are shown,
whereas performance comparisons for decision and lifetime predictions are displayed
in Table 4. For all tables, we report the performance metrics as balanced accuracy (BA),
AUC, True Positive Rate (TPR), False Positive Rate (FPR) accuracy (Acc), precision
(P), recall (R), F-measure (F1), and Macro-Averaged Absolute Error (MMAE).

Results for RQ1

Reopening. DeepPull wins against the baseline in 22 of the 24 cases concerning balanced accuracy, AUC, TPR, and FPR. We observe improvements ranging from 17.92%
to 37.23% in balanced accuracy, 24.71% to 46.39% in AUC, and 25.68% to 52.75% in
TPR, while FPR results vary, with four cases showing improvement (up to 48.78%) and
two cases showing a decline compared to the baseline. On average, we outperform the
baseline in all cases. Specifically, DeepPull achieves a balanced accuracy of 0.632, an

AUC of 0.693, a TPR of 0.685, and an FPR of 0.421, compared to the baseline, which achieves only 0.500 for all metrics.

Decision. DeepPull outperforms the baseline in all of the 30 cases concerning accuracy, precision, recall, F-measure, and AUC. We observe improvements ranging from 39.08% to 72.13% in accuracy, 4.71% to 60.44% in precision, 38.48% to 84.71% in recall, 27.38% to 63.17% in F-measure, and 29.75% to 82.36% in AUC. On average, we also win against the baseline in all cases. To be specific, DeepPull achieves an accuracy of 0.767, a precision of 0.879, a recall of 0.797, an F-measure of 0.833, and an AUC of 0.778, compared to the baseline which gains only an accuracy of 0.500, a precision of 0.753, a recall of 0.500, an F-measure of 0.595, and an AUC of 0.500.

Lifetime. DeepPull surpasses the baseline in all of the six cases concerning MMAE. We observe improvements ranging from 24.79% to 30.40% in MMAE. On average, we also win the baseline in all cases. To be precise, DeepPull gets an MMAE of 1.149, while the baseline gains only an MMAE of 1.600.

> **Answer:** *Overall, DeepPull consistently outperforms the randomized baseline in all six programming languages; thus DeepPull is suitable for predicting pull request reopening, decision, and lifetime early at the submission time.*

Table 3. Performance comparison between the randomized baseline, the existing approach, and DeepPull for predicting pull request reopening.

Language	Approach	Reopening			
		BA	AUC	TPR	FPR
Python	Baseline	0.500	0.500	0.500	0.500
	Existing	0.618	0.705	0.500	**0.264**
	DeepPull	**0.639**	**0.732**	**0.679**	0.400
R	Baseline	0.500	0.500	0.501	**0.500**
	Existing	0.528	0.649	**0.765**	0.709
	DeepPull	**0.600**	**0.715**	**0.765**	0.564
Java	Baseline	0.500	0.500	0.501	0.500
	Existing	0.554	0.584	0.362	**0.254**
	DeepPull	**0.590**	**0.624**	**0.696**	0.515
Ruby	Baseline	0.500	0.500	0.500	0.500
	Existing	0.557	0.583	0.506	0.391
	DeepPull	**0.641**	**0.684**	**0.635**	**0.354**
PHP	Baseline	0.500	0.500	0.501	0.500
	Existing	0.665	0.699	**0.643**	0.313
	DeepPull	**0.687**	**0.725**	0.629	**0.256**
C++	Baseline	0.501	0.501	0.501	0.500
	Existing	**0.645**	0.659	**0.741**	0.450
	DeepPull	0.634	**0.675**	0.704	**0.436**
AVG	Baseline	0.500	0.500	0.500	0.500
	Existing	0.595	0.656	0.596	**0.407**
	DeepPull	**0.632**	**0.693**	**0.685**	0.421

Results for RQ2

Reopening. DeepPull wins against the existing approach in 19 of the 24 cases concerning balanced accuracy, AUC, TPR, and FPR. We observe improvements ranging from 24.71% to 46.39% in AUC, while balanced accuracy results vary, with five cases showing improvement (up to 15.00%) and one case showing a decline. Moreover, TPR results vary, with four cases showing improvement (up to 92.00%) and two cases showing the opposite, and FPR results vary, with four cases showing improvement (up to 20.41%) and two cases showing a drop. On average, we outperform the baseline in three of four cases. Specifically, DeepPull achieves a balanced accuracy of 0.632, an AUC of 0.693, a TPR of 0.685, and an FPR of 0.421, compared to the existing approach which achieves only balanced accuracy of 0.595, an AUC of 0.656, a TPR of 0.596, and an FPR of 0.407.

Table 4. Performance comparison between the randomized baseline, the existing approach, and DeepPull for predicting pull request decision and lifetime.

Language	Approach	Decision					Lifetime
		Acc	P	R	F1	AUC	MMAE
Python	Baseline	0.500	0.771	0.500	0.607	0.500	1.599
	Existing	0.681	**0.878**	0.681	0.767	0.708	1.270
	DeepPull	**0.719**	0.874	**0.742**	**0.803**	**0.716**	**1.171**
R	Baseline	0.500	0.835	0.500	0.625	0.500	1.600
	Existing	0.594	0.865	0.609	0.714	0.589	1.224
	DeepPull	**0.721**	**0.874**	**0.777**	**0.823**	**0.649**	**1.204**
Java	Baseline	0.500	0.523	0.500	0.511	0.500	1.600
	Existing	0.792	0.815	0.779	0.797	0.872	1.198
	DeepPull	**0.826**	**0.839**	**0.826**	**0.832**	**0.909**	**1.139**
Ruby	Baseline	0.500	0.883	0.500	0.638	0.500	1.600
	Existing	0.737	0.920	0.769	0.838	0.682	1.262
	DeepPull	**0.781**	**0.925**	**0.819**	**0.868**	**0.720**	**1.141**
PHP	Baseline	0.500	0.803	0.500	0.616	0.500	1.600
	Existing	0.629	**0.921**	0.588	0.718	0.756	1.206
	DeepPull	**0.696**	0.906	**0.693**	**0.785**	**0.764**	**1.114**
C++	Baseline	0.500	0.597	0.500	0.544	0.500	1.600
	Existing	0.842	0.846	0.898	0.871	0.909	1.155
	DeepPull	**0.861**	**0.855**	**0.924**	**0.888**	**0.912**	**1.129**
AVG	Baseline	0.500	0.753	0.500	0.595	0.500	1.600
	Existing	0.712	0.874	0.721	0.784	0.753	1.219
	DeepPull	**0.767**	**0.879**	**0.797**	**0.833**	**0.778**	**1.149**

Decision. DeepPull outperforms the existing approach in 28 of the 30 cases concerning accuracy, precision, recall, F-measure, and AUC. We observe improvements ranging from 2.28% to 21.38% in accuracy, 2.88% to 27.73% in recall, 1.91% to 15.20% in F-measure, and 0.36% to 10.20% in AUC, while precision results vary, with five cases showing improvement (up to 3.01%) and one case showing a decline. On average, we excel the baseline in three of four cases. To be specific, DeepPull achieves an accuracy of 0.767, a precision of 0.879, a recall of 0.797, an F-measure of 0.833, and an AUC of 0.778, compared to the existing approach, which gains only an accuracy of 0.712, a precision of 0.874, a recall of 0.721, an F-measure of 0.784, and an AUC of 0.753.

Lifetime. DeepPull surpasses the existing approach in all of the six cases concerning MMAE. We observe improvements ranging from 1.69% to 9.62% in MMAE. On average, we also win over the existing approach in all cases. Particularly, DeepPull gets an MMAE of 1.149, while the baseline gains only an MMAE of 1.219.

> *Answer: Overall, DeepPull outperforms the existing approach across all programming languages. We can, thus, conclude that utilizing deep learning-based approaches significantly enhances performance in predicting pull request reopening, decision, and lifetime.*

7.4 Further Findings

In addition to assessing DeepPull's effectiveness through standard performance metrics, we carried out further experiments to delve into the implications of the results and their relevance to the broader research question. To begin with, we highlight the benefits of employing oversampling with SMOTE in conjunction with VAE in comparison to using SMOTE alone. Additionally, we investigate the importance of various features.

Comparing Oversampling Techniques. We discuss the advantages of using SMOTE in combination with VAE compared to using SMOTE alone. To illustrate this, we will present example cases through PCA plots. Figures 5 and 6 display 2-dimensional PCA plots for original reopening samples and synthetic reopening samples generated by SMOTE and SMOTE combined with VAE in Python and PHP. In the matter of oversampling techniques, we will state the advantage of oversampling using SMOTE combined with VAE compared to using only SMOTE.

Comparing the synthetic samples generated by SMOTE (in orange) and SMOTE combined with VAE (in green) in Figs. 5(b) and 6(b), we observe distinct differences in their distribution. SMOTE introduces some noise and synthesizes samples with consideration for outliers, potentially leading to overfitting. This can hinder generalization performance on unseen data. In contrast, synthetic samples generated by SMOTE combined with VAE exhibit a more even distribution, closely resembling the original sample distribution without considering outliers. Consequently, oversampling using SMOTE combined with VAE proves to be a superior approach compared to using SMOTE alone.

Measuring Feature Importance. We assessed feature importance in both the pull request reopening and evaluation stages using sensitivity analysis, a gradient-based attribution method [1, 18]. This method quantifies the contribution of each input feature to the model's predictions by analyzing the gradients of the loss function with respect to these features.

Specifically, we considered a deep neural network (DNN) with an input vector x and an output vector $S(x)$. The attribution method aimed to determine the contribution

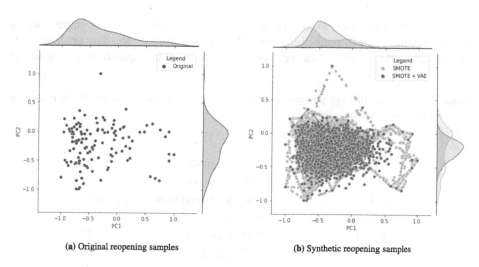

Fig. 5. PCA plots comparing original reopening samples and synthetic reopening samples created using both SMOTE and SMOTE combined with VAE in the Python language.

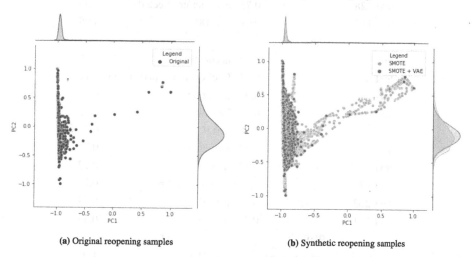

Fig. 6. PCA plots comparing original reopening samples and synthetic reopening samples created using both SMOTE and SMOTE combined with VAE in the PHP language.

R^c of each input feature x_i to a specific target output S_c. In sensitivity analysis, we computed attributions by taking the absolute value of the partial derivative of the target output S_c with respect to the inputs x_i, as expressed in Eq. 1 below:

$$R_i^c(x) = \left| \frac{\partial S_c(x)}{\partial x_i} \right| \qquad (1)$$

Larger absolute gradient magnitudes for a feature indicate greater importance in influencing the model's predictions. We calculated the average absolute gradient magnitude across the training data for each feature to provide a quantitative measure of

Table 5. List of top 10 most important features with their normalized weight in the reopening stage for each programming language.

Python		R	
is first pr	1.00	contributor age	1.00
text 425	0.95	has pr link	0.15
text 117	0.86	% of commits made by pr	0.12
# of events in pr	0.82	text 44	0.07
text 570	0.79	is core team	0.07
text 687	0.77	text 62	0.06
text 582	0.77	text 18	0.06
text 563	0.75	text 99	0.06
text 128	0.73	is recent pr rejected	0.06
text 111	0.69	text 181	0.05
Java		Ruby	
text 63	1.00	is core team	1.00
text 67	0.94	% of commits made by pr	0.91
text 38	0.90	has pr link	0.90
text 182	0.89	has test	0.85
text 12	0.88	text 9	0.79
text 72	0.87	# of commits	0.78
text 181	0.87	text 23	0.77
text 73	0.85	# of deleted lines	0.75
text 262	0.74	text 35	0.74
text 221	0.74	text 48	0.73
PHP		C++	
% of commits made by pr	1.00	text 210	1.00
has pr link	0.10	text 26	0.89
has test	0.03	text 87	0.83
is core team	0.03	text 90	0.83
is recent pr rejected	0.03	text 174	0.79
text 100	0.03	text 101	0.78
text 61	0.02	text 166	0.77
text 120	0.02	text 147	0.76
text 91	0.02	text 213	0.75
text 145	0.02	text 175	0.75

feature importance. Tables 5 and 6 present the top 10 most significant features and their corresponding normalized weights for the reopening and evaluation stages in specific programming languages. These weights were normalized from 0 (least important) to 1 (most important) to offer a relative measure of importance. As can be seen, textual features dominated 71 of 120 cases, indicating their crucial role in predicting pull request reopening, decision, and lifetime. Additionally, the reopening probability, an output of the reopening stage used as a predictor in the evaluation stage, appeared in the top 10 feature list for multiple languages, emphasizing its importance. These findings underscore the suitability of our architecture, where we first predict pull request reopening and subsequently forecast pull request decision and lifetime.

7.5 Threats to Validity

In this section, we will outline threats to internal, external, construct, and conclusion validity, and detail the steps taken to minimize their impact on our results.

Internal Validity. We have implemented several measures to minimize bias and errors throughout our study to ensure internal validity. A critical aspect of DeepPull is using actual pull request outcomes from real integrators, providing us with authentic and reliable data. By incorporating real-world data, we aim to capture the practical aspects and challenges associated with pull request reopening, decision, and lifetime in open-source projects on GitHub. In addition, we have meticulously processed and analyzed only the information available at the time of the pull request submission. We accomplished this by scraping the GitHub website, allowing us to extract pertinent features while safeguarding against potential information leakage.

Table 6. List of top 10 most important features with their normalized weight in the evaluation stage for each programming language.

Python		R	
contributor age	1.00	text 52	1.00
file rejected proportion	0.21	text 257	0.80
% of commits made by pr	0.14	text 282	0.79
reopening prob	0.08	text 299	0.78
reputation	0.07	text 249	0.75
text 111	0.05	text 273	0.74
is core team	0.05	contributor age	0.73
text 117	0.05	text 212	0.73
text 160	0.05	text 21	0.71
text 66	0.05	text 261	0.71

(continued)

Table 6. (*continued*)

Java		Ruby	
contributor age	1.00	file rejected proportion	1.00
% of commits made by pr	0.47	contributor age	0.65
file rejected proportion	0.40	% of commits made by pr	0.63
text 10	0.35	reputation	0.46
reopening prob	0.29	text 299	0.42
reputation	0.27	text 732	0.41
# of merged pr	0.20	reopening prob	0.32
# of rejected pr	0.19	text 342	0.29
has test	0.17	text 105	0.29
# of commits prev pulls	0.16	text 676	0.26
PHP		C++	
contributor age	1.00	contributor age	1.00
file rejected proportion	0.58	text 176	<0.01
% of commits made by pr	0.15	text 51	<0.01
reputation	0.10	text 227	<0.01
# of commits	0.08	text259	<0.01
is core team	0.08	text 103	<0.01
reopening prob	0.04	text 96	<0.01
text 61	0.04	text 251	<0.01
has pr link	0.04	text 55	<0.01
# of changed src files	0.04	text 241	<0.01

External Validity. Our study provides a broad range of perspectives by analyzing 83 real-world open-source projects across six popular programming languages on GitHub. However, our findings may not be representative of all programming languages and all types of software projects, especially those in commercial settings. To address this limitation, we plan to expand our experiments to include industrial software projects.

Construct Validity. We have adopted standard evaluation metrics commonly utilized in classification tasks. These metrics have also found application in prior software engineering research, enabling us to compare and validate our results effectively. However, evaluating the prediction of reopening poses a challenge due to highly imbalanced data and limited prior work addressing this specific issue. Therefore, we employ common metrics used in other domains to assess the performance of our approach to this task. Additionally, as a measure to further enhance construct validity, we include a randomized baseline and utilize an existing approach, which is a common practice, as a benchmark for evaluating the predictive performance of our approach. However, we constructed an alternative approach that closely followed the methodology of previous work because they did not explicitly provide their approach's implementation, which might not perfectly replicate all aspects of their approaches.

Conclusion Validity. We approach drawing conclusions from the extracted features in the studied project repositories with meticulous care and caution. It is essential to note that lifetime may not always accurately reflect the actual review and integration time of a pull request, as other factors, such as the integrator's workload or limited interaction with the contributor, may influence it [7]. Additionally, the reopening of a pull request may not always signify genuine reopening, as it can occasionally occur due to accidental closure [12].

8 Conclusions and Future Work

GitHub's pull-based development model plays a significant role in managing software complexity for modern software development teams. In the context of large projects, the overwhelming volume of pull requests can burden integrators, necessitating efficient workload management. Previous studies have employed traditional machine learning techniques with tabular data to build predictive models, but these methods may overlook valuable information. Furthermore, relying solely on decision and lifetime predictions may not fully address the needs of integrators.

In this paper, we proposed DeepPull, a novel deep learning-based approach designed to predict pull request reopening, decision, and lifetime in open-source software projects hosted on GitHub. Our method combines tabular and textual data, using advanced pre-trained models to extract meaningful text representations. We employ SMOTE and VAE for oversampling and leverage the advantages of the relationship between outcomes through shared learning. We conducted an extensive evaluation of six well-known programming languages, demonstrating that DeepPull significantly outperforms random guessing and showcases its advantages over the existing approach. Moreover, we performed additional experiments to highlight the insightful advantages of DeepPull's components in enhancing prediction accuracy.

For future work, we plan to validate our approach in industrial software projects. We aspire to explore novel sources of information that can more effectively characterize pull requests, including code changes, with the goal of improving predictive performance, especially for the reopening task. We also plan to integrate our approach as a tool within the GitHub platform to gather user feedback that enables further analysis and approach refinement.

References

1. Ancona, M., Ceolini, E., Öztireli, C., Gross, M.: Towards better understanding of gradient-based attribution methods for deep neural networks. In: Proceedings of 6th International Conference on Learning Representations (ICLR 2018) (2018)
2. Banyongrakkul., P., Phoomvuthisarn., S.: Multi-output learning for predicting evaluation and reopening of GitHub pull requests on open-source projects. In: Proceedings of the 18th International Conference on Software Technologies (ICSOFT 2023), pp. 163–174. INSTICC, SciTePress (2023)

3. Bird, C., Rigby, P.C., Barr, E.T., Hamilton, D.J., German, D.M., Devanbu, P.: The promises and perils of mining git. In: Proceedings of 6th IEEE International Working Conference on Mining Software Repositories, pp. 1–10. Vancouver, BC, Canada (2009)
4. Bojanowski, P., Grave, E., Joulin, A., Mikolov, T.: Enriching word vectors with subword information. CoRR (2016)
5. Chen, D., Stolee, K., Menzies, T.: Replication can improve prior results: a GitHub study of pull request acceptance. In: Proceedings of IEEE International Conference on Program Comprehension. vol. 2019-May, pp. 179–190. IEEE Computer Society, Montreal, QC, Canada (2019)
6. Dabbish, L., Stuart, C., Tsay, J., Herbsleb, J.: Leveraging transparency. IEEE Softw. **30**(1), 37–43 (2013)
7. de Lima Júnior, M.L., Soares, D., Plastino, A., Murta, L.: Predicting the lifetime of pull requests in open-source projects. J. Softw. Evol. Process **33**(6), e2337 (2021)
8. Devlin, J., Chang, M., Lee, K., Toutanova, K.: BERT: pre-training of deep bidirectional transformers for language understanding. In: Burstein, J., Doran, C., Solorio, T. (eds.) Proceedings of the 2019 Conference of the North American Chapter of the Association for Computational Linguistics: Human Language Technologies (NAACL-HLT 2019), pp. 4171–4186. Association for Computational Linguistics (2019)
9. Gousios, G., Pinzger, M., Deursen, A.V.: An exploratory study of the pull-based software development model. In: Proceedings of International Conference on Software Engineering, pp. 345–355. No. 1 in ICSE 2014, IEEE Computer Society, Hyderabad, India (2014)
10. Gousios, G., Storey, M.A., Bacchelli, A.: Work practices and challenges in pull-based development: the contributor's perspective. In: Proceedings of International Conference on Software Engineering. vol. 14-22-May-2016, pp. 285–296. IEEE Computer Society, Austin, TX, USA (2016)
11. Gousios, G., Zaidman, A., Storey, M.A., van Deursen, A.: Work practices and challenges in pull-based development: the integrator's perspective. In: Proceedings of 2015 IEEE/ACM 37th IEEE International Conference on Software Engineering. vol. 1, pp. 358–368. Florence, Italy (2015)
12. Jiang, J., Mohamed, A., Zhang, L.: What are the characteristics of reopened pull requests? A case study on open source projects in GitHub. IEEE Access **7**, 102751–102761 (2019)
13. Jiang, J., Teng Zheng, J., Yang, Y., Zhang, L.: CTCPPre: a prediction method for accepted pull requests in GitHub. J. Cent. S. Univ. **27**(2), 449–468 (2020)
14. McKee, S., Nelson, N., Sarma, A., Dig, D.: Software practitioner perspectives on merge conflicts and resolutions. In: 2017 IEEE International Conference on Software Maintenance and Evolution (ICSME), pp. 467–478 (2017)
15. Mikolov, T., Others: Distributed representations of words and phrases and their compositionality. In: Advances in Neural Information Processing Systems, pp. 1–9 (2013)
16. Mohamed, A., Zhang, L., Jiang, J.: Cross-project reopened pull request prediction in GitHub. In: García-Castro, R. (ed.) Proceedings of The 32nd International Conference on Software Engineering and Knowledge Engineering, SEKE 2020, pp. 435–438. KSI Research Inc., USA (2020)
17. Mohamed, A., Zhang, L., Jiang, J., Ktob, A.: Predicting which pull requests will get reopened in GitHub. In: Proceedings of Asia-Pacific Software Engineering Conference (APSEC). vol. 2018-Decem, pp. 375–385. IEEE Computer Society (2018)
18. Nielsen, I.E., Dera, D., Rasool, G., Ramachandran, R.P., Bouaynaya, N.C.: Robust explainability: a tutorial on gradient-based attribution methods for deep neural networks. IEEE Signal Process. Mag. **39**(4), 73–84 (2022)
19. Khadke, N.: Ming Han Teh. Predicting Acceptance of GitHub Pull Requests, M.S. (2012)

20. Ortu, M., Destefanis, G., Graziotin, D., Marchesi, M., Tonelli, R.: How do you propose your code changes? Empirical analysis of affect metrics of pull requests on GitHub. IEEE Access **8**, 110897–110907 (2020)
21. Soares, D., Limeira, M., Murta, L., Plastino, A.: Acceptance factors of pull requests in open-source projects. In: Proceedings of the 30th Annual ACM Symposium on Applied Computing, pp. 1541–1546. Association for Computing Machinery, New York, NY, USA (2015)
22. Tsay, J., Dabbish, L., Herbsleb, J.: Influence of social and technical factors for evaluating contribution in GitHub. In: Proceedings of International Conference on Software Engineering, pp. 356–366. No. 1 in ICSE 2014, IEEE Computer Society, Hyderabad, India (2014)
23. Yu, Y., Wang, H., Filkov, V., Devanbu, P., Vasilescu, B.: Wait For It: determinants of pull request evaluation latency on GitHub. In: 2015 IEEE/ACM 12th Working Conference on Mining Software Repositories, pp. 367–371 (2015)
24. Yu, Y., Yin, G., Wang, T., Yang, C., Wang, H.: Determinants of pull-based development in the context of continuous integration. Sci. China Inf. Sci. **59**, 1–14 (2016)
25. Zhang, X., Yu, Y., Gousios, G., Rastogi, A.: Pull request decision explained: an empirical overview. IEEE Trans. Softw. Eng. **49**, 849–871 (2022)
26. Zhang, X., Yu, Y., Wang, T., Rastogi, A., Wang, H.: Pull request latency explained: an empirical overview. Empirical Softw. Eng. **27**, 126 (2021)

On the Relevance of Graph2Vec Source Code Embeddings for Software Defect Prediction

Diana-Lucia Miholca[ORCID] and Zsuzsanna Oneţ-Marian[✉][ORCID]

Department of Computer Science, Babeş-Bolyai University, No. 1, Mihail Kogalniceanu Street, Cluj-Napoca, Romania

zsuzsanna.onet@ubbcluj.ro

Abstract. Software defects prediction is a crucial activity related to software development and an extensively studied subject that remains challenging. One of the difficulties lies in the fact the most prevalent software metrics are not sufficiently relevant for accurately predicting defects. In this paper we propose employing the Graph2Vec embeddings unsupervisedly learnt from the source code, as well as a novel suite of syntactic coupling metrics derived from Graph2Vec embeddings, named SYNMET, as a foundation for software defect prediction. The dependability of the Graph2Vec embeddings is evaluated in contrast to that of the alternative embeddings based on Doc2Vec and LSI. The assessment is conducted through multiple experiments performed on 16 versions of Apache Calcite. Three distinct classification models, namely FastAI as a deep learning model, Multilayer Perceptron as an untuned conventional model, and Random Forests with hyperparameter tuning as a tuned conventional model, are employed in the experimental study. The findings indicate a synergistic relationship among Graph2Vec, Doc2Vec, and LSI-based embeddings. When comparatively assessing the performance of the three classifiers, the empirical results underscore the supremacy of tuned Random Forests over FastAI and Multilayer Perceptron. This observation substantiates the effectiveness of hyperparameter optimization. The relevance of the SYNMET suite is also assessed through multiple comparative analyses, the results confirming that they enhance the software defect prediction performance and reconfirming the interplay between software coupling and defect proneness.

Keywords: software defect prediction · Doc2Vec · Graph2Vec · LSI · Hyperparameter tuning · Deep learning · Software coupling metrics

1 Introduction

Software defect prediction (SDP) involves identifying defective software components so as to concentrate testing efforts on them. As testing resources are invariably constrained, accurate SDP models can optimize software quality within the available resources. Given its critical role, it is unsurprising that SDP is an actively explored problem, featuring a plethora of Machine Learning-based approaches proposed in the literature.

To construct a Machine Learning (ML) model for SDP, having a uniform representation (feature vector) for all software entities (such as classes, methods, etc.) is essential.

H.-G. Fill et al. (Eds.): ICSOFT 2023, CCIS 2104, pp. 124–154, 2024.
https://doi.org/10.1007/978-3-031-61753-9_7

This common representation serves as input for ML algorithms. The earliest and most common approaches involv using software metrics for this purpose.

Initially, the metrics considered for SDP exclusively pertained to procedural code, but they have subsequently been substituted or supplemented by object-oriented and code change metrics. However, more recent approaches have emerged for constructing software features by directly or indirectly taking into account the source code, often leveraging the Abstract Syntax Tree (AST).

In a recent study [26], a comprehensive set of conventional software metrics has been compared with conceptual software features directly extracted from the source code using Doc2Vec and LSI. The study concludes that, on average, software features derived from Doc2Vec and LSI surpass traditional metrics in terms of their reliability in predicting defect-proneness. Notably, in the extraction of Doc2Vec and LSI-based features, the source code is treated as textual data, and the actual structural information captured by the Abstract Syntax Tree (AST) is not factored into consideration.

Consequently, in this present paper, we aim to extend the research conducted by Miholca et al. [26], while also leveraging on the structure of the source code. In pursuit of this goal, we introduce an additional representation unsupervisedly learned from AST of the source code using Graph2Vec [27]. Graph2Vec is a neural embedding framework capable of learning a fixed-length feature vector, known as *embedding*, for an entire graph.

The Graph2Vec-based embeddings will be assessed for their discriminative ability in classifying software entities as defective or non-defective. Given the intuition of a potential complementarity between the Graph2Vec-based embeddings, which leverage software structure, and the Doc2Vec and LSI-based embeddings, which leverage the semantics of the source code (particularly comments and identifiers), we will also explore whether combining them enhances SDP performance. Consequently, we formulate the following research questions:

- **RQ1.** What is the relative relevance of the embedding learnt using Graph2Vec in the context of SDP?
- **RQ2.** Does the combination of the Graph2Vec, Doc2Vec and LSI embeddings enhance the performance of SDP?

Miholca et al. [26] conducted experimental comparisons of multiple classifiers, with FastAI emerging as the top performer, closely followed by a feed-forward artificial neural network, specifically a Multilayer Perceptron (MLP). Building upon their findings, we also employ FastAI as our deep learning model. However, recent studies, such as [11, 19], suggest that deep learning may not be necessary for many learning tasks, as they consume more resources. These studies, even if not considering SDP, demonstrate that simpler ML algorithms, with proper hyperparameter tuning, can achieve comparable performance without the need for extensive training data and longer run times associated with deep learning.

In the context of SDP, Tantithamthavorn et al. [37] explored the impact of automated parameter optimization and found that for most classification techniques, significant performance improvement can be attained through hyperparameter optimization. Based on this insight, we have decided to also employ the Random Forest (RF) classifier with optimized parameters. Consequently, we formulate a third research question:

- **RQ3.** How does the SDP performance of FastAI compare to that of RF with optimized parameters for the considered representations?

The RF classifier has a large number of parameters, and even if we only consider a few values for each, there are too many possibilities, so performing a complete gridsearch is not feasible. We used an adaptation of the *random search-based hyperparameter tuning*, which only checks a predefined number of randomly selected hyperparameter points. While this method was shown to have similar performance to other parameter tuning approaches in [37], it checks only a fraction of the hyperparameter space and might miss the best hyperparameter. Consequently, we add another research question, targeting the hyperparameter tuning process and its results:

- **RQ4.** Does performing a local search around the best hyper-parameters lead to hyper-parameters which improve the performance of RF?

The literature [7] asserts that a high percentage of software defects stems from violated organizational and technical dependencies. Of these, technical dependencies are expressed through coupling measures.

The Abstract Syntax Tree (AST) of the source code is a tree representation of the syntactic structure of the code, but it also contains information about the types of the nodes (statements, variables, etc.). Since Graph2Vec is capable of learning embeddings from any graph, passing it an AST will result in embeddings that capture aspects related to the syntactic structure of the source code. Consequently, the similarity between the Graph2Vec embeddings of two different software entities captures their degree of syntactic (or structural) coupling. A literature review study [31] has concluded that structural coupling metrics have been reported by numerous studies [32] to be successful in predicting software defects.

Moreover, in a previous paper [24], we have introduced a new suite of conceptual coupling measures derived from Doc2Vec and LSI embeddings and we have assessed them for SDP, the results confirming their superiority when compared to both the Doc2Vec and LSI embeddings, but also the widely used Promise metrics [35].

Therefore, as an additional original contribution, we propose taking a step further from proposing the direct use of Graph2Vec embeddings for SDP by defining a new suite of 18 Graph2Vec-based syntactic coupling metrics, named SYNMET, to be used for representing software entities in the context of SDP. Accordingly, we formulate a last research question to be addressed in the current study:

- **RQ5.** What is the relative relevance of the SYNMET suite of syntactic coupling metrics derived from Graph2Vec embeddings for SDP?

This paper is an extended version of the paper [25], presented at the International Conference on Software Technologies in 2023. Compared to [25], we have extended the analysis for RQ1 - RQ3 (which were addressed in that paper) and we have added RQ4 and RQ5. More specifically, in [25] we have introduced the use of the Graph2Vec embedding as a new representation to the benefit of SDP and proposed combining the Graph2Vec-based embedding with the Doc2Vec-based and the LSI-based embeddings proposed in [26]. We have also evaluated the effectiveness of parameter optimization in the context of SDP by comparing a tuned Random Forest to the FastAI deep classifier, while using the proposed software embeddings as inputs. While [25] only presented the results of this comparison, in this paper we extend it with a detailed analysis of the hyperparameter tuning process and the returned hyperparameters. Moreover, we try to improve the results of the hyperparamter tuning process by adding a local search step to it. An additional original contribution of this paper consists in proposing novel syntactic coupling metrics, computed based on the Graph2Vec embedding representation of the software entities, that are relevant for discriminating between defective and non-defective software components.

The rest of this paper is structured as follows. Section 2 briefly presents a selection of existing SDP approaches that are pertinent to the current study. The next sections are based on the research questions of this study. Section 3 deals with RQ1 and RQ2, presenting the embeddings that we have considered, the ML models, case studies and evaluation methodologies, together with the results and their analysis. Section 4 focuses on RQ3, presenting the details of the hyperparameter tuning process, the results of comparing the performance of the tuned RF with the performance of untuned FastAI and an analysis of the hyperparameter tuning process. Section 5 analyzes whether adding a genetic algorithm based step to the hyperparameter tuning will lead to hyperparameters with improved performance. Section 6 defines the new syntactic coupling metrics derived from Graph2Vec source code embeddings and assesses their relevance for SDP. Finally, in Sect. 7, conclusions are drawn and directions for further research are outlined.

2   Related Work

A vast body of literature addresses the SDP problem. Over the years, researchers have put forth numerous approaches employing supervised and unsupervised machine learning, deep learning, ensemble methods, and more.

A survey conducted in 2011 [12] reviewed 208 papers published between 2000 and 2010. A more recent survey from 2020 focusing especially on approaches with unsupervised learning, [18], analyzed 49 papers. Another study, from 2021, focusing on ensemble learning-based approaches found 46 relevant studies [21]. Therefore, there is a huge number papers on SDP, but in the following our focus will be narrowed to only a selection of papers that are most pertinent to the central theme of our study: various software representations to be considered in SDP.

The majority of existing studies conduct experimental evaluations using SDP data sets available in the Promise Software Engineering Repository [35], now known as SeaCraft (*Software Engineering Artifacts Can Really Assist Future Tasks*) [1]. Consequently, many SDP approaches rely on the Promise metrics, which consist of static Object-Oriented (OO) metrics or traditional metrics associated with the quality of procedural source code. Literature reviews [20] indicate that approximately 87% of case studies in this domain utilize such procedural or object-oriented metrics, while having the primary focus on proposing accurate classifiers.

Nevertheless, more recent studies have initiated a new and highly active research direction in the realm of Software Defect Prediction (SDP): the design of novel, pertinent features to facilitate the discrimination between defective and non-defective software entities. This research direction stems from the realization that existing software features are either inadequate or insufficiently relevant for SDP, rendering it a persistently challenging problem. In the subsequent discussion, we will concentrate on presenting state-of-the-art approaches that are most closely aligned with our own approach.

Numerous approaches introducing new features consider the AST of the source code. One notable approach is proposed by Wang et al. in [39, 40]. They employ Deep Belief Networks (DBNs) to automatically learn semantic features from the AST. These resultant features have been subject to a comparative evaluation against traditional metrics regarding their relevance for SDP, using open-source projects from the Promise repository as case studies. The evaluation results substantiate that the proposed semantic features outperform traditional SDP features.

Li et al. [17] have introduced a comparable methodology, employing Convolutional Neural Networks (CNNs) in lieu of DBNs. They combine the features extracted through this process with some traditional ones. The combined representation is assessed for its efficacy in SDP using the Logistic Regression (LR) classifier. The experimental results confirm that AST-based features surpass traditional ones, and the combination of the two yields even superior performance.

Another study leveraging AST-based features for SDP has been conducted by Dam et al. [8]. They have introduced a tree-structured network comprising Long-Short Term Memory (LSTM) units as an SDP model fed with AST embeddings. Employing the same set of 10 case studies as Wang et al. [40], they train two traditional classifiers, LR and Random Forest, on the features generated by the LSTM.

Aladics et al. [3] introduced an approach where the AST of the source code has been parsed in a depth-first order, and the sequence of nodes has been recorded and treated as a document on which Doc2Vec has been applied. Their experimental evaluation, involving several ML algorithms, indicated that these embeddings might not surpass traditional source code metrics individually, but combining the two improves the SDP performance.

An SDP model utilizing a Convolutional Graph Neural Network has been put forth by Sikic et al. in [36]. The neural network architecture is specifically designed for graph data, allowing AST data to be fed into it. In the experimental evaluation, 7 SDP data sets from the Promise repository have been employed. The results demonstrated that the proposed model surpasses standard SDP models and is comparable to state-of-the-art AST-based SDP models, including [39].

Another direction of defining features derived from the source code, without involving AST, is proposed by Miholca et al. [24], who introduced the COMET metrics suite. This suite starts from the representations of the source code learnt using LSI and Doc2Vec. However, these representations are not directly employed for SDP. Instead, for each entity, various statistical measures are computed between its representation and the others (all or just the defective or non-defective ones). These statistical measures together provide the representation of an entity. The experimental evaluation has been performed on 7 Promise data sets and the COMET metrics suite turned out to outperform the traditional Promise metrics.

Doc2Vec and LSI vectorial representations of the source code have been directly used for SDP in a study by Miholca et al. [26]. The authors have compared them to an extensive set of 4189 metrics containing static code metrics, clone metrics, warning-based metrics, changes-based and refactoring-based metrics, AST node counts and code churn metrics. As experimental case study, multiple versions of a software system have been considered. Different combinations of the metrics subsets have been evaluated in terms of their relevance for SDP. The experimental results led to the conclusion that combining Doc2Vec and LSI produces a predominantly superior performance of SDP when compared to the 4189 software metrics, as well as to the separate use of Doc2Vec and LSI representations.

Following the introduction of BERT, an advanced language representation model, researchers have begun exploring its applicability in predicting software defects. Pan et al. [29] utilized CodeBERT, a BERT model pre-trained on open-source repositories, while Uddin et al. [38] independently pre-trained a BERT model on source code. For enabling proper training, Cong et al.'s approach involves over-sampling, while the data used by Uddin et al. have been augmented. In both approaches, code comments have been eliminated in the pre-processing phase. In contrast, our approach, presented in the following, intentionally retains code comments, considering them as potential carriers of semantic information that might benefit SDP.

3   The Relevance of the Graph2Vec Embedding for SDP

In this section we want to find the answer to our first two research questions: how does the performance of SDP models trained on embeddings learnt using Graph2Vec compare to the performance of models trained on embeddings learnt using Doc2Vec and LSI, and whether combining all three embeddings improves the performance of the models. Since these two research questions are strongly connected to each other, we are not presenting separately the analysis for Graph2Vec (which would be required to answer RQ1) and then the one for the combined representation (required to answer RQ2). Instead, we present both the methodology and the evaluation together and analyze the results separately.

Before presenting the analysis and its results, we will describe the considered embeddings and the representation we have built based on them (Sect. 3.1), followed by a presentation of the ML models used for building the predictors (Sect. 3.2) and the case study on which the experiments were performed (Sect. 3.3). Finally, we will present the evaluation methodology of the results in Sect. 3.4.

3.1   Proposed Representations

Instead of considering static structural or code churn metrics like the vast majority of SDP approaches, in this paper we consider three different embeddings constructed (directly or indirectly) from the source code of a software system.

The first embedding is unsupervisedly learnt by **Doc2Vec** [16], a prediction-based model for representing texts (in our case, source code) as a fixed-length numeric vector.

It is a MLP based model that extends Word2Vec and an alternative to traditional models such as bag-of-words and bag-of-n-grams. The main advantage of Doc2Vec over traditional models is that it considers the semantic distance between words [16].

The second embedding is extracted by **LSI** [9], a count-based model for representing texts (in our case, source code). LSI builds a matrix of occurrences of words in documents and then uses singular value decomposition to reduce the number of words while keeping the similarity structure between documents.

The third embedding is based on **Graph2Vec**, a model which can create a fixed-length vector of an entire graph, using unsupervised learning [27]. The basic idea behind the algorithm is to view an entire graph as a document and its rooted subgraphs around the nodes as the words of the document and apply document embedding models (more exactly, Doc2Vec) to learn graph embeddings. Source code can easily be parsed into AST which is in fact a graph, for which an embedding can be generated using Graph2Vec.

For any embedding, the software entities are represented as numeric vectors. These are composed of numerical values corresponding to a set $\mathcal{F} = \{f_1, f_2, \ldots, f_s\}$ of s features learned from the source code directly (in case of Doc2Vec and LSI) or indirectly, through the AST (in case of Graph2Vec).

Therefore, a software entity se is represented as an s-dimensional vector in an emb space:

- $se^{emb} = (se_1^{emb}, \cdots, se_s^{emb})$, where se_i^{emb} $(\forall 1 \leq i \leq s)$ denotes the value of the i-th feature computed for the entity se by using embedding emb, $emb \in \{Doc2Vec, LSI, Graph2Vec\}$.

For extracting the conceptual vectors, we have opted for $s = 30$ as the length of the embedding. In case of Doc2Vec and LSI, the source code (including comments) afferent to each class was filtered so as to keep only the tokens presumably carrying semantic meaning. So, operators, special symbols, English stop words or Java keywords have been eliminated. For both Doc2Vec and LSI, we have used the implementation offered by Gensim [33]. For Graph2Vec we have used the implementation from *Karateclub* [34], with the number of epochs set to 100 and the flag to consider the labels of the AST-nodes set to True.

The experimental results of previous studies [23] [22] [26] revealed that combining Doc2Vec and LSI is appropriate and increases the performance of SDP, while, to the best of our knowledge, Graph2Vec was not used previously for SDP. Consequently, we have decided to use the following three representations in our experimental evaluation (a more formal definition of them is available in [25]):

- *Doc2Vec + LSI* - each software entity se is represented as a $2 * s$-dimensional vector built by concatenating the embeddings provided by Doc2Vec and LSI.
- *Graph2Vec* - each software entity se is represented as the embedding provided by Graph2Vec for it.
- *Doc2Vec + LSI + Graph2Vec* - each software entity se is represented as $3 * s$-dimensional vector, the concatenation of all three embeddings for it.

The third representation is inspired by the intuition that the *Doc2Vec + LSI* embedding captures semantic (or conceptual) information contained by the source code, including the comments, while overlooking the structural information, whereas the *Graph2Vec* embedding also captures data related to the syntactic structure of the source code. Consequently, we intend to experimentally verify whether or not joining them enhances the SDP performance.

3.2 The Considered ML Models

In the literature many different ML models have been applied for the problem of software defect prediction, and there is no clear conclusion regarding the best approach. Consequently, we have decided to use three classification models for our experiments: FastAI, a deep learning model that proved to be the best-performing one in [26], Multilayer Perceptron, an untuned conventional model that proved to be the second best-performing classifier in [26] and Random Forest with hyperparameter optimization, as a tuned conventional classifier.

FastAI. FastAI, the first classification model employed in the supervised analysis, is a deep learning classifier implemented in the FastAI machine learning library [15]. It comprises an artificial neural network with embeddings of the input layer. The architecture includes 1 input, 1 output and 2 hidden layers. In comparison to other deep learning models, particularly Convolutional Neural Networks, FastAI is very small and fast, with training times under 2 min on our data set and inference time under 1 s per instance at runtime. This characteristic renders it suitable for real-time usage scenarios. The model is trained using the FastAI *fit one cycle* method, with a learning rate that varies according to a specific pattern: first it increases, then it decreases and the process is repeated for each epoch.

Multilayer Perceptron. The second classification model employed is a Multilayer Perceptron. We used the scikit-learn implementation for this model, opting for one single hidden layer and a rectified linear unit activation function. The model was trained using a stochastic gradient-based optimizer with a constant learning rate of 0.001 and for a maximum of 2000 epochs.

Random Forest. The third classification model used in this analysis is Random Forest [6], an ensemble learning method, which builds a set of decision trees and uses a majority voting mechanism to make a prediction for an unseen instance. Each decision tree is built considering only a random selection of features from the data set and, in general, using only a subset of the training instances, sampled randomly with replacement. RF have previously been used extensively for SDP [21]. In order to find the best parameters for RF we have performed a parameter tuning process, whose details are presented in Sect. 4.1.

3.3 Case Study

As a case study, we chose 16 releases of the Apache Calcite software system, an open-source dynamic data management framework [5]. Details about the considered versions

of Calcite are presented in Table 1. For each Calcite version, the total number of software instances, the number of defective software instances, and the defective rate are
provided.

We started from the Calcite data sets provided by Herbold et al. [13], that have been
generated by an extended version of the SZZ-RA [28] algorithm and contain the value
of 4189 software metrics, but we have only used the class labels and added them to our
representations, matching instances based on the class name.

Table 1. Number of non-defective and defective instances, total number of instances and rate of
defective instances for all Calcite versions [25].

Version	Non-defective	Defective	Total	Defective rate	Version	Non-defective	Defective	Total	Defective rate
1.0	897	178	1075	0.166	1.8	1200	101	1301	0.078
1.1	990	113	1103	0.102	1.9	1220	90	1310	0.069
1.2	982	126	1108	0.114	1.10	1226	84	1310	0.064
1.3	1003	112	1115	0.100	1.11	1251	80	1331	0.060
1.4	1004	123	1127	0.109	1.12	1334	81	1415	0.057
1.5	1073	103	1176	0.088	1.13	1222	53	1275	0.042
1.6	1086	107	1193	0.090	1.14	1255	53	1308	0.041
1.7	1124	128	1252	0.102	1.15	1307	45	1352	0.033

3.4 Evaluation Methodology

In assessing the performance of the three supervised models, when fed with different
vectorial representations, scaled in [0,1] using Min-Max normalization, we employed
the following evaluation methodology. For FastAI and MLP the data was divided into
70% for training, 10% for validation (for early stopping) and 20% for testing. For RF
there was no early stopping, so the data was split into 80% for training and 20% for
testing. To ensure consistent results, 30 repetitions with different splits had been performed.

During this evaluation process, the confusion matrix for the binary classification
task has been computed for each of the 30 testing subsets. Based on the confusion
matrix, the *Area under the ROC curve* (AUC) has been calculated as a performance
indicator. The reported values have been averaged over the 30 experiments.

We chose AUC as a performance evaluation measure because the SDP literature
indicates that AUC is suitable for evaluating the performance of software defect prediction models [10]. Its value ranges from 0 to 1, higher values indicating better classification performance. The computation method for AUC is presented in [25].

3.5   Results and Analysis

Difficulty Analysis. Before training the supervised classification models presented in Sect. 3.2 we have decided to perform an unsupervised learning based analysis considering the *difficulty* of the representations.

As defined by Zhang et al. [41], the difficulty of a class c, in a binary classification context, is the proportion of data instances belonging to class c for which the nearest neighbor (computed using the Euclidean distance, when ignoring the class label) belongs to the opposite class. In our case, the two difficulty measures are computed for the defective (positive) and for the non-defective (negative) classes. Intuitively, the difficulty of a class indicates how challenging it is to distinguish the instances belonging to that class from the others.

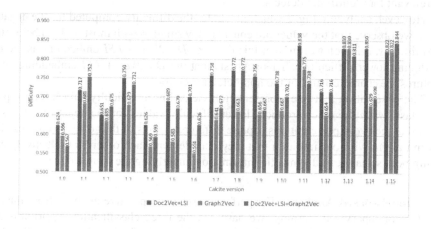

Fig. 1. Difficulty values for the three vectorial representations considering only the defective class [25].

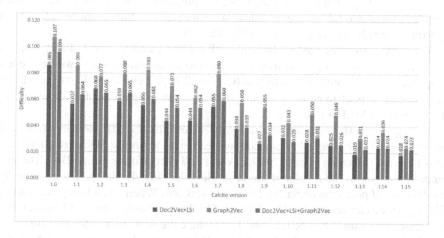

Fig. 2. Difficulty values for the three vectorial representations considering only the non-defective class [25].

The computed difficulty values for the defective class are illustrated in Fig. 1, and those for the non-defective class are depicted in Fig. 2.

Upon analyzing Fig. 1, where, for a clearer presentation of the differences, the y-axis labels start from 0.5, it becomes evident that the difficulty of the positive class is quite high. Most values hover around 0.6–0.7, with the minimum at 0.551 and, for some versions and representations, reaching as high as 0.83. This suggests that, on average, around two-thirds of the defective instances are closer to a non-defective instance than to a defective one, posing a considerable challenge for the accurate prediction of defective entities.

Comparing the values for different embeddings, it can be seen that for 12 out of 16 versions, the *Graph2Vec* representation yields a lower difficulty than the other two. This suggests that the *Graph2Vec* embedding captures structural information that may be relevant for identifying defects.

However, analyzing Fig. 2 which illustrates the difficulty computed for the negative class, we observe that the values are considerably smaller, with most of them below 0.1. Additionally, it is noteworthy that this time the *Doc2Vec + LSI* embedding is the one producing lower difficulties. This suggests that the *Doc2Vec + LSI* embedding better captures the characteristics of the non-defective entities.

The observation that one representation yields lower difficulty values for the positive class, while the other produces lower difficulty values for the negative class, suggests that the two representations capture different aspects of the software entities. This finding aligns with our intuition that they complement each other by collectively capturing both semantic and syntactic information underlying the source code.

ML Models-Based Analysis. For performing the comparative analysis from the perspective of supervised learning, we have run the three classification algorithms presented in Sect. 3.2 on all 16 versions of Calcite while feeding them with the three embeddings proposed in Sect. 3.1.

Due to the large number of values, we are presenting the results visually, instead of putting them into tables. Nevertheless, a document with the complete values for all algorithms and all runs is available on Figshare [2].

The AUC values for FastAI, MLP and RF are depicted on Figs. 3, 4 and 5, respectively. While we did not put them on the figures to avoid visual overcrowding, we have computed the 95% confidence intervals (CI) for all AUC values. For FastAI and RF the margin of error is at most 0.03 (although there is one single case for RF where it is 0.08), while for MLP it is at most 0.02.

As regards RQ1, considering the FastAI algorithm (Fig. 3), we can see that the *Graph2Vec* and *Doc2Vec + LSI* embeddings lead to quite similar SDP performance, but almost always (15 cases out of 16) *Doc2Vec + LSI* outperforms *Graph2Vec*. The same stands if we look at the results of the MLP classifier (Fig. 4): the values are close, but *Doc2Vec + LSI* performs better for 14 Calcite versions. When considering the results of RF (Fig. 5), we can notice that *Doc2Vec + LSI* is better in only 8 cases. Moreover, there are 4 cases (versions 1.5, 1.6, 1.11 and 1.15) where the AUC values for *Doc2Vec + LSI* are a lot lower than the ones for *Graph2Vec*. This aspect will be discussed in Sect. 4.

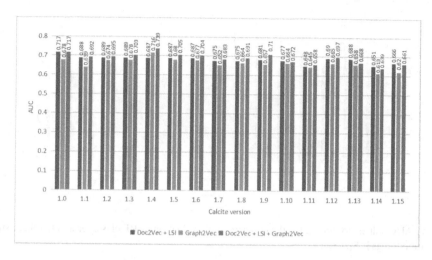

Fig. 3. AUC values computed for the experimental evaluation of the FastAI classifier and the three studied embeddings [25].

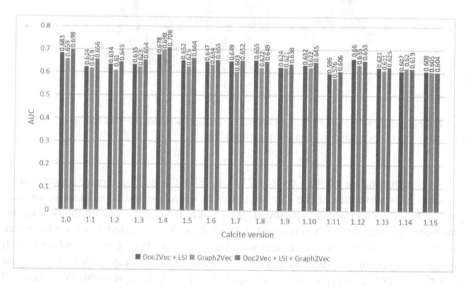

Fig. 4. AUC values computed for the experimental evaluation of the MLP classifier and the three studied embeddings [25].

In conclusion, our answer for RQ1 is that the *Graph2Vec* embedding performs comparably to *Doc2Vec + LSI*, but in most cases, regardless of the classification algorithm used, it is outperformed by *Doc2Vec + LSI*.

To address RQ2, we refer to Figs. 3, 4, and 5 once more. We can see that, for all three algorithms, the *Doc2Vec + LSI + Graph2Vec* is the best-performing one in 12 out of 16 cases. This is summarized in Fig. 6.

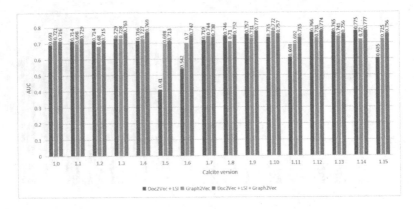

Fig. 5. AUC values computed for the experimental evaluation of RF classifier and the three studied embeddings [25].

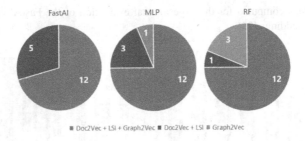

Fig. 6. The number of best-performing vectorial representations for the 16 versions of the Calcite software system, for each classification algorithm [25].

To further validate whether the *Doc2Vec + LSI + Graph2Vec* representation indeed captures information about the characteristics of defective and non-defective entities, we conducted an additional experiment. We run the RF classifier (with the best hyperparameter selected for each version of the Calcite software system), but we have randomly shuffled the class labels. In this way, we try to learn from a *corrupted* data set. If the classifier produces results on this corrupted data that are comparable to the ones on the original data, it suggests that only random noise has been learned. We employed the same methodology as for the other experiments, where 20% of data have been randomly selected for testing (the labels being randomly shuffled). For each version, the experiment was repeated 30 times to account for randomness in the classifier. The average AUC values obtained for the 16 versions range between 0.478 and 0.521, so significantly below the AUC values for the original data set, which are above 0.71. This confirms that the *Doc2Vec + LSI + Graph2Vec* embedding captures aspects carrying discriminative information that enables differentiation between defective and non-defective software entities.

Therefore, our answer for RQ2 is that the *Graph2Vec* and *Doc2Vec + LSI* embeddings improve the performance of the SDP model.

In order to see if the conclusions of the two research questions are statistically significant, we have first considered the 48 AUC values for each source code embedding (16 values for each classifier). According to the Kolmogorov-Smirnov test (with Lilliefors' method) all three variables (i.e. set of AUC values for code embeddings) are normally distributed so we have used a one-way repeated measures ANOVA test. Mauchly's test indicated that the assumption of sphericity had been violated, therefore degrees of freedom were corrected using Greenhouse-Geisser estimates of sphericity. The results of ANOVA show that the AUC values for the three embeddings differ significantly. Post hoc tests revealed that the *Doc2Vec + LSI + Graph2Vec* representation has significantly higher AUC values than both other representations. However, there is no significant difference between *Doc2Vec + LSI* and *Graph2Vec* embeddings. Consequently, only the answer to RQ2 is statistically significant.

4   FastAI Versus Tuned Random Forest as Defect Prediction Models

In this section we try to answer our third research question, regarding the performance of the Random Forest model for which hyperparameter tuning was performed compared to the performance of FastAI, a deep learning model, without hyperparameter tuning. We will first describe the hyperparameter tuning process in Sect. 4.1, followed by the comparison between FastAI and RF in Sect. 4.2. Finally, we will analyze the results of the hyperparameter tuning process in Sect. 4.3 and the best hyperparameters in Sect. 4.4.

4.1   Hyperparameter Tuning

RF was one of the classifiers used in a study about the effect of hyperparameter tuning for SDP models [37], but only one parameter, the number of classification trees, was tuned. The conclusions of that study were that RF is not that sensitive to hyperparameter values when AUC is used as a performance measure. Since we use different data sets and different representations than the ones used in [37], we have decided to see if their conclusions are valid for our data as well and to try and find the best set of parameters for the RF classifier.

Table 2. Hyperparameters of the Random Forest algorithm and the values used for tuning [25].

Parameter	Description	Values considered for tuning
n_estimators	number of trees to build	50, 75, 100, 150, 200
criterion	function used to measure the quality of the split	gini, etropy, log_loss
max_depth	maximum depth of a tree	3, 5, 7, 9
max_features	number (fraction) of features to check for the best split	log2, sqrt, 0.25, 0.5, 0.75, 0.95
bootstrap	whether to use bootstraping	True, False
class_weight	weights assigned for the classes	None, balanced, balanced_subsample
ccp_alpha	parameter used for determining which subtree to prune	0, 0.01, 0.02, 0.03, 0.04
max_samples	the maximum fraction of samples to use if bootstrap is True	0.5, 0.6, 0.7, 0.8, 0.9

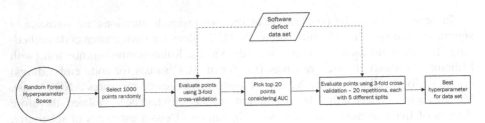

Fig. 7. Steps of the hyperparameter tuning process [25].

We have used the implementation for RF from the *scikit learn* library [30], where there are a set of parameters related to building the trees that can be used to find the best model. We have decided to tune 8 of them, that are presented in Table 2 together with the considered values. We would like to mention that the *scikit learn* implementation has some parameters that we have left out of the hyperparameter tuning and for which the default values were used. These are mainly parameters related to the minimum number of instances required for a leaf node or for a split or the maximum number of leaf nodes. Since SDP data sets tend to be highly imbalanced, we considered that it is best to keep the default, low, values for these parameters.

Out of the parameter values from Table 2 not all possible combinations are valid: if the value of *bootstrap* is set to *False*, the value of *max_samples* has to be set to *None*. Considering this restriction, the total number of valid parameter combinations for the RF algorithm is 32.400. Checking such a large number of parameter combinations using grid search is not possible, especially since some of the parameters (for example *bootstrap* and *max_features*) introduce randomness in the process, so in order to get a more accurate view of the performance of a point from the hyperparameter space, several runs for that point should be executed. In order to balance the total run time and the exploration of the hyperparameter space, we have decided to use a two-step parameter tuning process, which is presented on Fig. 7.

For each of the 16 data sets and each of the three representations, first we have selected 1000 random hyperparameter points and evaluated them using a single run of a 3-fold cross validation on the current data set using the AUC measure. This is called *random search-based hyperparameter tuning* and is an alternative for grid search which was shown in [37] to perform just as well as grid search for SDP. Out of the 1000 points, 833 were generated setting the value of *bootstrap* to *True*, while the remaining 167 points were generated for *bootstrap* set to *False*. These values were selected to be proportional to the size of the considered hyperparameter space for the two possible values of *bootstrap*, 27000 and 5400 points, respectively.

In the second step of the process, the 20 points with the highest *AUC* from the first step were selected and re-evaluated. The 3-fold cross validation was repeated 20 times and for each repetition 5 different random splittings into the 3-folds were considered. Consequently, for every point, we had the value of *AUC* for 100 evaluations. The average of these values was considered to be the evaluation value of that hyperparameter point. Finally, the point with the highest *AUC* was selected as the best hyperparameter for the given data set and representation.

4.2 Comparison of FastAI and Random Forest

To address our third research question, we examined the results presented in Sect. 3.5 from a different perspective. Rather than comparing the performance obtained by the same classifier for different embeddings, we compared the performance of the two classifiers for the same embeddings. We provide a summary of the comparisons in Fig. 8.

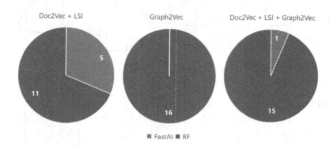

Fig. 8. The number of best-performing classifiers for the 16 versions of the Calcite software system, for each embedding [25].

As illustrated in Fig. 8, the tuned RF classifier outperforms FastAI for all representations. This confirms the conclusions presented in [11, 19], asserting that properly tuned simpler models can outperform deep learning models. To verify the significance of parameter tuning, we have repeated the experiments for the $Doc2Vec + LSI + Graph2Vec$ representation (since, according to the conclusions of RQ2, this is the best-performing representation) considering the default parameters of RF from *scikit-learn*. The results were all less than 0.56, which is significantly lower than the AUC values achieved for the tuned RF, all of which are above 0.71.

Our findings about how much parameter tuning matters for RF differ from the findings of Tantithamthavorn [37], who concluded that RF is not sensitive to hyperparameter tuning (although they only tuned the parameter denoting the number of trees). The reason for this discrepancy might be given by the difference in the considered features: we have used embeddings learned from the source code, while in [37], structural, complexity, and size metrics are used. There is another observation regarding RFs in [37]: they are not among the top-performing classifiers. In our study, RFs had the best performance, but we compared only three approaches, and only the parameters of RF were tuned, while Tantithamthavorn et al. compared 26 classifiers, so it is possible that even better performance can be achieved by considering other classifiers.

In order to test if the difference between the performance of FastAI and RF is statistically significant, we have compared the 16 AUC values for the two classifiers for the $Doc2Vec + LSI + Graph2Vec$ embedding. Since the Kolmogorov-Smirnov test showed that both variables are normally distributed, we used a one-way repeated measures ANOVA again (even if we had only two variables) whose results show that the AUC values for RF are significantly higher than those for FastAI. Consequently, we can conclude that the results for RQ3 are statistically significant.

4.3 Analysis of the Hyperparameter Tuning Process

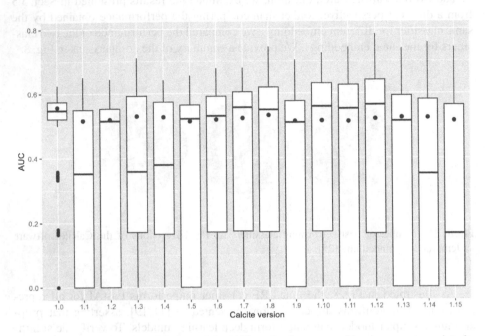

Fig. 9. Box plot with the AUC values of the 1000 randomly generated hyperparameter points for the *Doc2Vec + LSI + Graph2Vec* representation. The red dots show the performance of RF with default parameters.

The previous experiment demonstrated that default parameters perform quite poor on the *Doc2Vec + LSI + Graph2Vec* representation, so we have decided to look at the initially generated 1000 hyperparameter points for all representations.

For all data sets and representations there were hyperparameter points with an AUC value of 0 (at least 97, at most 462) and a lot of points with an AUC value below 0.5 (at least 162 and at most 995). Actually, there were 4 versions of the Calcite data set, when for the *Doc2Vec + LSI* representation there was an exceptionally high number of hyperparameter points with an initial AUC value below 0.5: version 1.5 (995 points), 1.6 (903), 1.11 (844) and 1.15 (929). On Fig. 5 we can see that these are exactly the versions with an AUC value a lot less than the other versions and representations. This is probably the result of a random search which produced a lot of hyperparameter points with very poor performance. This suggests that in some cases, random search might not generate good enough points, and probably the number of points should be increased in such cases.

Considering that overall the *Doc2Vec + LSI + Graph2Vec* representation had the best performance, we have decided to analyze the initially generated 1000 hyperparameter points for this representation, to see how varied their AUC values are. The boxplot for the 1000 AUC values for each version of the software system are presented on Fig. 9.

The red dots show the performance of a separately trained RF classifier using the default parameters.

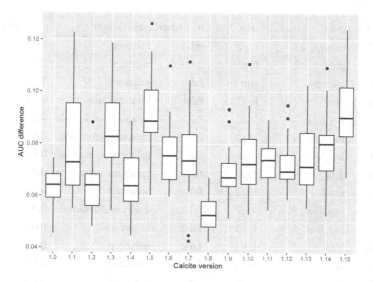

Fig. 10. Box plot with the difference in AUC values during the re-evaluations of the best 20 hyperparameter points for the *Doc2Vec + LSI + Graph2Vec* representation.

Figure 9 demonstrates that different hyperparameters can lead to big differences in the performance of the RF classifier. Next, we wanted to see how this performance changes if we evaluate the same hyperparameter repeatedly. In the second step of the hyperparameter tuning process, we have re-evaluated 100 times the best performing 20 hyperparameters using different random seeds and random train-test splittings. For each hyperparameter we have computed the difference between the maximum and minimum AUC achieved during these re-evaluations, to see how much the AUC changes. The box-plot for the differences is presented on Fig. 10.

Analyzing the plots from Fig. 10, we can see that the AUC differences belong to a smaller interval, they rarely pass 0.12 and the medians are all less than or equal to 0.09. This suggests that the performance of one hyperparameter is relatively stable (compared to the spread of values for the initial 1000 points). Considering the results from the two box-plots, we can conclude that while the first step of our hyperparameter tuning process is crucial, this second step is not so important, and in case of limited resources, effort should be focused on covering a larger number of points. Nevertheless, an AUC difference of even 0.09 might be important, since on Fig. 5 in some cases the difference between two representations is less than that value.

Table 3. The best hyperparameters for the 16 versions of the Calcite system for the RF algorithm for the *Doc2Vec + LSI + Graph2Vec* representation. Abbreviations: V. - version, max_e. - max_estimators, crit. - criterion, max_d. - max_depth, max_feat. - max_features, max_s. - max_samples.

V.	max_e.	crit.	max_d.	max_feat.	bootstrap	class_weight	ccp_alpha	max_s.
1.0	200	entropy	7	log2	false	balanced	0.02	None
1.1	50	gini	7	log2	false	balanced	0.02	None
1.2	150	entropy	7	sqrt	false	balanced	0.04	None
1.3	200	gini	7	log2	false	balanced_subsample	0.03	None
1.4	100	log_loss	7	log2	false	balanced_subsample	0.03	None
1.5	200	log_loss	9	log2	false	balanced_subsample	0.04	None
1.6	150	log_loss	7	sqrt	false	balanced_subsample	0.04	None
1.7	150	gini	9	log2	false	balanced_subsample	0.02	None
1.8	150	log_loss	5	log2	false	balanced	0.04	None
1.9	200	log_loss	5	log2	false	balanced_subsample	0.04	None
1.10	150	log_loss	5	log2	false	balanced	0.04	None
1.11	200	gini	7	log2	false	balanced	0.03	None
1.12	150	gini	7	log2	false	balanced	0.03	None
1.13	200	gini	7	log2	false	balanced	0.04	None
1.14	100	gini	5	sqrt	false	balanced	0.04	None
1.15	150	gini	5	log2	false	balanced	0.03	None

4.4 Analysis of the Best Hyperparameters

The best hyperparameters for the 16 versions of Calcite for the *Doc2Vec + LSI + Graph2Vec* representation are presented in Table 3. We can see that each version has its own best hyperparameter, with the exception of versions 1.8 and 1.10, which share the same best hyperparameter.

While there is no universal best hyperparameter for the Calcite versions, we can see that all versions have the value *false* for bootstrapping (and consequently *None* for the maximum number of samples). For the other parameters, different values were found to be the best for different versions. For the criterion parameter, for example, all three possible values (entropy, gini, log_loss) appear, while for other parameters, only some of them are present among the best hyperparameter values, which means that we might see some trends. For example, the number of estimators seems to be high: only one version has 50 estimators and no version has 75, the larger values (100, 150 and 200) are preferred. Similarly, higher values seem to be preferred for max_depth (the value 3 is missing) and ccp_alpha (0 and 0.01 are missing). Regarding class_weight it seems clear that some form of weighting is beneficial, but not clear which one. And interestingly, the max_features is either log2 or sqrt. In the *Doc2Vec + LSI + Graph2Vec* representation, we have 90 features, so the logarithm and square root means that only 6-9 features are enough.

Considering that almost all versions have distinct best hyperparameters, but these are quite close to each other, we have decided to analyze the *transferability* of the best hyperparameter from one Calcite version to another. In order to do this, we have trained on the *Doc2Vec + LSI + Graph2Vec* representation of each Calcite version a RF model for each of the 16 best hyperparameters. We have used the same methodology as described in Sect. 3.4. The results are presented on the heatmap from Fig. 11, where the rows show the versions whose hyperparameter was used and the columns show the version which was used for testing. For example, the first row contains the AUC values when the best hyperparameters from version 1.0 were used for each Calcite version.

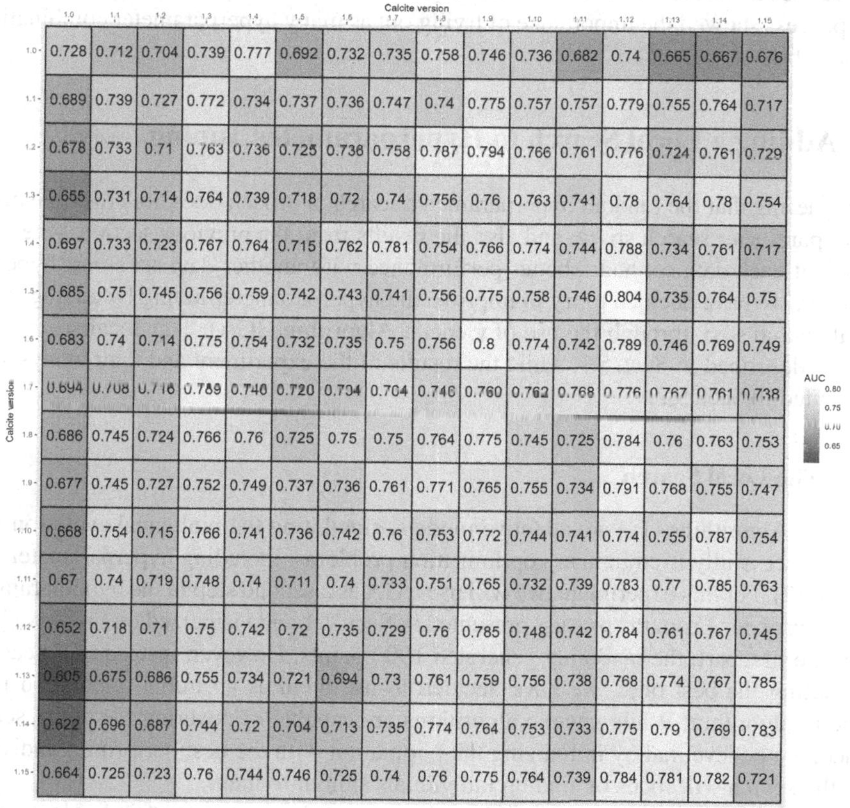

	1.0	1.1	1.2	1.3	1.4	1.5	1.6	1.7	1.8	1.9	1.10	1.11	1.12	1.13	1.14	1.15
1.0	0.728	0.712	0.704	0.739	0.777	0.692	0.732	0.735	0.758	0.746	0.736	0.682	0.74	0.665	0.667	0.676
1.1	0.689	0.739	0.727	0.772	0.734	0.737	0.736	0.747	0.74	0.775	0.757	0.757	0.779	0.755	0.764	0.717
1.2	0.678	0.733	0.71	0.763	0.736	0.725	0.736	0.758	0.787	0.794	0.766	0.761	0.776	0.724	0.761	0.729
1.3	0.655	0.731	0.714	0.764	0.739	0.718	0.72	0.74	0.756	0.76	0.763	0.741	0.78	0.764	0.78	0.754
1.4	0.697	0.733	0.723	0.767	0.764	0.715	0.762	0.781	0.754	0.766	0.774	0.744	0.788	0.734	0.761	0.717
1.5	0.685	0.75	0.745	0.756	0.759	0.742	0.743	0.741	0.756	0.775	0.758	0.746	0.804	0.735	0.764	0.75
1.6	0.683	0.74	0.714	0.775	0.754	0.732	0.735	0.75	0.756	0.8	0.774	0.742	0.789	0.746	0.769	0.749
1.7	0.694	0.708	0.716	0.789	0.746	0.720	0.734	0.704	0.746	0.760	0.762	0.768	0.776	0.767	0.761	0.738
1.8	0.686	0.745	0.724	0.766	0.76	0.725	0.75	0.75	0.764	0.775	0.745	0.725	0.784	0.76	0.763	0.753
1.9	0.677	0.745	0.727	0.752	0.749	0.737	0.736	0.761	0.771	0.765	0.755	0.734	0.791	0.768	0.755	0.747
1.10	0.668	0.754	0.715	0.766	0.741	0.736	0.742	0.76	0.753	0.772	0.744	0.741	0.774	0.755	0.787	0.754
1.11	0.67	0.74	0.719	0.748	0.74	0.711	0.74	0.733	0.751	0.765	0.732	0.739	0.783	0.77	0.785	0.763
1.12	0.652	0.718	0.71	0.75	0.742	0.72	0.735	0.729	0.76	0.785	0.748	0.742	0.784	0.761	0.767	0.745
1.13	0.605	0.675	0.686	0.755	0.734	0.721	0.694	0.73	0.761	0.759	0.756	0.738	0.768	0.774	0.767	0.785
1.14	0.622	0.696	0.687	0.744	0.72	0.704	0.713	0.735	0.774	0.764	0.753	0.733	0.775	0.79	0.769	0.783
1.15	0.664	0.725	0.723	0.76	0.744	0.746	0.725	0.74	0.76	0.775	0.764	0.739	0.784	0.781	0.782	0.721

Calcite version

AUC
0.80
0.75
0.70
0.65

Fig. 11. Heatmap with the AUC values for the RF classifier considering each Calcite version and each best hyperparameter on the *Doc2Vec + LSI + Graph2Vec* representation.

Since lighter colors represent higher AUC values, if the main diagonal has the lightest colors, it means that for each version their own hyperparameter provides the best results. This is true for version 1.0 (first column) where the best AUC value is achieved for the hyperparameters for version 1.0, but not for the other versions. For version 1.1, there are 6 other cases where another hyperparameter leads to better results than 0.739.

This phenomenon can be observed for the other versions as well: at least 1, but in some cases more than 10 other versions have higher AUC values. This suggests that the hyperparameter tuning process was not sufficient, there are other, better hyperparameters for each version.

Consequently, our answer for RQ3 is that, for our data sets, the RF classifier with the best hyperparameter setting outperforms FastAI in most cases. Nevertheless, the parameter tuning process is far from being perfect: there were 4 identified cases when the random search parameter tuning approach could not identify good enough parameters for the *Doc2Vec + LSI* representation and in these cases the performance of FastAI was better than that of RF. Considering the *Doc2Vec + LSI + Graph2Vec* representation where the results seemed to be the best in general, further analysis of the parameter tuning process showed the importance of trying out as many hyperparameter combinations as possible.

5 Adding a Local Search to Hyperparameter Tuning

Considering that the random hyperparameter search approach does not cover the entire hyperparameter search space, and also the results from the previous section, where we saw that each data set had a better performance with another data set's best hyperparameter, we have decided to try to improve the hyperparameter tuning by adding to it a local search step, through the use of Genetic Algorithms (GA). This local search process is described in Sect. 5.1, while the results of the experiment and their analysis are presented in Sect. 5.2.

5.1 The Local Search

Genetic Algorithms [14] are adaptive models, simulating the biological evolution process, successfully used in many optimization problems, including hyperparameter tuning [4, 37]. For this experiment, we will use a GA as a second step in the hyperparameter tuning process. From the process presented in Sect. 4.1 and visualized on Fig. 7 we have kept the first part, the randomly generated 1000 points. However, instead of repeatedly evaluating the best ones, we have decided to use them as an initial population for a genetic algorithm. While genetic algorithms are capable of covering the entire search space, we believe that by initializing the population with the best performing individuals, the search will focus on finding individuals similar to them.

The genetic algorithm starts with an initial population, made of individuals, each having a fitness value, showing how good that particular individual is. This population is then evolved for a predefined number of epochs, nr_epochs. During every epoch, the following process is repeated until a new population is created: two individuals are selected from the current population, in such a way that individuals with higher fitness have a higher chance of being selected. With a probability $p\_crossover$ these two individuals are recombined creating two new individuals. On each individual mutation happens with a probability $p\_mutation$. The resulting individuals are added into a new population and when this new population has enough members, it will replace the old one and a new epoch starts. Optionally, an elitism mechanism can also be used, which simply copies the best individual(s) from one epoch to another to make sure that they are not lost.

In our case, each individual is a hyperparameter combination of the RF model, an array containing 8 elements, one value for each parameter from Table 2. Their fitness is the average AUC value of the repeated evaluations. For selection, we have used the tournament selection procedure, where we randomly selected t individuals out of which the two best ones are returned as parents. Crossover was performed using one randomly generated cutpoint in the array and recombining the two halves. Mutation was performed on each parameter (i.e. element of the array) separately and as a result a new value was randomly chosen for that parameter. We have used the elitism as well.

Table 4. Parameters of the Genetic Algorihm parameter tuning process.

Parameter	Value
Nr. of epochs	20
Population size	41
Nr. of individuals in tournament	5
Probability of crossover	0.75
Probability of mutation	0.1
Nr. of elits	1
Nr. of shuffle splits	3
Nr. of random checks	10

The parameters of the GA algorithm are presented in Table 4. Due to the repeated evaluations of each individual, running the Genetic Algorithm takes a lot of time. Considering the results of the analysis from Sect. 4.3, namely that it is better to evaluate more points than to evaluate one point many times, we have decided to consider the best 41 points, instead of just 20, but we have reduced the number of repeated evaluations: instead of doing 20 repetitions for 5 random splittings, we have used 10 repetitions with 3 random splittings.

5.2 Results and Analysis

We have decided to run the GA only on the *Doc2Vec + LSI + Graph2Vec* representation (since this had the best performance in the previous experiments) and we have selected only 6 versions of the Calcite data sets, since running the GA on all versions would have taken far too long. We have tried to select some representative versions: 1.0 and 1.2 since they have the highest defective rates; 1.14 and 1.15 since they have the lowest defective rates; 1.5 and 1.9 since RF had the worst and best AUC for them on the experiments from Sect. 3.5 (in case of best performance 1.9 and 1.14 had the same value, but 1.14 was already selected).

Once we had the best hyperparameters, we have evaluated them in same way, in which the evaluation was performed for the other experiments: 30 repetitions and 80%-20% train-test splitting. The results are presented in the second column of Table 5,

Table 5. AUC results for the best hyperparameters achieved with random search-based hyperparameter tuning, with and without the Genetic Algorithms-based local search step.

Version	With GA	Without GA
1.0	0.719	0.716
1.2	0.719	0.715
1.5	0.742	0.713
1.9	0.766	0.777
1.14	0.788	0.777
1.15	0.775	0.756

where the third column contains the results for the best hyperparameter obtained with the initial hyperparameter tuning process. We can see that with the exception of version 1.9 the AUC value was improved. However, if we look at the AUC values from Fig. 11 obtained by using the best hyperparameters from other versions, we can see that for each version (except 1.14) there are higher AUC values achieved by other hyperparameters.

In conclusion, our answer for RQ4 is that adding the local search can find better hyperparameters, but considering the time it takes to run the genetic algorithm, it might not be the best option.

6 The Relevance of SYNMET Metrics for SDP

This section introduces our SYNMET metrics suite consisting of syntactic coupling metrics derived from Graph2Vec embeddings, in Sect. 6.1, and addresses our last research question, RQ5, regarding their relative relevance for SDP, in Sect. 6.2.

6.1 The SYNMET Metrics Suite

To derive metrics characterizing a software entity, se, in relation to multiple others, the individual syntactic coupling values (i.e. the ones computed independently, for se in relation to each of the other software entities considered) need to be aggregated. One approach for such summarization is using descriptive statistics. So, attributes of software entities, derived from their syntactic couplings with other software entities, can be obtained by computing measures of central tendency, such as the *mean*, and of variability, like the *maximum* and the *standard deviation*. This approach results in a new suite of syntactic coupling metrics derived from Graph2Vec-based embeddings.

So, after extracting the Graph2Vec embeddings and representing each software entity se as: $se^{Graph2Vec} = (se_1^{Graph2Vec}, \cdots, se_s^{Graph2Vec})$, where $se_i^{Graph2Vec}$ ($\forall 1 \leq i \leq s$) denotes the value of the i-th feature computed for the entity se by using Graph2Vec, we compute the syntactic coupling value (SC) between each pair of software entities, se_i and se_j ($1 \leq i < j \leq n$), as the *similarity* between their Graph2Vec embedding vectors. For quantifying the closeness of two high-dimensional vectors, we employ both *euclidean* (Formula (2)) and *cosine* (Formula (1)) similarities.

$$SC^{cosine}(se_i, se_j) = \frac{\left| \sum_{k=1}^{m} (se_{ik} \cdot se_{jk}) \right|}{\sqrt{\sum_{k=1}^{m} (se_{ik} \cdot se_{ik})} \cdot \sqrt{\sum_{k=1}^{m} (se_{jk} \cdot se_{jk})}} \tag{1}$$

$$SC^{euclidean}(se_i, se_j) = \frac{1}{1 + \sqrt{\sum_{k=1}^{m} (se_{ik} - se_{jk})^2}} \tag{2}$$

The subsequent step involves constructing, for each software entity se_i, a numerical sequence comprising the entity's syntactic coupling values (SC) computed with respect to:

1. all the other entities from the software system, $Seq^{all}(se_i)$:

$$Seq^{all}(se_i) = \{SC(se_i, se_j) | \, j = 1 \ldots n, j \neq i\} \tag{3}$$

2. the other software entities that are *defective*, $Seq^{defective}(se_i)$:

$$Seq^{defective}(se_i) = \{SC(se_i, se_j) | \, j = 1 \ldots n, j \neq i, \, se_j \text{ is defective}\} \tag{4}$$

3. the other software entities that are *non-defective*, $Seq^{non-defective}(se_i)$:

$$Seq^{non-defective}(se_i) = \{SC(se_i, se_j) | \, j = 1 \ldots n, j \neq i, se_j \text{ is non-defective}\} \tag{5}$$

The final step performed involves defining the software metrics from the SYNMET suite as the *mean* (Formula (6)), *maximum* (Formula (7)) and *standard deviation* (Formula (8)) descriptive statistic measures computed for the numerical sequences $Seq(se_i)$ (Formulae (6)-(8)) built at the previous step for each software entity se_i. By $Seq_j(se_i)$ we denote the j-th element in the sequence $Seq(se_i)$.

$$mean(Seq(se_i)) = \frac{\sum_{j=1}^{|Seq(se_i)|} Seq_j(se_i)}{|Seq(se_i)|} \tag{6}$$

$$max(Seq(se_i)) = \max_j \{Seq_j(se_i), \, 1 \leq j \leq |Seq(se_i)|\} \tag{7}$$

$$stdev(Seq(se_i)) = \sqrt{\frac{\sum_{j=1}^{|Seq(se_i)|} (Seq_j(se_i) - mean(Seq(se_i)))^2}{|Seq(se_i)|}} \tag{8}$$

Our motivation for including standard deviation as a measure of spread stems from evidence in the literature stating that software entities highly coupled with others that are also highly inter-coupled tend to have lower chances of being defective [7]. Consequently, there might be a positive impact of such a measure on correctly classifying non-defective instances, particularly considering that Graph2Vec-based embeddings demonstrated maximum difficulty for the negative class compared to other embeddings, as indicated in the results presented in Sect. 3.5. A possible explanation for the observation that highly inter-coupled software entities are less likely to contain defects is that, as consistently inter-coupled software components emerge, developers become more aware of such dependencies. This increased awareness enables them to understand how changes propagate and where to focus their attention, ultimately reducing the probability of introducing defects [7].

Following the methodology described above, 18 $(3 \cdot 3 \cdot 2)$ software metrics are obtained, as described in Table 6. They compose the SYNMET suite of Graph2Vec-based syntactic coupling software metrics that can be fed into defect predictors.

We mention that the methodology of obtaining the SYNMET suite is similar to that employed for defining the COMET conceptual coupling metrics suite we have introduced in a previous paper [24].

6.2   SYNMET's Relevance for SDP Analyses

When assessing the relevance of the SYNMET metrics, our primary focus is on comparing SYNMET to Graph2Vec embeddings in terms of their discriminative power when it comes to differentiating between defective and defect-free software entities, so as

Table 6. SYNMET metrics suite.

Descriptive statistic measure	Syntactic coupling are computed with respect to:	Similarity measure used for computing the syntactic coupling	SYNMET metric
Mean	all other software entities	euclidean	mean_SC_all_euclidean
		cosine	mean_SC_all_cosine
	all other software entities that are defective	euclidean	mean_SC_defective_euclidean
		cosine	mean_SC_defective_cosine
	all other sofware entities that are defect-free	euclidean	mean_SC_non-defective_euclidean
		cosine	mean_SC_non-defective_cosine
Maximum	all other software entities	euclidean	max_SC_all_euclidean
		cosine	max_SC_all_cosine
	all other software entities that are defective	euclidean	max_SC_defective_euclidean
		cosine	max_SC_defective_cosine
	all other sofware entities that are defect-free	euclidean	max_SC_non-defective_euclidean
		cosine	max_SC_non-defective_cosine
Standard deviation	all other software entities	euclidean	stdev_SC_all_euclidean
		cosine	stdev_SC_all_cosine
	all other software entities that are defective	euclidean	stdev_SC_defective_euclidean
		cosine	stdev_SC_defective_cosine
	all other sofware entities that are defect-free	euclidean	stdev_SC_non-defective_euclidean
		cosine	stdev_SC_non-defective_cosine

to argue the added value brought by taking a step further from proposing the use of Graph2Vec embeddings for SDP and defining a new syntactic metrics suite based on them.

Difficulty Analysis. In order to assess the relative relevance of the SYNMET metrics for SDP we have started with a comparative difficulty analysis, performed according to the methodology described in Sect. 3.5.

We have computed the difficulties of the 16 SDP data sets (i.e., one for each considered version) generated when representing the software entities as numeric vectors consisting of the values for the 18 syntactic coupling metrics composing the SYNMET suite. The resulting difficulty values have been compared to those obtained when considering the Graph2Vec embeddings directly.

The numeric results indicate that the difficulties computed for the defective class are reduced for only 4 versions, being kept constant for other 2 versions, when replacing the Graph2Vec embedding-based representations with the SYNMET-based representations. However, as depicted in Fig. 12, the difficulty values computed for the non-defective class, for which Graph2Vec proved to perform the worst of the considered embeddings, are reduced for 15 out of 16 versions (all excepting version 1.2) when considering the SYNMET metrics for representing the software entities. This confirms our intuition that syntactic coupling might facilitate alleviate misclassification of defect-free software components.

When it comes to the overall difficulty, computed for both the defective and the non-defective class, the SYNMET metrics still reduce the difficulty of the SDP task for most of the versions. The comparison is depicted in Fig. 13. For 13 out of 16 versions (1.0, 1.1, 1.3, 1.4, 1.6, 1.7, 1.8, 1.9, 1.11, 1.12, 1.13, 1.14 and 1.15), replacing the Graph2Vec embedding with the SYNMET-based representation leads to a lower overall difficulty, while for one version (1.10) the difficulty remains the same. Therefore, only for two versions (1.2 and 1.5) the Graph2Vec embeddings produce better (i.e., lower) overall difficulties.

As a conclusion of the difficulty analysis, the numerical results indicate the potential of the SYNMET syntactic coupling metrics, derived from Graph2Vec embeddings, to positively impact the performance of SDP by reducing the difficulty of discriminating between defective and non-defective software entities, especially by contributing to the correct classification of the non-defective ones.

Supervised Analysis. The second analysis we have performed in order to asses the relative relevance of the SYNMET metrics suite for SDP is based on supervised ML. We selected RF with optimized parameters as ML classification model, given its superior performance when compared to the alternative ML models considered in the current study.

Therefore, using the same initial hyperparameter tuning and evaluation methodology as in the case of the supervised analysis comparing the different embeddings (see Sect. 4.1), RF has been evaluated as a SDP model when fed with the values for SYNMET software metrics instead of software embeddings.

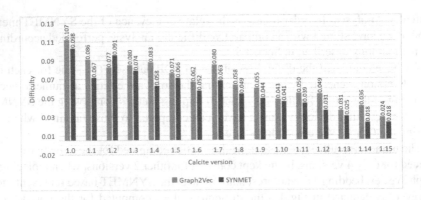

Fig. 12. Difficulty values for Graph2Vec versus SYNMET considering only the non-defective class.

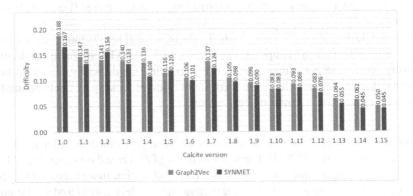

Fig. 13. Overall difficulty values for Graph2Vec versus SYNMET.

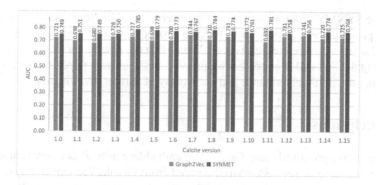

Fig. 14. AUC values computed for the experimental evaluation of the RF classifier when using SYNMET metrics versus Graph2Vec embeddings for representing the software entities.

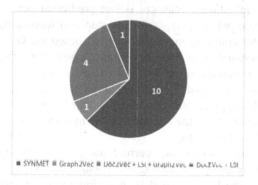

Fig. 15. The number of best-performing representations for the 16 versions of Calcite software system, when using RF with optimized parameters as classifier.

The obtained AUC values are depicted comparatively in Fig. 14. As it can be observed, excepting only one version, 1.10, RF achieves better classification performance, as measured via AUC, when fed with SYNMET instead of Graph2Vec embeddings. The improvement brought by SYNMET is non-negligible, reaching 12.8% for version 11 and being of 6.1% on average, while for the only version for which the AUC decreases, namely 1.10, the AUC is reduced only by about 2.1%.

Moreover, when compared to all the embedding-based representations, the SYNMET-based representation lead to the highest AUC for most Calcite versions. The comparison is visually summarized in Fig. 15. In 10 out of the 16 software version the SYNMET-based representation proves to be the best-performing one, being followed by the one that combines Doc2Vec, LSI and Graph2Vec embeddings and that wins for 4 other versions. The Graph2Vec embedding and the one that combines only Doc2Vec and LSI win for just one version, each.

In conclusion, the results of the supervised learning analysis confirm the relevance of the SYNMET structural coupling metrics for SDP and reconfirm the interplay between software coupling and defect-proneness.

As the SYNMET metrics prevalently produce better AUC than multiple embedding-based representations, which, in turn, have proved in [26] to be superior to a very extended set of software metrics, we can deduce that the new syntactic coupling metrics, composing the SYNMET suite, that we propose in the current paper, have the potential of boosting the SDP performance and are worthy of further investigation.

7   Conclusions

In this paper, we proposed using Graph2Vec embedding as well as a new syntactic coupling metrics suite, named SYNMET, derived from Graph2Vec embeddings, as novel representations of software entities in software defect prediction models. Results from several experimental analyses have validated the significance of the proposed representations in detecting defect proneness. The synergy of Graph2Vec embedding with Doc2Vec and LSI embeddings enhances defect prediction performance due to their complementary nature, while taking a further step and feeding the defect prediction model with syntactic coupling metrics computed based on Graph2Vec embedding, instead of the unprocessed Graph2Vec embedding, significantly increases the accuracy of discriminating between defective and defect-free software entities. In our comparative analysis, we have employed three classification models, including the FastAI deep learning model and a hyperparameter-tuned Random Forest, the latter outperforming the former, which underscores the effectiveness of hyperparameter optimisation in the realm of software defect predictors.

To bolster the conclusions of our current study we aim to broaden the scope of our experimental analyses by considering additional open-source software systems and exploring other machine learning models. Additionally, we envision delving into the efficacy of CodeBERT and graphCodeBERT for SDP and conducting a reliable comparison of it with our current approach, but also to deepen the study on the interplay between Graph2Vec-based syntactic coupling and defect proneness. In particular, we envision proposing new suites of aggregated coupling metrics, considering conceptual coupling in addition to syntactic coupling, and of aggregated cohesion, so as to more comprehensively capture the quality of software design to the benefit of software quality assurance, including software defect prediction.

Acknowledgements. This work was supported by a grant of the Ministry of Research, Innovation and Digitization, CNCS/CCCDI - UEFISCDI, project number PN-III-P4-ID-PCE-2020-0800, within PNCDI III.

References

1. The Seacraft Repository of Empirical Software Engineering Data (2017)
2. Source-Code Embedding-Based Software Defect Prediction - Data Sets and Detailed Results (2023). https://figshare.com/s/d5a7e8126ccd94181511
3. Aladics, T., Jász, J., Ferenc, R.: Bug prediction using source code embedding based on Doc2Vec. In: Computational Science and Its Applications, pp. 382–397 (2021)

4. Alibrahim, H., Ludwig, S.A.: Hyperparameter optimization: comparing genetic algorithm against grid search and Bayesian optimization. In: 2021 IEEE Congress on Evolutionary Computation (CEC), pp. 1551–1559 (2021). https://doi.org/10.1109/CEC45853.2021.9504761
5. Begoli, E., Camacho-Rodríguez, J., Hyde, J., Mior, M.J., Lemire, D.: Apache calcite: a foundational framework for optimized query processing over heterogeneous data sources. In: Proceedings of the International Conference on Management of Data, pp. 221–230 (2018). https://doi.org/10.1145/3183713.3190662
6. Breiman, L.: Random forests. Mach. Learn. **45**, 5–32 (2001)
7. Cataldo, M., Mockus, A., Roberts, J.A., Herbsleb, J.D.: Software dependencies, work dependencies, and their impact on failures. IEEE Trans. Softw. Eng. **35**(6), 864–878 (2009)
8. Dam, H.K., et al.: A deep tree-based model for software defect prediction (2018)
9. Deerwester, S.C., Dumais, S.T., Landauer, T.K., Furnas, G.W., Harshman, R.A.: Indexing by latent semantic analysis. J. Am. Soc. Inf. Sci. **41**, 391–407 (1990)
10. Fawcett, T.: An introduction to ROC analysis. Pattern Recogn. Lett. **27**(8), 861–874 (2006). https://doi.org/10.1016/j.patrec.2005.10.010
11. Fu, W., Menzies, T.: Easy over hard: a case study on deep learning. In: Proceedings of the Joint Meeting on Foundations of Software Engineering, pp. 49–60 (2017)
12. Hall, T., Beecham, S., Bowes, D., Gray, D., Counsell, S.: A systematic literature review on fault prediction performance in software engineering. IEEE Trans. Softw. Eng. **38**(6), 1276–1304 (2011)
13. Herbold, S., Trautsch, A., Trautsch, F., Ledel, B.: Problems with SZZ and features: an empirical study of the state of practice of defect prediction data collection. Empiric. Softw. Eng. **27**(2) (Jan 2022). https://doi.org/10.1007/s10664-021-10092-4
14. Holland, J.H.: Genetic algorithms. Sci. Am. **267**(1), 66–73 (1992)
15. Howard, J., et al.: fastai (2018) https://github.com/fastai/fastai
16. Le, Q.V., Mikolov, T.: Distributed representations of sentences and documents. Comput. Res. Reposit. 1–9 (2014). https://doi.org/10.1145/2740908.2742760
17. Li, J., He, P., Zhu, J., Lyu, M.R.: Software defect prediction via convolutional neural network. In: IEEE International Conference on Software Quality, Reliability and Security, pp. 318–328 (2017). https://doi.org/10.1109/QRS.2017.42
18. Li, N., Shepperd, M., Guo, Y.: A systematic review of unsupervised learning techniques for software defect prediction. Inf. Softw. Technol. **122**, 106287 (2020)
19. Majumder, S., Balaji, N., Brey, K., Fu, W., Menzies, T.: 500+ times faster than deep learning: a case study exploring faster methods for text mining stack overflow. In: Proceedings of the 15th International Conference on Mining Software Repositories (MSR 2018), pp. 554–563. (2018)
20. Malhotra, R.: A systematic review of machine learning techniques for software fault prediction. Appl. Soft Comput. **27**, 504–518 (2015). https://doi.org/10.1016/j.asoc.2014.11.023
21. Matloob, F., et al.: Software defect prediction using ensemble learning: a systematic literature review. IEEE Access **9**, 98754–98771 (2021)
22. Miholca, D., Onet-Marian, Z.: An analysis of aggregated coupling's suitability for software defect prediction. In: 2020 22nd International Symposium on Symbolic and Numeric Algorithms for Scientific Computing, pp. 141–148. IEEE Computer Society (2020). https://doi.org/10.1109/SYNASC51798.2020.00032
23. Miholca, D.L., Czibula, G.: Software defect prediction using a hybrid model based on semantic features learned from the source code. In: Knowledge Science, Engineering and Management: 12th International Conference, Part I, pp. 262–274 (2019). https://doi.org/10.1007/978-3-030-29551-6_23

24. Miholca, D.L., Czibula, G., Tomescu, V.: Comet: a conceptual coupling based metrics suite for software defect prediction. Procedia Comput. Sci. **176**, 31–40 (2020). https://doi.org/10.1016/j.procs.2020.08.004. Knowledge-Based and Intelligent Information and Engineering Systems: Proceedings of the 24th International Conference KES2020
25. Miholca., D., Oneţ-Marian., Z.: Source-code embedding-based software defect prediction. In: Proceedings of the 18th International Conference on Software Technologies - ICSOFT, pp. 185–196. INSTICC, SciTePress (2023). https://doi.org/10.5220/0012129600003538
26. Miholca, D.L., Tomescu, V.I., Czibula, G.: An in-depth analysis of the software features' impact on the performance of deep learning-based software defect predictors. IEEE Access **10**, 64801–64818 (2022). https://doi.org/10.1109/ACCESS.2022.3181995
27. Narayanan, A., Chandramohan, M., Venkatesan, R., Chen, L., Liu, Y., Jaiswal, S.: Graph2vec: learning distributed representations of graphs (2017)
28. Neto, E.C., da Costa, D.A., Kulesza, U.: The impact of refactoring changes on the SZZ algorithm: an empirical study. In: 2018 IEEE 25th International Conference on Software Analysis, Evolution and Reengineering (SANER), pp. 380–390 (2018)
29. Pan, C., Lu, M., Xu, B.: An empirical study on software defect prediction using CodeBERT model. Appl. Sci. **11**(11), 4793 (2021). https://doi.org/10.3390/app11114793
30. Pedregosa, F., et al.: Scikit-learn: machine learning in python. J. Mach. Learn. Res. **12**, 2825–2830 (2011)
31. Radjenović, D., Heričko, M., Torkar, R., Živkovič, A.: Software fault prediction metrics: a systematic literature review. Inf. Softw. Technol. **55**(8), 1397–1418 (2013). https://doi.org/10.1016/j.infsof.2013.02.009
32. Rathore, S.S., Kumar, S.: A study on software fault prediction techniques. Artif. Intell. Rev. **51**(2), 255–327 (2019)
33. Řehůřek, R., Sojka, P.: Software framework for topic modelling with large corpora. In: Proceedings of the LREC 2010 Workshop on New Challenges for NLP Frameworks, pp. 45–50. ELRA (2010)
34. Rozemberczki, B., Kiss, O., Sarkar, R.: Karate club: an API oriented open-source python framework for unsupervised learning on graphs. In: Proceedings of the ACM International Conference on Information and Knowledge Management, pp. 3125–3132. ACM (2020)
35. Sayyad, S., Menzies, T.: The PROMISE repository of software engineering databases. School of Information Technology and Engineering, University of Ottawa (2015). http://promise.site.uottawa.ca/SERepository
36. Sikic, L., Kurdija, A.S., Vladimir, K., Silic, M.: Graph neural network for source code defect prediction. IEEE Access **10**, 10402–10415 (2022). https://doi.org/10.1109/ACCESS.2022.3144598
37. Tantithamthavorn, C., McIntosh, S., Hassan, A.E., Matsumoto, K.: The impact of automated parameter optimization on defect prediction models. IEEE Trans. Softw. Eng. **45**(7), 683–711 (2019). https://doi.org/10.1109/TSE.2018.2794977
38. Uddin, M.N., Li, B., Ali, Z., Kefalas, P., Khan, I., Zada, I.: Software defect prediction employing BiLSTM and BERT-based semantic feature. Soft Comput. **26**, 1–15 (2022). https://doi.org/10.1007/s00500-022-06830-5
39. Wang, S., Liu, T., Nam, J., Tan, L.: Deep semantic feature learning for software defect prediction. IEEE Trans. Softw. Eng. **46**(12), 1267–1293 (2020). https://doi.org/10.1109/TSE.2018.2877612
40. Wang, S., Liu, T., Tan, L.: Automatically learning semantic features for defect prediction. In: Proceeding of the International Conference on Software Engineering, pp. 297–308 (2016)
41. Zhang, D., Tsai, J., Boetticher, G.: Improving credibility of machine learner models in software engineering. In: Advances in Machine Learning Applications in Software Engineering, pp. 52–72 (2007). https://doi.org/10.4018/978-1-59140-941-1.ch003

Author Index

H.-G. Fill et al. (Eds.): ICSOFT 2023, CCIS 2104, p. 155, 2024.
https://doi.org/10.1007/978-3-031-61753-9

Author Index

Printed in the United States
by Baker & Taylor Publisher Services